The Jewish People in
Classical Antiquity

The Jewish People in Classical Antiquity

From Alexander to Bar Kochba

JOHN H. HAYES
and SARA R. MANDELL

Westminster John Knox Press
LOUISVILLE
LONDON · LEIDEN

Scripture quotations from the Revised Standard Version of the Bible are copyright 1946, 1952, © 1971, 1973; Apocrypha © 1957, 1977, by the Division of Christian Education of the National Council of the Churches of Christ in the U.S.A. and are used by permission.

Quotations from Josephus are reprinted by permission of the publishers and the Loeb Classical Library, from Josephus: *The Jewish War,* translated by H. J. Thackeray, Cambridge, Mass.: Harvard University Press, 1976–79, and Josephus: *Jewish Antiquities,* vol. I–X, translated by H. J. Thackeray (vol. 4–5), Ralph Marcus (vol. 6–8), and Louis Feldman (vol. 9–10), Cambridge, Mass.: Harvard University Press, 1978–81.

Quotations from *Greek Historical Documents: The Hellenistic Period,* by R. S. Bagnall and P. Deron, 1981, are reprinted by permission of the publishers, Scholars Press, Atlanta, Georgia.

Book and cover design by Jennifer K. Cox
Cover illustration courtesy of The Stock Market

First edition
Published by Westminster John Knox Press
Louisville, Kentucky

This book is printed on acid-free paper that meets the American National Standards Institute Z39.48 standard. ♾

PRINTED IN THE UNITED STATES OF AMERICA
01 02 03 04 05 06 07—10 9 8 7 6 5 4 3 2

Library of Congress Cataloging-in-Publication Data

Hayes, John Haralson, date.
    The Jewish people in classical antiquity : from Alexander to Bar
Kochba / John H. Hayes and Sara R. Mandell.
        p.   cm.
    Includes bibliographical references and index.
    ISBN 0-664-25727-5
    1. Jews—History—586 B.C–70 A.D.   2. Jews—History—168 B.C.–135
A.D. 3. Judaism—History—Post-exilic period, 586 B.C.–210 A.D.
I. Mandell, Sara, date. II. Title.
DS121.65.H39 1998
933—dc21   97-41868

Contents

Charts, Maps, and Texts

CHARTS

MAPS

TEXTS

Preface

This work is a companion volume to J. M. Miller and J. H. Hayes, *A History of Ancient Israel and Judah* (Philadelphia/London: Westminster Press/SCM Press, 1986). It continues the historical account at the point where the earlier volume terminated. The focus of the present volume is the Judean–Jerusalem community and therefore does not discuss Jewish life in the Diaspora.

Abbreviations

Ant.	*Jewish Antiquities* by Josephus. Loeb Classical Library, 10 vols. Cambridge, Mass./London: Harvard University Press/ William Heinemann, 1926–1965.
CAH	*Cambridge Ancient History,* 2d ed. Cambridge: Cambridge University Press.
DSST	*The Dead Sea Scrolls Translated-The Qumran Texts in English.* 2d ed. By F. Garcia Martinez. Leiden/Grand Rapids: E. J. Brill/Wm. B. Eerdmans Publishing Co., 1996.
EDRL	*Encyclopedic Dictionary of Roman Law.* By A. Berger. Philadelphia: American Philosophical Society, 1953.
GHD	*Greek Historical Documents: The Hellenistic Period.* By R. S. Bagnall and P. Deron. Chico, Calif.: Scholars Press, 1981.
GLA	*Greek and Latin Authors on Jews and Judaism: Edited with Introductions, Translations and Commentary.* By M. Stern. 3 vols. Jerusalem: Israel Academy of Sciences and Humanities, 1974–84.
HW	*The Hellenistic World from Alexander to the Roman Conquest: A Selection of Ancient Sources in Translation.* By M. M. Austin. Cambridge: Cambridge University Press, 1981.
LSJ	*A Greek-English Lexicon.* By H. G. Liddell, R. Scott, and H. S. Jones. Oxford: Clarendon Press, 1940.
MPAT	*A Manual of Palestinian Aramaic Texts (Second Century B.C.–Second Century A.D.).* By J. A. Fitzmyer and D. J. Harrington. Rome: Biblical Institute, 1978.
OGIS	*Orientis Graeci inscriptiones selecta.* 2 vols. Edited by W. Dittenberger. Leipzig: S. Hirzel, 1903–05.
War	*War* by Josephus.

Introduction

Ideology rather than an attempt to ascertain what really happened often colors the study of Jewish Palestine and its inhabitants from the Restoration era to the conclusion of the Second Jewish Revolt. The history of the Jews is often treated as a chronicle of a totally unique people, chosen by the one and only real deity. The Jews of the land of Palestine and those living beyond its borders in the Diaspora are presumed to have formed a singular Yahwistic community, whose antecedents go back to the creation of everything as depicted in Genesis 1 and 2. This "chain of being" predicates that, even when its members were exiled from the Land, the character and continuity of the community never ceased to exist. So, from this perspective, in 538 B.C.E., when Cyrus conquered the Babylonians and permitted those exiled in Babylonia to return to their native lands, he really allowed the true community of Judahites to return to Jerusalem and reestablish their Temple state. By their own self-definition, the returnees were the only surviving community with the right to call themselves the Sons of Israel.

As viewed by those Jews of the Temple state who saw themselves as the heirs of this "unique" Yahwistic tradition, this reading of their history was more than an interpretation: it was what really took place. Consequently, it was ideologically and theologically proper. With the exception of scholars, who acknowledge the difference between ideology and history, most people who view the history of this era from a Jewish or Christian faith perspective adopt a similar attitude. So it is not surprising that most of what is construed as specifically ancient "Jewish" literature that survives, including works that are from mutually different political and/or theological camps, agrees in at least one matter in its theo-political slant: the Jerusalemite community was the normative representative of all Jews everywhere. Some of these works take it for granted that almost all Jews were in agreement with one another both theologically and politically. They also suggest that only a few renegades and radicals were in opposition to what until recently was treated as "normative Judaism." We now know, however, that there was no such thing as normative Judaism. There were both theologically based and politically based parties in the Temple state from its earliest days onward, and they did not belong to a unified faith community.

From the time of the Restoration of the Jews from exile in Babylon onward, there existed or came into being a number of different Jewish communities. In addition to which, various factions, both political and religious, developed within those communities. These communities and factions coexisted in Palestine, and they were Jewish insofar as they were Yahwists. Some of the Yahwistic groups represented political alignments or parties, whereas others represented religious alignments or sects. Although our knowledge about the various factions and sects within the Jerusalemite community is greater by far than that of any other community in Palestine within the period of the Persian, Greek, Greco-Roman, and Roman periods, we do have some information about certain other communities situated there, such as the Samaritans, the Qumran Covenanters, and early Jewish Christian sects, for example.

These communities were not mutually isolated, and they occasionally interacted with one another. Their relationship to one another was not always peaceable and mutually accepting. Where we do have primary evidence, it at times supports the opposite hypothesis. On the other hand, both artifactual, scriptural, and literary-historical material indicate that the Jews of necessity interacted with foreigners in the Macedonian (and other) Greek, Greco-Roman, and Roman non-Jewish world. They may well have interacted with more peoples and states in the Ancient Near East than we realize, but we cannot ascertain this with any degree of certainty. Problems arise in understanding these Jewish communities and their interaction among themselves and with foreigners because much of our data do not always report the specific information we seek. This does not mean that this information is not inherent in the available texts and artifactual remains. Rather, it is frequently there, and we must "exegete it."

Aside from the works that treat the Jerusalem Temple state itself, we have some material that helps us to know about the Samaritans; some that helps us to know about the Qumran Covenanters; and some that helps us to know about the followers of Bar Kochba, the leader of the revolt with which our study ends. We also have the great body of early rabbinic literature that treats the Temple state as the rabbinic "theological" state's linear predecessor. But the Rabbinates themselves did not evolve in a linear manner, and there were sectarian factions within their camp. It is thus meaningful that rabbinic literature presents itself as having an antecedent theological and sociocultural unity, and it does so in such a way that even when it acknowledges differences within its own camps, it still depicts an ideal that there was and always had been a unified normative Judaism.

There is a century and a half between the Persian period and the rise of the Hasmonaean family. Nevertheless, we do not have any primary historical literature treating the Yahwistic community in Judah and Jerusalem during this period. This does not mean that this information had been forgotten. Various Jewish circles had a knowledge of the major historical events and international developments that occurred during this time. This is attested to by such works as the book of Daniel, especially chapter 11, the *Damascus Document*, and statements in a few other second-century B.C.E. writings, such as Ben Sira (Ecclesiasticus), as well as by the first-century C.E. works of Josephus. All of these works must be considered secondary because they were composed later.

This lack of what we would consider primary works is not due to the absence of literary activity in Yahwistic circles, even those in Judah and Jerusalem. A great amount of biblical and deutero-canonical but not specifically historical literature comes not only from the Persian period but also even later. In fact, some scholars think that the greatest portion of the canonical text, including major portions of Genesis through 2 Kings, comes from the Second Temple era, that is, after 538 B.C.E..

We have more extant literary-historical information for the Hellenistic era, with which we begin our study, through the Second Jewish Revolt, with which we close it, although there is no all-encompassing work that deals with the entire period. We have the major accounts—(the *Antiquities*, but also the *War*, the *Life*, and the *Contra Apion*)—of the sometime Jewish historian, sometime Roman apologist Josephus, which are focused on Jews and on Jewish Palestine from the beginning through the period of the First Jewish Revolt, as well as the major accounts in 1 and 2 Maccabees. Information also comes from Greek and Roman historians. Because the Roman world outside of Palestine is often not seen as relevant to understanding what transpired in Palestine, Roman writings have often been ignored. This precludes incorporating into the analysis of events data that shed light on how Rome viewed her sociocultural and historical interactions with others. These interactions, however, must be used in conjunction with the eastern data to lead to a balanced understanding of Rome's role in Jewish Palestine. Moreover, although Roman literature may only incidentally mention Jews or Jewish Palestine, these sources do provide data that allow us to see how Jews and Jewish Palestine fared under their Greco-Roman hegemons.

While there are a number of Greek and Roman authors upon whose works we draw for particular material, there are only a few of major significance for any part of the period we study. Most important are Josephus (noted above), Polybius, Marcus Tullius Cicero, Livy, and, to a limited extent, Tacitus. Polybius was a second-century B.C.E. pro-Roman historian of

Greek origin, who wrote his *History* so as to show by what means Rome fulfilled her fate and destiny of becoming the ruler of the world. Despite the Greek Polybius's *pro-Roman bias*, his analysis of events is in many cases determinative for our understanding of the history of Rome's interaction with the East. Cicero, the oratorical "giant" and patriot, even when he was not politically astute, lived and wrote during the mid–first century B.C.E. Although he was serving the ideology of the party he so dearly loved, the *Optimates* (Best Men), his political orations and letters, in spite of his partisan position, give invaluable data about Rome and its world. In particular we find evidence concerning Rome's treatment of those under Roman suzerainty, about the exercise of Roman domestic law—both civil and criminal, which do not always seem to be distinct from one another—and Roman understanding of international law, particularly as to how it pertains to the interaction between different nations, thereby suggesting how Rome itself could govern the world, and so on. Livy is often discounted because he is late and an ideologue. As a first-century B.C.E.–first-century C.E. Roman historian, Livy wrote his *History of Rome: From the Founding of the City* after Augustus had brought about his new world order, with himself (Augustus) as *princeps* (that is, first among equals or at least ideologically so). Moreover, Livy was in the service of Augustus, and his great opus had as its intent the advancement of Augustus's own teleologically defined self-image. Livy intended his work to show that all of the histories of Rome was fated to occur as it did so as to bring about the Principate of Augustus. Finally, there is the first-century C.E. historian Tacitus. In his *Annals*, he tells us virtually nothing about Jewish Palestine, and in his *Histories* he tells us so little about it that it too can be construed as virtually nothing. On the other hand, in both works, Tacitus tells us so much about Rome under the emperors that we can understand something of the nature of how Rome ruled.

There are yet other Roman or Greco-Roman writers who contribute a fact here and the description of an event there. They are of lesser historical importance, in general, and frequently of lesser reliability than even Tacitus—who does seem to get his underlying facts right even when his bias and his propensity to "yellow journalism" so color his presentation that the reader does not want to believe him but finds he must do so. In any case, although it is a given that we must be extremely careful in analyzing even the major (non-Jewish) Greco-Roman writing precisely because we are often extracting data that were not included so as to illustrate either the relationship of the Greeks or the Romans to the Jews of the Temple state, we must also be careful to account for the authors' respective ideological bias toward Rome itself or toward the individual parties at Rome.

There is yet another problematic in studying the history of Jews in

Palestine, and particularly in the Temple state, during the Hellenistic era through the Second Jewish Revolt. The extant literature does not clearly note and depict the interaction of that state with Rome until a far later period than when it actually commenced. Reconstruction of some of that interaction is possible, however, because the literature does remark upon it in an obfuscated manner. Given the nature of the literature, this is not surprising. The difficulties in understanding the kind of events in the Temple state that emanate from this lack of direct reference to Rome are compounded by the fact that the Greco-Roman literature that survives does not pay attention to Jewish Palestine, except when it figures into either Greek or Roman history in an important or active manner.

At any rate, the difficulty caused by the lack of what either those in antiquity or we could construe as a history of Jewish Palestine containing primary sources (other than 1 and 2 Maccabees and Josephus's *Antiquities* and *War,* which themselves are not primary but secondary sources for most of the periods they cover) causes grave problems in reconstructing what really happened.

When, in 538 B.C.E., the Judahites were permitted to return to Judah (in the Persian province [satrapy] known as "Across the River") the newly emerging Temple state came into being as a "chartered" state, subject to priestly rule. At first this newly chartered state, like the remainder of the region, was subject to Persia, but subsequently, in what is called the Hellenistic era (beginning in 333 B.C.E.), it and the rest of Coele-Syria became subject to the Macedonian Greek states, first under Seleucid dominion, then Egyptian. It remained in Egypt's hands from 301 B.C.E. until it was regained by the Seleucid monarch in 200 B.C.E.

One remarkable characteristic of the period in question, particularly of the Hellenistic era, is that an offshoot of another type of "chartered state," the Greek city-state, began to be established in the East, including Palestine. These city-states were largely populated with hellenized local populations rather than, or at least more than, with Hellenic people. The chartered Greek city-states were governed apart from, and independent of, the territorially defined region that constituted what we think of as "Jewish Palestine." The latter itself consisted of more states, including Temple states, and regions than that of the Temple state of Judah and Jerusalem. (Nevertheless, for convenience, we shall refer to Judah and Jerusalem as *the* Temple state.) There were states in Jewish Palestine that were neither part of the Temple state nor Greek city-states. Other "Jewish" states, such as that of the Samaritans (which was also a Temple state), for example, had not been established, patterned on, or chartered as a Greek city-state. Those given citizenship in the city-states were Greek, or they were hellenized Greek (that is, assimilated native) people. Such citizenship was highly prized, as it entitled its holders to certain rights and privileges that were otherwise unavailable; at the same time it placed certain obligations on them. Although it is ideologically predicated that real Jews—that is, Yahwists—could be represented as a unified entity that would not have any part in the rights, privileges, or duties of these city-states, this is historically invalid.

Toward the beginning of the period in which the Temple state had come under the suzerainty of the Seleucids, it also came under the hegemony of Rome (196 B.C.E.). At least it did so from the Roman perspective. This does not mean that the Seleucid monarch, Antiochus the Great, accepted this Roman hegemony over what he deemed his dominion willingly. It may be of great importance to realize that when he had been defeated by Rome (190/189 B.C.E.), he may not even have acknowledged it publicly. This lack of acknowledgment would, of course, affect his relationship with those still subordinate to him. We do not have data to know just how he reacted. But we do have evidence, both literary (primary) and exegetic (secondary) based on the nature of historical events, that supports the belief that the people in the Temple state were well aware of the meaning of Roman foreign policy for them. Moreover, it is clear that some sectarian groups used it to their own advantage in their interaction with their Seleucid hegemon. Nevertheless, we do not have the day-to-day (or even year-to-year) type of knowledge of the way in which the geopolitics of this pyramidal type of rule, whereby the Temple state was subject to the Seleucid monarchy, which was itself subject to Rome, affected the Temple state and its development.

As we shall see, it was exactly this pyramidal relationship that allowed Judas Maccabeus to obtain a diplomatic relationship with Rome (ca. 161 B.C.E.) and thus gird up his newly won right to rule the Temple state (see 1 Maccabees 8). Once this relationship (called an *amicitia,* "friendship") had been negotiated, Judas and his state became a Roman client—a relationship that characterized Rome's interaction with foreign states just as it characterized the Roman aristocracy's interaction with lower-class (plebeian) Romans themselves. Polybius shows that all parts of the known (i.e., civilized) world had been brought under Roman control. This was accomplished by a single effort, the oneness of which is itself discernible. Moreover, the fixed period of time in which it occurred shows a beginning and end, each of which is clearly set and notable (Polybius III.1.4–5).

Being a client of Rome was useful to the Temple state. It gave its people specific standing in the Roman geopolitical world. So Rome's hegemony and subsequent suzerainty within the pyramidal relationship, whereby the Seleucid monarch was subject to Rome and the Hasmonaeans were subject to both but also had recourse to either, gave the Hasmonaeans a degree of protection from their Seleucid master. This relationship was basic to the Hasmonaean dynasty's continued interaction with both the Seleucid kings and the Romans. It was also basic to the intervention of Pompey the Great in the dispute between Hyrcanus II and Aristobulus II over the kingship. It was Pompey's understanding of what was required of him as the holder of *imperium maius* (rather great power) or even *imperium infinitum* (unlimited power) in the East, rather than the greedy desire to add a new subject to Rome's dominion, which resulted in his taking of Jerusalem in 63 B.C.E. So, although we like to think of the Temple state as having won freedom from the Seleucid monarchy when the Jews in their revolt celebrated a victory and cleansed the Jerusalem Temple of its "pagan" profanation (generally assumed to be 164 B.C.E.), this is not historically valid. The Temple state remained subject to the Seleucids. But it took on new internal rulers: the Hasmonaean dynasty, beginning with Judas Maccabeus. It does not matter that the early Hasmonaeans did not take the title "king": they ruled as if they were kings, and later Hasmonaeans took that title.

At first the Romans permitted the Hasmonaeans to hold a client kingship, whether or not they called themselves kings. This was Rome's preferred method of extending its dominion, and Rome only took on the responsibilities of direct rule—that is, annexation (physical or territorial provincialization)—when given no other choice. Basically, it was cheaper and easier for the Roman Senate to allow others to do their work for them. Rome did not interfere in the Temple state's expansion, we presume because no Roman interests were threatened thereby. However, when the succession in the Hasmonaean dynasty led to civil war (65–63 B.C.E.), Rome had to intervene and eventually to take on the responsibility of direct rule. But the Romans got rid of this onerous chore when circumstances in Jewish Palestine and in Rome made it feasible to do so. The Romans designated a new client kingdom, with Herod the Great placed in charge (40 B.C.E.) and finally made king (38 B.C.E.). But when the Herodian dynasty also became factionalized, the Roman *princeps*, Augustus, who had long since been accorded almost unbounded power, divided their kingdom into separate kingdoms, annexing only part of it under direct Roman rule (4 B.C.E.–6 C.E.). Ultimately, however, Rome had to annex the remainder of Jewish Palestine, with Augustus consolidating major portions of what had been Palestine under the new Roman province of Judea (6 C.E.).

Despite ideology to the contrary, the Romans did not willingly rule their empire directly. This is even the case after the establishment of the Principate (the Roman Empire [three dates are given for this: 30, 27, and 23 B.C.E.; each is in some way correct, and historians differ as to which is the best choice since each represents a major grant of power to Augustus. This has been well discussed in works devoted to Roman history, and in any case is beyond the scope of our study]). So when it was expedient, under the Emperor Claudius, Rome reestablished the province of Judea as a client state under a new Herodian dynasty (40 C.E.). This too failed, and its failure was part of the lengthy antecedents of the First Jewish Revolt, which led to the fall of the Temple (70 C.E.) and the end of the Temple state (73 C.E.), although not of Jewish Palestine itself save when that land is defined ideologically as under the sovereignty of those who claimed to be the successors in a chain emanating from Moses. Clearly then, although the ruler of the Temple state changed from time to time, and there were client kings for the greater part of its existence during the Hellenistic and Roman eras, there was hardly a time in which it was independent in the modern sense of the term.

To understand the relationship of the Temple state to its hegemons or suzerains, we must understand something of the nature of the religion(s) practiced in that state and in Palestine as a whole. The Temple state is not to be construed as the only "Jewish" state in Palestine. It was only one of a number of communities in Palestine that practiced some form of Yahwism. This worship of a common deity, however, did not guarantee a commonality of means and practices in which the god was worshiped. Likewise, it did not guarantee a commonality of nationality, ethnicity, sectarian adhesion, or social class and/or affiliation, nor the same level of integration with and/or assimilation to non-Yahwists or to the ways of life emanating from the non-Yahwistic, especially the Greco-Roman, world.

In fact, even within the Temple state itself there were various sectarian and/or social groups. These frequently differed from one another in both societal structure, historical background, ethnicity, and integration with and/or assimilation to non-Yahwists or at least to precepts and ways of life emanating from the non-Yahwistic, especially from the Greco-Roman, world. They also differed in the manner in which they worshiped their common deity. Occasionally, however, there was some type of overlapping, be it societal, historical, or manner of worship. To put this another way, the commonality of the Yahwistic faith—where such commonality existed—was not usually sufficient to form a societal juncture bridging the differences between the different groups. This is not absolute, however, since on occasions, such bridges were joined. At times, the differences between these groups were such that they could not be classified as being different sectarian factions within one nation, that of Jewish Palestine, but rather they were different nations living in Palestine and sharing a common but differently practiced Yahwistic faith.

It is not always easy or even possible to distinguish between various groups in Palestine, and particularly those within the Temple state, because the extant literary data are ideologically slanted so as to portray the citizens of that Temple state as if they were unified in culture and belief, as we have already noted. At times, this slanting is such that some members of that state were treated as outsiders. So those who did not agree with what the author or redactor of the document(s) deemed the "mainstream" socioreligious practices and way of life were depicted as few, as being of radical if not criminal bent, and even as being non-Jews. (We have no way of knowing whether the authors/redactors knew that this was a theo-political ideological perspective or whether they were "true believers.") But, whatever they knew or believed, we must remember theirs is an ideolog-ical rather than a historical perspective.

Likewise we do not know how the changes in boundaries that occurred from time to time affected or even were perceived by those in Palestine, or by their overlords, since most of our data regarding them comes from sources favorable to the Temple state itself (1 and 2 Maccabees, and Jose-phus's writings) or from archaeological data. What we do know is that different areas in Palestine were incorporated into the Temple state at dif-ferent times. So the boundaries differed accordingly. The Persian province Judah, located in the central area of Palestine, was small. During the early Hellenistic era, these boundaries changed, but the state still did not extend beyond the central area. Subsequently, particularly during the Has-monaean era, other regions of Palestine were incorporated into the Temple state, frequently by conquest.

Many of the difficulties inherent in our inability to make the distinctions that are necessary to understand fully the people and the events in which they were involved are compounded by problems in terminology. Al-though some of these problems are modern, many of them are ancient. For example, we call the entire area we are studying Palestine, differentiating between Jewish and non-Jewish Palestine. First of all, the use of the term "Palestine," derived from Roman usage, to describe the land in question prior to Roman times, is anachronistic. It is traditional to use it, and we will also do so. Second, there is a problem in defining what is meant by Jewish Palestine. What we treat as non-Jewish Palestine may not necessarily be non-Jewish or at least totally non-Jewish; and, likewise, what we treat as Jewish may not necessarily be totally so. Third, there is a problem in nam-ing the Temple state. We, like other scholars, speak of the Temple state of Judah and Jerusalem, but sometimes we call it Judah or Judea. However, we must not forget that the Romans called the area that they would even-tually incorporate as a province Judea, and this cannot be presumed to have had the same boundaries in earlier times.

There is a great difficulty in the use of the term "Jewish," and the atten-dant specification of the land as "Jewish Palestine." Traditionally, scholars refer to all but the Greek city-states (*polis* [sing.], *poleis* [pl.]) that arose in Palestine during the Second Temple era as "Jewish Palestine," and to the

people in the Temple state or who those who dwelled elsewhere but ad-
hered to the cult practiced in Judah and Jerusalem as "Jews." However,
Yahwists who were not part of the Temple state of Judah and Jerusalem but
lived in Palestine are also referred to as Jews. This is in line with the way
in which we customarily translate the respective Greek and Latin terms de-
noting Judeans.

We use the term "Yahwistic" to refer to those who worshiped Yahweh-
Elohim, that is, the Lord God, by whatever title he may be called. It does
not matter whether those worshipers lived in or outside of the land that is
anachronistically called Palestine. (We will retain that denotation for two
reasons: first, because it causes no confusion, and second, because the borders of the various states that constitute Jewish Palestine, and particularly
those of the Temple state, varied during the course of their history.) One
group, that of the Samaritans, actually moved their state (from Samaria to
Shechem), whereas others had states or communities that were carved out
of existing states and territories by various hegemons or suzerains.

The terms "Jew" and "Jewish" are, generally speaking, problematic. For
the greater part of the period in question, the term "Jew" is primarily neither an ethnic nor a religious term, although it was frequently used as such.
Rather it is a term that denotes or merely connotes a person's or group's
place of origin as Judean. Even this is complicated by the fact that some
Yahwists who did not dwell in Palestine were defined as Judeans or Jews.
This practice often denoted the prejudice of "outsiders," for example, various Greek and Roman authors, be they historians or even poets. It also frequently denoted the prejudice of those "insiders" who wanted to advance
their own ideological precept that there was a mainstream or "normative"
type of Yahwistic worship that extended throughout the Diaspora, and
that this practice always corresponded to what was defined by certain factions or even a specific faction within the Temple state. Commonly, however (as attested by the need for the Christian movement, once it came into
existence, to define itself as the New and the True Israel), various Yahwists,
rather than calling themselves Jews, referred to and defined themselves as
the Sons of Israel or Israelites. These latter classifications are older denotations for those who joined together in the worship of Yahweh. What is
meaningful is that they never ceased to be used as a type of self-definition.

It is imperative, therefore, to distinguish between the different types of
Jews or Judeans living in Palestine. What is most difficult is that many foreigners classified certain but not all Yahwists as Jews or Judeans, wherever
they lived. For example, we know that the Flavian (Roman) Emperor
Domitian (ruled 81–96 C.E.) determined people's Jewish status by the presence of circumcision, as both the poet Martial and the pseudo-historian
Suetonius have shown. That is, by the Flavian Principate, which began un-

der the rule of Vespasian in 69 C.E., Jewish status, allegedly noted for taxation purposes, was dependent on circumcision, not on Yahwistic worship per se or on having historical antecedents in Palestine. Not all Jews were circumcised, just as not all Jews accepted the version of scriptures that led to what we now treat as canonical in the Masoretic tradition.

We stress, therefore, that when the term "Jew" is applied to those who had roots in the Temple state, it does not matter whether they lived in that state or elsewhere or whether they thought of themselves as adhering to that state's cult. What is important is how people defined themselves and how they were defined by others. So whereas "outsiders" might refer to the people as Jews or Judeans, the people generally considered themselves Israelites, but this did not classify them as an ethnicity (Greek: *ethnos*) as we would define that term today.

In this book we will use the term *ethnos* as it was used in antiquity. Many scholars frequently misinterpret Roman literature, thinking that *ethnos* was sometimes treated as the equivalent of the Latin term *gens*, which means "a major group (clan) of several families really or supposedly descending from a common ancestor" (*EDRL* 482), but is just as often used to denote a nationality as that term is now understood. So, for instance, the Judahites as an entirety may be so denoted, but so may the Jews of Judah and Jerusalem, and so may the Samaritans, and others. Even subgroupings within these nationalities may also be classified as *gentes* (Latin pl. of *gens*). But as it is generally used, the Greek category *ethnos* is closer to the Roman category "tribe" (Latin: *tribus*), which at first was a territorially delimited classification, but which later partially lost its territorial demarcation.

The term *ethnos*, then, denotes a "number of people living together, company, body of men," and so on (*LSJ*), and after Homer it also took on the meaning of a "nation" or "people" (becoming the equivalent of the Greek category denoted by *laos*), which leads to confusion when dealing with the distinction between a territorial nation and a sphere of influence or an area over which a Roman magistrate exercised power. In fact, *ethnos* is often the equivalent of the Roman term *provincia* (*LSJ*), which is not restricted to a territorial usage but frequently represents a magisterial assignment.

Most important, *ethnos* denotes a "class of men, caste, tribe" or order, such as orders of priests as opposed to the entirety of a priestly cast. But it can also denote the entirety of a priestly cast or a priestly association. Moreover, it is not limited to what is devoted to the sacred. So it also denotes other, secular types of associations and guilds that may or may not be tied into trade. What the term *ethnos* does not mean is "race," although it is frequently incorrectly translated as such, particularly when it is viewed as the equivalent of the Greek term *laos* (which also does not mean "race").

The term *ethnos* had, therefore, a different meaning—both denotation and connotation—than does the term "ethnicity" today. This meaning was localized. Often it represented a political or theo-political faction. This usage as such came into practice because such factions had some type of clan or tribal allegiance that was thought to be derived from their "common worship of a divinity as a special protector of the *gens* and common cult ceremonies" (*EDRL* 482). So, for example, a scholar responsible for collecting and annotating Greek inscriptions has defined the term *ethnos* as "a class of men who have a common mode of living defined by duty and civil condition" (*OGIS* 90 line 17 [the Latin term *victus* not only denotes "a common mode of living" but also denotes "eating together"]). Like the Latin *gens*, the *ethnos* was political in nature. Hence, the term *ethnos*, as used during the period we are studying, is a legal term rather than an anthropological one. It denotes a group or community that is bonded together for governance and/or religious or obligatory purposes. Therefore, it is important that the Jews as an entity comprised more than one *ethnos*, including the priestly orders or *ethnoi* (pl. of *ethnos*), even when certain *ethnoi* thought of themselves as constituting all Jews and therefore as *the Ethnos of the Jews*.

On that account, although most scholars call various people Jewish, and they talk of Second Temple Judaism, we stress that this appellation must be scrutinized whenever it is used. This is particularly the case because three of our most important literary sources, Josephus and 1 and 2 Maccabees, use the term "Jew" (actually they use the term "Judean") to refer to one culturally and theologically delimited people, sometimes called the *ethnos* of the Jews. But sometimes they refer to the *ethnos* of the Jews in such a way that it is clear that they envision that *ethnos* as itself broken down into differing *ethnoi* in accordance with the varied denotations of that category in antiquity. In any case, these separate *ethnoi* that form the *ethnos* of the Jews also could include one particular group that was given the same name as the larger constituency: *ethnos* of the Jews.

The term *princeps* (first among equals) rather than emperor is used to designate Augustus's rank. Although the latter term, "emperor," is a title that had traditionally been accorded a victorious Roman general, its later use to designate the ruler of Rome is anachronistic during the early Principate. So when Augustus did assume that title, incorporating it into his name, it still reflected its honorific-military origins.

CHAPTER 1

The Jewish Community
under Ptolemaic and Seleucid Rule

Alexander the Great, Hellenization,
and Ultimately Rome

The Hellenistic era in Jewish Palestine, as elsewhere in the eastern world, began with Alexander the Great's conquests. Hellenism itself (that is, the taking on of Greek ways, culture, and the Greek language), however, did not really begin to develop in those lands to any great extent until the end of the fourth century B.C.E., when Alexander's former generals, the so-called Diadochi ("successors"), had established their rule in the East. The nature of the respective societies they "founded" placed a premium on being Greek (a Hellene) or, in some cases, being Greek-like (hellenized). At one time it was thought that hellenization was limited and in some realms hardly encouraged at all by the Macedonian Greek monarchs or by those who were Greek by birth rather than hellenized. We now know that this is invalid. Hellenization was widely pervasive. It was resisted or possibly simply ignored only by certain classes or groups of people, particularly the urban masses along with the serfs or peasants in various outlying areas and backwater regions.

When the Hellenistic era began, it was necessary for someone who wished to be thought of as hellenized to speak Greek and participate in the gymnasium and other Greek institutions. Eventually it was only demanded that a person speak Greek, so it became easier for a non-Greek person to be treated as Greek. There was great incentive for people to become hellenized, whether or not participation in the gymnasium and other Greek institutions were requisite conditions. Most important, hellenization allowed non-Greeks to fit into or, more often, to advance within the governmental class of the newly forming societies.

Whatever the basis for hellenization, not only major realms such as that of the Seleucids but also small kingdoms and states became hellenized. For example, even in Ptolemaic Egypt, despite propaganda to the contrary, hellenized natives played a role in government, albeit not a major one. Clearly there was far more hellenization in the Jewish Temple state than 1 or 2 Maccabees or even Josephus openly acknowledged. In fact, the extent to which hellenization occurred anywhere in the eastern world depended on the valuation of that status by those who sought upward mobility—the "trickle up" factor—and on the need to incorporate native talent by those who sought to administer the state—the "trickle down" factor. The importance of hellenization for trade was not nearly as significant an issue as was the politically motivated seeking of status. Nonetheless, trade played its own role in the assimilation of non-Greeks into the Greek world.

When there is documentation that allows for something like a full-blown depiction of life—early in the second century—of the Judean community that formed a Temple state, often referred to as Judah and Jerusalem or simply as Judah or Judea, that community appears as a minor entity in the general Hellenistic world. Nevertheless, it must not be construed as a "backwater community." A degree of sophistication, particularly in Jerusalem, is obvious to whoever reads Josephus. It was certainly obvious to the author of Ecclesiastes, who rails against it, albeit without specifically naming the object of his wrath. Neither the size nor the status, be it that of a province or a client state, of Judah and Jerusalem argues against the sophistication or the hellenization of those in Jerusalem.

After the Restoration, Judah formed a part of the Persian province (satrapy) called "Across the River" (*'aber nahara*, or Trans-Euphrates) by the Persians as well as by Ezra-Nehemiah. Judah was a small region in the central area of Palestine. With the commencement of the Hellenistic era, Judah and Jerusalem were still under foreign domination, but now they were subordinate to the Macedonian Greek rulers, not to the Persians. For most of its history from the Restoration onward, the Temple state was not free as we would construe that status. All of Palestine, including the "free" Greek city-states, owed allegiance to the respective Greek city-state or to whatever monarch that had chartered them.

Concomitant with Rome's rise to power after the successful conclusion of the Second Punic War (the Hannibalic War) in 202 B.C.E., the political and socioeconomic machinations between the various groups of Jews, particularly those of the Grecophiles (who may or may not have been limited to the aristocracy), became more important than they had previously been. This importance was amplified by the newly found status of the Temple state after 196 B.C.E., when it, like the rest of the Hellenistic world, fell under Rome as an additional (not a replacement) hegemon if not suzerain. In other words, there was now a pyramidal relationship, whereby Judah and Jerusalem were subject to Rome as well as to their Macedonian monarch, whether or not they or their Macedonian monarch admitted it. By this time those Macedonian Greeks, who had become subordinated to Rome *de facto* albeit not *de jure*, willy-nilly became subordinated to Rome—acting as their "protector"—insofar as Rome was concerned (Polybius III.1.4–5). This factor became basic to Roman ideology, which stressed Rome's role as protector of Greek "freedom" *(patrocinium libertatis Graecorum).*

So it does not matter whether this subordination was already in effect and acknowledged. For example, Polybius (II.11.5–15) shows that the people of Corcyra, Apollonia, and others as well had accepted Roman protection, and Epidamnus, Issa, and others came under Roman protection during the third century B.C.E. Livy (e.g., XXXVI.4.1–3; XXXVII.3.9–11) shows that Egypt, which, like a number of other states had been sending envoys, gifts, and even promises of aid in war to Rome, and which was following the dictates of the Roman Senate as it had done for some time prior to 196 B.C.E., and which had also been rewarded by Rome for its attentive attitude (Livy XXXVII.3.11), was clearly a Roman client state. This suggests that wherever and whenever possible, at least up until 168 B.C.E. (with the defeat of Perseus at Pydna) or possibly 146 B.C.E. (with the burning and salting of Carthage and Corinth), although possibly even until the beginning of the Empire, the Romans did adhere to their own ideological representation of the relationship between themselves and their client kings, whereby it was the "everlasting custom of the Roman people to augment the eminence *(maiestas)* of allied kings with every honor" (Livy XXXVII.35.8 [all translations of Livy are by Sara R. Mandell]). This of course refers to those clients or presumed clients who understood Rome's *Realpolitik* and, therefore, did not give offense to their "patron."

Rome ultimately waged a terrible war with Antiochus the Great. (Technically there was only one war since there was only one declaration of war [in 191 B.C.E., Livy XXXVI.1.5, 2.1–2, 3.7–12]. The Romans were precluded by their religious beliefs from fighting a war that had not been declared according to religious stipulations.) The Romans did not see what had transpired as two separate wars (Livy XXXVI.51). Rather they viewed it as two conjoined wars: one for Greece and Europe, which caused the second, for Asia. Because ideology and reality were not yet one and the same, this was construed as a war against a sovereign, not a rebellion of a subject against his Roman suzerain. Rome's purpose in going to war with Antiochus was to bring about in reality the hegemony that the Romans had already established in principle in the "Isthmian Doctrine" (Polybius XVIII.46.13–15; Livy XXXIII.33). Livy delineates Hannibal's alleged viewpoint, which is clearly a historically valid perspective, namely, that the Romans would be "striving for dominion over the entire world" when war broke out in Asia (Livy XXXVI.51.5). So, in accord with this aim and ideology, Livy presents the consul Manius Acilius as stating:

> Then Asia and Syria and all the richest kingdoms as far as the rising sun will open up to Roman Rule. What (territory) then will be

missing [from our domain] so that we cannot establish our boundaries, (stretching) from Gades to the Red Sea at the Ocean that (itself) bounds the earth, and so that every human community cannot
venerate the Roman name, second only to the gods. (Livy
XXXVI.17.14–15)

Exactly what Livy's Hannibal predicated was accomplished in actuality.
It came about not only when Antiochus not only suffered defeat at Magnesia in 190 B.C.E. but also with the humiliation of the terrible peace
Rome imposed, at Apamaea, in 188 B.C.E. (Livy XXXVIII.38). Antiochus
was deprived of that part of his kingdom that lay beyond the Taurus
Mountains (Livy XXXVII.55.5–6; XXXVIII.38). By virtue of the actuality
of acquiring Rome as a suzerain, he was no longer totally free to exercise his sovereignty with impunity even in that part of his kingdom that
he was permitted to control. What is most important for understanding
events in Judah and Jerusalem is that the Romans wanted or rather pre-
tended that they wanted "all the cities that are in Asia to be freed just as
all Greece had been freed" (Livy XXXVII.35.10). Accordingly, they set
this ideological precept as part of the peace terms offered to Antiochus
in 190 B.C.E., because they knew he would fight rather than accept it. Antiochus, who would have made peace as an equal, was thereby forced to
go to war against the Romans, who could then justify their own hegemony over the monarch of such a great empire. They were able to bring
Antiochus to the position they wished, diminishing his empire at the
same time as they made him a Roman client, whether he wished it or not
(Livy XXXVII.45.14).

It is important to understand that, at this time, a political entity such as
a state or a city-state could be free and yet subject to another state. In Greco-
Roman antiquity "free" does not mean what we today would construe it
to mean. Rather, it denoted a status of nominal freedom, a status granted
by a state's overlord. It does not however even hint that the state in question was no longer subordinated to that same overlord. Frequently the
freedom a state enjoyed was compounded by an additional type of freedom: that of exemption from external taxation. This latter freedom was
generally categorized as "immunity," a status that was also granted by a
state's overlord. Even this freedom from taxation was relative since there
were certain types of monies that were due the hegemon of "free" or "free
and immune" states. Thus it represented freedom from certain types of
taxation.

In any case, this new Hellenistic-Roman context was the product of the
confrontation and blending of the East (the Persian and national cultures),
with the West (the invading Macedonian version of Greek culture). The latter was itself being altered by, at the same time as it was altering, Roman

culture. The inauguration of this new state of affairs represented by Macedonian-Greek hegemony officially began with the conquest of Alexander the Great. This conquest, for Syria-Palestine at least, marked the end of ancient times and the dawn of domination by the "Classical" Western civilizations of Greece and ultimately Rome. But the hegemony by the latter, that is, Roman rule, although in actuality a continuation of an old state of affairs, may ideologically be deemed an inauguration of yet a new state of affairs as represented by Roman supervision. The commencement of Rome's hegemony in the East officially began in 196 B.C.E., when Flamininus issued the Isthmian Proclamation (Polybius XVIII.46.5; Livy XXXIII.32.5) and put into effect the Isthmian Doctrine (Polybius XVIII.46.15; Livy XXXIII.33), which became the basis for Rome's dominion in the eastern world. According to the Isthmian Proclamation, Rome became the protector of all Greeks dwelling in both Europe and Asia. Those who heard the proclamation, according to Livy (XXXIII.33.7), interpreted it as meaning "all Greek and Asian cities were given liberty." There is no indication that they had to live in a *polis,* although we may assume that it was characteristically Greek to do so. Thus, Livy's report suggests a basic misunderstanding that is actually representative of subsequent Roman policy. This can be seen in Livy's (XXXIII.34.5) report regarding what has been called the Isthmian Doctrine. Here Flamininus and his ten-man advisory board (*decemviri*) told Antiochus's representatives that "all Greek cities everywhere should exist in peace and freedom." It is important that the Isthmian Doctrine actually arose from the Roman Senate, not from Flamininus. The Senate passed a decree (*Senatus Consultum:* decree of the Senate) as to how the peace with Philip was to be applied in Rome's foreign policy. This decree of the Senate held that it was its (that is, Rome's, and therefore the Senate's) prerogative "to organize the affairs of Greece, and to secure Greek freedom" (as noted by Polybius XVIII.44; Livy XXXIII.30). In effect, this gave Rome the right to protect Hellenes anywhere.

What is noteworthy is that the Isthmian Doctrine afforded Rome's clients or other types of subjects less protection than the Isthmian Proclamation had given, but it still allowed them some protection. At the same time, it gave Rome no less leeway to extend its "protectorate." In particular, it allowed Rome to grant diplomatic instruments (*amicitiae:* friendship) to city-states or other types of states that were still subject to foreign kings or monarchs, with or without the permission of those monarchs. The state that was granted a Roman diplomatic instrument was thereby made to feel that it had a powerful "protector." Frequently, however, the state did not realize that no matter what legal terminology the Roman Senate used in its diplomacy, anyone under Rome's protection was actually a Roman client, which was something of a masked vassalage. After the Senate changed a state's *amicitia* into a *societas et amicitia* (alliance and friendship) for its own convenience, as it ultimately did with all *amicitiae* it had granted, the client state status became a more open type of vassalage. There is no doubt that this vassalage was thinly disguised so as to preempt the need for Rome to enforce her rule. What is most important is that this came about as a consequence of the Isthmian Doctrine and the decree of the Roman Senate on which it was based. The first tenet of the decree of the Senate (Livy XXXIII.30) was that all Greek cities in both Europe and Asia were to have *libertas* (freedom) and *autonomia* (autonomy). That is, they were to be free, while under Rome's protection. At the same time they had the right to live under their own laws, again while under Rome's protection. It must be stressed that neither freedom nor autonomy meant then what they mean today. Protection was a "two-edged sword." It was valuable when needed, but it reduced those who had it to some type of vassalage.

So "Greekness" is very important in understanding the Jewish Temple state's place and role in the Hellenistic and the Hellenistic-Roman worlds, and it is particularly important in understanding that state's relationship to Rome after 196 B.C.E. Similarly, it matters that there had been Greek influence in Palestine well before 196 B.C.E. Despite the official commencement of the Hellenistic era with the eastern ventures of Alexander the Great, Greek influence in Palestine had begun well before the last third of the fourth century B.C.E. Archaeological data suggest that commerce between the Greek world and Judah had begun by the eighth–seventh century B.C.E. or perhaps earlier. What Alexander's conquest did was merely to effect a change of the Temple state's suzerain. It removed a Persian sovereign who used Aramaic as the language of governance and imposed a Macedonian sovereign who used Greek as the language of governance. What the Isthmian Doctrine did was to impose over the entire ancient Near East, including the Temple state, a Latin-speaking, and most often a Latin- and Greek-speaking, politically factionalized sovereign, whose parties respectively reverenced or scorned "Greek" and the Greeks. This sovereign used Greek as the language of governance, no matter what the preference of any allegedly dominant faction or theologically sectarian group within the state.

There were theological changes as well. Several centuries earlier, under Cyrus the Persian, various gods and religious practices of the people of the nations in his domain were treated with respect. In the Cyrus Cylinder, Cyrus brags that he returned the icons that used to "live" in the sanctuaries prior to their destruction; he established "permanent sanctuaries" for those icons, and he restored the people who once lived in the sacred cities whose icons he returned. Moreover, except for Cambyses, the same was true of Cyrus's successors. But it was particularly characteristic of Darius

I (522–486 B.C.E.), who as part of his benevolent religious policy (as noted in Ezra 6) enabled the Judahites, or those of the Judahites restored by Cyrus, to rebuild their Temple. (We must not presume that all the Judahites in exile in Babylon left there and returned to Palestine at the time of the Restoration.) In fact, although the newly restored Judahites (now the Judeans/Jews) had first been given permission to build their Temple by Cyrus, this had been interrupted during the reign of Cambyses. It was Darius who permitted the Jerusalem Temple to be rebuilt.

The Macedonian monarchs, insofar as the extant data informs us, did not seem to pay attention to the religious practices of those under their dominion save when those practices were baneful to the state or to the monarchy. Some seemed to have some respect for those natives who became hellenized, whereas some did not; and, in fact, some may not even have encouraged hellenization. (Until recently, for example, it was believed that the Ptolemaic rulers of Egypt discouraged it. Now we know that this is untrue.) Generally speaking, none of the Roman factions or parties, whose political maneuvers greatly affected senatorial policy in the Roman world, had any respect for either eastern natives who abided by their own culture or those eastern natives who became hellenized. Nevertheless, the Romans did follow through on their policy of using the very existence of hellenized people and states to justify their exercise of power over them so as to advance their own ideological and geopolitical ends. They did so under the guise of protecting all Greeks everywhere, as expressed in the Isthmian Doctrine.

Pre-Alexandrian Greek Influence

Greek influence in the eastern Mediterranean including Palestine was not a phenomenon that suddenly burst on the scene with the conquest of Alexander the Great in 333 B.C.E. In about 738 B.C.E. during the reign of Tiglath-pileser III, an Assyrian official in Phoenicia wrote to his master that Ionian Greeks were raiding coastal cities (text ND 2370; see *Iraq* 25 [1963], pp. 76–77; *CAH* III/3, p. 15). Early Greek settlements along the northern Syrian coast, at such sites as Al Mina and Tell Sukas, probably date from the eighth century, if not earlier. Significant but not numerous references to Greeks appearing in Assyrian and Babylonian texts indicate that they were widespread in the East both as raiders and as captives. So it is not surprising that the Egyptian pharaoh Psammetichus I (664–610 B.C.E.) relied strongly upon Greek as well as other mercenaries in his military forces. Egypt at this time and subsequently was a haven for Greek traders as well as soldiers of fortune. There is evidence that Greeks fought on behalf of both Egypt and Babylon at Carchemish in 605 B.C.E.

From the seventh century B.C.E. on, Greek mercenaries, traders, and even tourists became significant in eastern Mediterranean life. Greek conscripts and, later, mercenaries played an important role in the Persian military, and Greek doctors practiced at the Persian court. The Greek language may have become as widely read as it was spoken, but this is purely speculative. On the other hand, there was a bilingual heritage among the eastern Greeks. Those who participated in the Persian governmental enterprises in their own *poleis* learned Aramaic, the lingua franca that the Persians used to govern in the West. Herodotus, who knew both Greek and Aramaic (he was from a family of the bureaucratic level at Halicarnassus) traveled in the mid–fifth century in Egypt, Phoenicia, Babylonia, Judah, and other parts of the Persian Empire. He was able to talk with people, because in all these places he found persons able to communicate mainly in Aramaic, but frequently in Greek as well.

Despite widespread assumptions to the contrary, Palestine was not untouched by Greek influence, even as early as the eighth century B.C.E. But subsequent to that time, both Persian and Egyptian forces that passed through and bivouacked in Palestine certainly included Greeks. Their influence remained whether or not they themselves did, as the fourth-century Yahud coins (minted in imitation of the Attic drachma) themselves suggest. Judahite soldiers probably served alongside Greek troops in Neco's armies during the late seventh century. Judahite soldiers certainly served in the same garrison as did Greeks at Elephantine, an island on the first cataract of the Nile used as a defensive fortress, from the early fifth century B.C.E. onward. At various times in the fourth century, contingents of Greek troops were stationed in Palestinian coastal towns.

Merchants, even more than soldiers, were the ancient bearers of culture, establishing and relying upon continuing and mutually beneficial relationships. Palestine, particularly the portion that until 722 B.C.E. had formed the northern state of Israel, lay along the major trade routes that linked not only Egypt, Phoenicia, Syria, and Mesopotamia but also South Arabia and the ports on the Mediterranean coast. Archaeological excavations show that there had been trade from the eighth century onward, as we have already noted, with an increasing amount of Greek pottery evidenced throughout Palestine from the sixth century onward. And this alone testifies to the vigorous trade between the East and the Aegean.

The Phoenicians, who had long had contact with the Greeks, were strongly influenced by and adopted many aspects of Greek culture and became its disseminators in the region. Those areas in Palestine most open to Phoenician influence, the coastal region and Galilee, were probably most touched by unmediated Greek influence. The demand for Greek merchandise even led to the production of local imitations. Early postexilic biblical texts know the Greeks (Yavan) primarily as traders (Ezek. 27:13–19; Isa.

66:10; Joel 3:6). Judean coins, from at least as early as the fourth century, were strongly influenced by Greek coinage. They bear the Hebrew word *YHD*, written in archaic Hebrew script, and the figure of the Athenian owl as well as of a bearded, helmeted God. Glyptic art on seals and other items as well as statuettes reflects strong and direct Greek influence. To say that Alexander the Great did not introduce Greek culture into Palestine but found it already there is historically accurate. It would be misleading, however, to overemphasize this fact, particularly since Hellenistic culture was decidedly different from the various forms of Greek culture that preceded it.

Alexander's Conquest

With Alexander's decisive victory over the Persian forces under Darius III (336–330 B.C.E.) at the Battle of Issus in 333 B.C.E., a new chapter opened in Near Eastern history. After humiliating the Persian army and capturing most of the royal family, Alexander moved down the eastern Mediterranean coast, cutting off the Persian naval forces from their home ports. Tyre, with its offshore island base and strong naval support, put up a determined but desperate resistance. After seven months the city fell, the island having been joined to the mainland by a causeway. Gaza resisted but succumbed more quickly, and Alexander marched triumphantly into Egypt. The Egyptians offered no opposition but greeted him as a liberator from their hated Persian masters. The pharaonic title "Son of Amon-Ra" was conferred upon him by Egyptian priests. Alexander reciprocated with respect for the Egyptian gods and with the same consideration for the native Egyptian leaders that he showed all native leaders in his effort to bring about world unity, under his own dominion.

In 331 B.C.E., Alexander marched out of Egypt, headed east, and smashed the newly raised army of Darius III at Gaugamela, east of the Tigris. In flight, Darius was killed by one of his own officials. Persepolis, the capital of the Persian Empire, was taken, looted, and its royal palace burned. Diodorus (XVII.70–72), a late and occasionally trustworthy Sicilian historian, has preserved an account of the Macedonian looting of the city. The city held enormous hoards of gold and silver that had been collected as taxes and tribute by the Persians but which had then been stored in the royal treasury and thus removed from circulation (see *HW* 20–21). With his triumph, Alexander declared himself the successor of the "Great King" and pushed forward to subdue the remainder of his newly acquired kingdom. In the next six years, the Macedonian forces moved eastward to the Indus Valley, although remaining within the old boundaries of the Persian Empire. Returning to Babylon by way of southern Persia, Alexander died there on 10 June 323 B.C.E., just before his thirty-third birthday.

CHART I. The Early Hellenistic Period

Assassination of Philip and accession of Alexander (336 B.C.E.)
Beginning of Alexander's invasion of Asia (334)
Battle of Issus (333)
Alexander rejected Darius's peace offers (332)
Siege of Tyre (332)
Alexandria founded in Egypt (331)
Destruction of Persepolis (330)
Death of Alexander in Babylon (323)

Ptolemaic Rulers	*Major Events*	*Seleucid Rulers*
323–283 Ptolemy I Soter		
	Seleucus recovered Babylon (312)	312–281 Seleucus I Nicator
	Defeat of Antigonus at Ipsus (301)	
	Founding of Antioch on the Orontes (300)	
283–246 Ptolemy II Philadelphus Soter		281–261 Antiochus I
	First Syrian War (274–271)	
		261–246 Antiochus III Theos
	Second Syrian War (260–253)	
	Zenon's tour of Palestine	
246–222 Ptolemy III Euergetes I	Callinicus	246–226 Seleucus II
	Third Syrian War (246–241)	
	War between Seleucus and Antiochus Hierax (241–235)	
	Seleucus campaigned against Parthians (231)	
		226–223 Seleucus III Ceranus
222–204 Ptolemy IV Philopator		223–187 Antiochus III the Great

Fourth Syrian War
(219–217)
Ptolemaic victory at
Raphia (217)
Alliance of Hannibal of
Carthage and Philip
of Macedonia (215)
Antiochus campaigned
in the East (212–205)

204–180 Ptolemy V Epiphanes

Antiochus campaigned
in Asia Minor (204–203)
Possible pact between
Antiochus and Philip V
against Ptolemy V
(203–202)
Fifth Syrian War (202–200);
Antiochus conquered
Coele-Syria and Palestine
Isthmian Proclamation (196)
Peace between Antiochus III
and Ptolemy V (195)
War of Rome against
Antiochus III (192–188)
Antiochus III defeated at
Magnesia (189)
Treaty of Apamaea (188)

187–175 Seleucus IV
Philopator

180–145 Ptolemy VI Philometor

Heliodorus visited Jerusalem

175–164 Antiochus
IV Epiphanes

Jason appointed high
priest (about 174)
Menelaus replaced Jason
as high priest (about 171)
Ptolemy VIII Euergetes II
challenged his brother
Ptolemy VI for joint
rule (170)
Sixth Syrian War
(170–168)
Antiochus IV

Ptolemaic Rulers	Major Events	Seleucid Rulers
	campaigned against Egypt on two occasions Jason's uprising against Menelaus (probably 169) Antiochus attacked Jerusalem and looted the Temple (probably 169) Seleucid forces took over Jerusalem (168 or 167)	

Alexander and the Community in Judah and Jerusalem

No detailed and reliable account of the initial encounter of the Macedonian invaders with the Yahwistic community in Judah and Jerusalem is extant. In a highly legendary story, Josephus (*Ant*. XI.326–39) reports that Alexander was greeted, after some hesitation, by Jaddua, the ornately robed high priest, and his subordinates, who presented the monarch with the community's word of capitulation. Josephus claims that Alexander then visited Jerusalem, offered sacrifice in the Temple, and read the book of Daniel in which his conquest had been predicted. This tradition, greatly embellished in rabbinic sources, as well as the legend about Alexander's removal of the bones of Jeremiah to the newly founded Egyptian city of Alexandria to guard it from snakes and crocodiles, at least displays no evidence of conflict between Greeks and Yahwists. At most, it suggests that the transition from Persian to Greek rule went smoothly for the Jerusalemite community.

Tradition has it that Alexander, without visiting Jerusalem, accepted and left intact the political and religious structures and privileges that the Jews had enjoyed under the Persians. Josephus says that when the high priest requested of Alexander

> that they might observe their country's laws and in the seventh [the sabbatical] year be exempt from tribute, he granted all this. Then they begged that he would permit the Jews in Babylon and Media also to have their own laws, and he gladly promised to do as they asked. And, when he said to the people that if any wished to join his army while still adhering to the customs of their country, he was ready to take them, many eagerly accepted service with him. (*Ant*. XI.338–39)

Alexander and the Samarians

The situation was quite different in the province of Samaria. Initially, perhaps before or during the siege of Tyre, Samaria submitted and sought to ingratiate itself with Alexander (*Ant.* XI.321–22). The Samarian ruler, Sanballat (III?), contributed eight thousand troops to Alexander's forces. Shortly thereafter, perhaps while Alexander was in Egypt and following the death of Sanballat, the city, for unknown reasons, rebelled and burned alive Andromachus the Greek prefect over Syria (reported by Curtius Rufus; see *GLA* I.447–49). Either Alexander or Perdiccas, one of his commanders, destroyed the city. The recent discovery of legal and administrative Aramaic papyri, bearing dates from about 375 to 335 B.C.E., along with some two hundred skeletons (the estimated number of skeletons has varied) of persons of varying age in a Wady Daliyeh cave, eight and a half miles north of Jericho, is testimony of an attempted but futile flight of leading citizens from the city.

A Macedonian military colony was settled on the site. Archaeological data from Samaria include structures reflecting Greek style and testify to a Greek reconstruction of the city. According to Josephus, Sanballat requested and was granted permission from Alexander to build a new Yahwistic temple. His narrative reports that Manasseh, a brother of the Jerusalemite high priest Jaddua, had married Nikaso, the daughter of Sanballat (III?), governor of Samaria (*Ant.* XI.302–3). Such intermarriages were a common feature of the time (*Ant.* XI.312). At the insistence of his son-in-law, Sanballat proposed to build a temple on Mount Gerizim which would rival that of Jerusalem and to install Manasseh as high priest. When plans to secure such permission from Darius III were interrupted by Alexander's invasion, the latter was implored with the request to which he acceded (*Ant.* XI.306–12, 321–25), being assured by Sanballat that it would be to the king's advantage "that the power of the Jews should be divided in two, in order that the nation might not, in the event of revolution, be of one mind and stand together and so give trouble to the kings as it had formerly given to the Assyrian rulers" (*Ant.* XI.323). Unfortunately Josephus provides no description of the temple's actual construction.

Since the Jerusalemite-Samaritan schism played an important role in the later history of both Second Temple Yahwism and rabbinic Judaism, a summary of what can be known about the relationship between these two religious communities (Jerusalemite and Samaritan), both of which were situated in Palestine, prior to the end of the fourth century B.C.E., seems in order. (We use "Samarian" to refer to the political entity of the province of Samaria and "Samaritan" to denote the Yahwistic religious community and adherents.)

1. The Samaritan and the Jerusalemite communities shared many common features of Yahwistic faith. Samaritan theology, however, like its northern Israelite predecessor, did not share, and in fact strongly rejected,

the special emphasis on Jerusalem as the chosen city. Likewise, it did not acknowledge, and again strongly rejected, the house of David as the chosen dynasty. Both of these precepts, which characterized much Jewish theology within the Temple state of Judah and Jerusalem, were inheritances of those Judahites (the children of Israel from Judah) who had gone into exile in Babylon in 586 B.C.E. They were not part of the inheritance of the northern Israelites.

2. Both communities were accepted as authoritative religious entities by many Yahwists. After the Elephantine temple (that is, the Yahwistic temple at Elephantine, an island in the Nile on which there were Yahwistic mercenaries who considered themselves "Judahites" or Jews) was destroyed, for example, an appeal was made to both Jerusalem and Samaria for authority to rebuild the sanctuary (about 410 B.C.E.).

3. There was much interaction between the two Yahwistic communities. This is reflected in widespread intermarriage and a common sharing of the Pentateuch, albeit with minor differences, as authoritative scripture. The strict, exclusivistic Yahwists, like Nehemiah, Ezra, the Levites, and their supporters who favored Judean isolation and absolute devotion to their sectarian vision of the Jerusalemite cult, were not representative of all Jews, and certainly not of all Yahwists, some of whom were monotheistic but not exclusivistic, and others who were neither monotheistic nor exclusivistic.

4. According to Josephus (*Ant*.XI.312, 322, 340, 346), many of the founders and adherents of the new cultic center on Mount Gerizim were Jews from the Temple state, among whose number were many priests. He reports that "the elders of Jerusalem" opposed Manasseh's high post in the Jerusalemite priesthood and, with Jaddua's consent, barred him from the altar (*Ant*. XI.306–9). At issue was Manasseh's marriage to someone who was not part of the Temple state.

> But, as many priests and Israelites were involved in such marriages, great was the confusion which seized the people of Jerusalem. For all these deserted to Manasseh, and Sanballat supplied them with money and with land for cultivation and assigned them places wherein to dwell, in every way seeking to win favour for his son-in-law. (*Ant*. IX.312)

Behind such inner-Judean conflicts obviously lay some of the same tensions that had plagued the community since the return from exile.

5. Presumably, the Yahwistic cultic center in Samaria was destroyed when the city was attacked by the Macedonians. With the establishment of a Macedonian military colony at Samaria, Shechem, an old and sacred

Yahwistic holy place at the foot of Mount Gerizim (see Deut. 11:29), became the primary religious center of northern Yahwists. The new Yahwistic temple, probably constructed early in the Hellenistic period, was built on Mount Gerizim, a sacred mountain with its own theological and mythological associations. Archaeological evidence demonstrates that the old city of Shechem was rebuilt early in the Hellenistic period, and remains of the new sanctuary apparently have been found on Gerizim underneath the ruins of a Roman-age temple.

6. Even the construction of a new Yahwistic temple on Mount Gerizim did not produce any irrevocable break between the southern religious community of the Temple state of Judah and Jerusalem and the northern religious Samaritan Yahwistic community. As late as the second century B.C.E., outsiders could refer to the two as members of a single religious group (see 2 Macc. 5:22–23; 6:1–2; see the quote from *Ant.* XI.323, above), and even the northerners could be referred to as "Judeans," that is, "Jews."

The Impact of Alexander's Conquest

With Alexander's conquest of the East, Syria-Palestine became demonstrably part of the Hellenistic world. The consequences of this new situation were many and significant.

1. Again, a new culture, emanating from foreigners, was superimposed upon the region. Even after Alexander's death, the rulers who succeeded him, the so-called Diadochi, were Greco-Macedonian in origin, although in some instances they continued to intermarry with natives as Alexander had first demanded. For the most part, the conquering Greeks certainly did not immediately amalgamate with the local cultures but considered themselves superior to the oriental "barbarians." (The Greek term "barbarian" denotes one who is "non–Greek-speaking." It does not necessarily have the later and even modern connotation of "noncivilized," and we should not infer from its usage that the conquerors thought the conquered uncivilized. In fact, "barbarian" was often used by Greeks to describe even the most civilized of peoples.)

2. Greek became the new language of governance, commerce, business, and communication. So it replaced Aramaic as the lingua franca of the western part of the Hellenistic Ancient Near East, just as it replaced Akkadian as the lingua franca of the eastern portion. (This does not mean, however, that native peoples ceased to use their own tongues or the respective linguae francae that had been in use prior to the spread of Greek in that capacity.)

3. Along with the staffing with Greeks (or those who took on Greek

ways, that is, became hellenized) of the old administrative structures of the Persians, Greek cities (*poleis*) were established throughout those areas of the East in which they had not previously existed. These cities functioned as both military and commercial centers and, in some respects, were granted favored status. Quite early in the Hellenistic period, cities such as Gaza and Ptolemais (the old town of Acco) along the coast, and Philadelphia, Pella, and Philoteria in Transjordan were established as independent Greek towns (see Map 1).

Most important, the Greek city-state (the *polis*) was organized around certain political institutions and physical features. These included a constitution; a body of youths, the Ephebeion, who were being initiated into young manhood and its concomitant responsibilities; the *gymnasium*, the place of education as well as of athletic events and social intercourse, and courts as well as temples. The city-states were frequently governed under the so-called unwritten law, that is, the *nomos agraphe*.

4. For members of the non-Greek, local population to make their way into and benefit from the new cultural and political conditions, adjustments and concessions had to be made to the new orders of the day. A knowledge of Greek and at least a nominal participation in the dominant culture, that is, becoming somewhat hellenized, were essential.

The Period of Ptolemaic Dominance

When Alexander's sudden and mysterious illness cut short his auspicious career, he had made no plans for a successor and left no real candidate from the family line—only an illegitimate, half-witted half-brother named Philip and an unborn son carried by his eastern, Bactrian wife Roxane. Neither was to rule in his own right. So it is not surprising that both were eventually put to death amid the struggles for power among Alexander's generals, who, for a time, sought to keep alive the unity of Alexander's kingdom and even fought to realize this dream. But the efforts proved futile.

Because of their strategic location, Palestine and the small Yahwistic community nestled in the hills around Jerusalem were sucked into the maelstrom of post-Alexandrian politics. Ptolemy, the Macedonian general who became the ruler, what the Persians had called a "satrap," in Egypt made the recently founded city of "Alexandria beside Egypt" his capital. He then occupied Palestine and southern Syria in 320 B.C.E. He realized, like the pharaohs of old, that control of this area was Egypt's first line of

MAP 1.
EASTERN MEDITERRANEAN SEABOARD
DURING THE HELLENISTIC PERIOD

defense, and that control of the Syro-Palestinian port cities was a major source of commercial wealth.

During the next few years, as part of a more generalized war between the Diadochi, the Macedonian generals who were the successors of Alexander, Ptolemy struggled with the capable Antigonus Monophthalmus ("The One-Eyed") for control of the area. Conditions did not stabilize until after the Battle of Ipsus (301 B.C.E.), which concluded the war between the Diadochi in which various spheres of dominance were determined. The Macedonians Seleucus and Lysimachus defeated the octogenarian Antigonus and his son Demetrius, who were also Macedonians. Since Ptolemy was conspicuous by his absence from the battlefield, Syria-Palestine was assigned to his old comrade-in-arms Seleucus, who also held the territory of Babylonia. Ptolemy, however, following the example of Antigonus and like Cassander in Greece, Lysimachus in Anatolia, and Seleucus in Asia, had assumed the title of king and moved to reoccupy Palestine and southern Syria. The Ptolemaic dynasty was to control the region for the next century, although the house of Seleucus never surrendered its claim to the area. Even though little detailed knowledge about life in the Temple state under Ptolemaic rule is available, there were important developments that had a bearing on the community.

Pro- and Anti-Ptolemaic Factions

Ptolemaic control over the area, always challenged by the Seleucids, tended to create pro-Ptolemaic and anti-Ptolemaic factions in the Temple state community. That is, diversity existed within the community over whether the best interests of the community were served by strong support of the Ptolemies. Josephus reports the following:

> Hecataeus [of Abdera; about 300 B.C.E.] goes on to say that after the battle of Gaza [perhaps in 312 B.C.E.] Ptolemy became master of Syria [but subsequently withdrew to Egypt], and that many of the inhabitants, hearing of his kindliness and humanity, desired to accompany him to Egypt and to associate themselves with his realm. "Among these (he says) was Hezekiah, a chief priest of the Jews, a man of about sixty-six years of age, highly esteemed by his countrymen, intellectual, and moreover an able speaker and unsurpassed as a man of business." (*Contra Apion* I.186–87; see *GLA* I.35–44)

This emigration of pro-Ptolemaic Judeans to Egypt suggests a definite polarization in the Temple state community. The existence of anti-Ptolemaic sentiment in Jerusalem is evidenced also by Josephus's report, allegedly drawn from Agatharcides of Cnidos (second century B.C.E.):

> The people known as Jews, who inhabit the most strongly fortified of cities, called by the natives Jerusalem, have a custom of abstaining from work every seventh day; on those occasions they neither bear arms nor take any agricultural operations in hand, nor engage in any other form of public service, but pray with outstretched hands in the temples until the evening. Consequently, because the inhabitants, instead of protecting their city, persevered in their folly, Ptolemy, son of Lagus, was allowed to enter with his army [probably in 302/1 B.C.E.]; the country was thus given over to a cruel master, and the defect of a practice enjoined by law was exposed. (*Contra Apion* I.209–10; see *Ant.* XII.5–6; see also *GLA* I.106–9)

Moreover, this movement of Jews of Jerusalem to Egypt, noted by Hecatacus, as well as Ptolemy's later need to recapture Jerusalem indicate that there was a strong anti-Ptolemaic party in Jerusalem which sympathized with Antigonus and subsequently with Seleucus. The author of the *Letter of Aristeas* reports that Ptolemy inflicted harsh treatment on the Jews, although the numbers given are probably exaggerated:

> When by a combination of good fortune and courage Ptolemy had brought his attack on the whole district of Coele-Syria and Phoenicia to a successful issue, in the process of terrorizing the country with subjection, he followed the old and established ancient Near Eastern tradition of transporting some of his foes and reducing others to captivity. The number of those whom he transported from the country of the Jews, that is Palestine, to Egypt amounted to no less than a hundred thousand. Of these he armed thirty thousand picked men and settled them in garrisons in the country districts. (*Letter of Aristeas*, 12–13)

Administration of the Region

Numerous changes in the administration of Syria-Palestine occurred during the early Hellenistic period. During the Persian period, the community in Judah and Jerusalem had been under the civil authority of a provincial governor, who was appointed by the foreign administration.

At the same time, it was under the religious authority of the Jewish high priest, who was not chosen at random. Rather he was the scion of a family, in whose line the high priesthood was hereditary. During the Persian era, the high priest was probably approved for the office by the foreign royal administration, as was the case during the Hellenistic era. After Ptolemy's takeover, the office of governor disappeared. Such a condition would have greatly enhanced the role and importance of the high priest, who had been approved for office by the Hellenistic monarch. Alongside the high priest and important priestly families was the *gerousia*, or senate or assembly. This group, probably the forerunner of the later Sanhedrin, had its roots in earlier Persian times when rulers of Judean districts, heads of major families, and wealthy nobles (see Neh. 3:12–27; 4:19) participated in administrative affairs. The *gerousia* was an aristocratic, not a democratically elected, body. Concomitant with this may have been one or more religious senates or assemblies, but this is not certain. If not, it is possible that the political *gerousia* was more a theo-political governing body than a secular one, but this too cannot be ascertained with any degree of certainty.

The Temple state, comprised of Judah and Jerusalem, was incorporated into the highly organized economic administration of the Ptolemies. The community was subject to the system of heavy taxation, royal monopolies, and land lease policy that the Ptolemies maintained. We have little direct evidence about the day-to-day realities of Ptolemaic administration in Palestine. Nevertheless, it can be assumed that many specific features of the administrative system found in Egypt were also operative in modified form in Palestine. These would have included: (1) the division of the region into subunits (*toparchies* and *hyparchies*), and (2) various types of appointed officials, such as finance ministers (the *dioiketoi*) and managers of royal financial affairs (the *oikonomoi*). These officials handled all matters except the military, which was under the charge of an official called the *strategos*. Probably Ptolemaic troops were stationed at various places in Palestine.

A few surviving Greek papyri provide information about administrative affairs in Palestine. A papyrus dating from 260 B.C.E. (see Text 1) contains an official ordinance regarding the registration of livestock and slaves in the area. It clearly illustrates the tight economic control and supervision exercised over the region. It also recognizes the role and importance of informants. The archives of a certain Zenon, an Egyptian officer who traveled through Palestine and Phoenicia between January 259 and February 258 B.C.E., illustrate additionally the economic and administrative conditions in the area. Zenon undertook his supervisory trip at the direction of the chief Egyptian minister of finance and economic affairs.

TEXT 1:
PTOLEMAIC ORDINANCE ON SLAVE
AND LIVESTOCK REGISTRATION

—to the *oikonomos* assigned in each hyparchy, within 60 days from the day on which the [ordinance] was proclaimed, the taxable and tax-free [livestock] . . . and take a receipt. And if any [do not do as] has been written above, [they shall be deprived of] the livestock and shall be [subject to the penalties] in the schedule. [Whatever] of the livestock was unregistered up to the proclamation of [the ordinance shall be free of taxes] for former years, of the pasture tax and crown tax and the other penalties, but from the 2[5]th year they shall pay the sum owing by villages. . . . As for those . . . who make a registration in the name of another, the king will judge concerning them and their belongings shall be confiscated. Likewise,—

Those holding the tax contracts for the villages and the komarchs shall register at the same time the taxable and tax-free livestock in the villages, and their owners with fathers' names and place of origin, and by whom the livestock are managed. Likewise they shall declare whatever unregistered livestock they see up to Dystros of the 25th year in statements on royal oath.

And they shall make each year at the same time declarations and shall pay the sums due as it is set out in the letter from the king, in the proper months according to the schedule. If any do not carry out something of the aforesaid, they shall be liable to the same penalties as those registering their own cattle under other names.

Anyone who wishes may inform (on violations), in which case he shall receive a portion of the penalties exacted according to the schedule, as is announced in the schedule, and of the goods confiscated to the crown he shall take a third part.

By order of the king: If anyone in Syria and Phoenicia has bought a free native person or has seized and held one or acquired one in any other manner—to the *oikonomos* in charge in each hyparchy within 20 days from the day of the proclamation of the ordinance. If anyone does not register or present him he shall be deprived of the slave and there shall in addition be exacted for the crown 6000 drachmas per head, and the king shall judge about him. To the informer shall be given . . . drachmas per head. If they show that any of the registered and presented persons were already slaves when bought, they shall be returned to

them. As for those persons purchased in royal auctions, even if one of
them claims to be free, the sales shall be vaild for the purchasers.

Whoever of the soldiers on active duty and the other military set-
tlers in Syria and Phoenicia are living with native wives whom they
have captured need not declare them.

And for the future no one shall be allowed to buy or accept as security native free persons on any pretext, except for those handed
over by the superintendent of the revenues in Syria and Phoenicia for
execution, for whom the execution is properly on the person, as it is
written in the law governing farming contracts. If this is not done,
(the guilty party) shall be liable to the same penalties, both those giving (security) and those receiving it. Informers shall be given 300
drachmas per head from the sums exacted. (*GHD* 95–96)

Moving throughout the area, he checked on local affairs and administrative procedures, dealt with trade relationships, handled disputes, and
looked in on local estates operated by Ptolemaic personnel. Two specific
taxes exacted in Ptolemaic Egypt itself may have been exacted in Jewish
Palestine as well. There was a capitation tax—which was defined as a salt
tax because of the great value of salt in antiquity—doing double service as
a census. There also was a property tax.

The Zenon archives make it clear that Palestine and Phoenicia were being exploited to the fullest through both taxation and trade. The impact of
Ptolemaic bureaucracy seems to be reflected also in the advice offered by
the author of Ecclesiastes:

If you see in a province the poor oppressed and justice and right violently taken away, do not be amazed at the matter; for the high official is watched by a higher, and there are yet higher ones over
them. But in all, a king is an advantage to a land with cultivated
fields. (Eccl. 5:8–9)

Under the Ptolemies, collection of taxes in Palestine and the surrounding
region was carried out through a system of tax farming. This is often overlooked because this same system was subsequently adopted by, and is now
treated as characteristic of, the Romans, frequently without consideration of
its antecedents. Under this system, during the period of Ptolemaic control,
the right to collect taxes in the various districts and cities was annually sold
at auction in Alexandria to the highest bidders (*Ant.* XII.155, 169, 175). Subsequently with the commencement of direct Roman taxation, which occurred at a considerably later date than that of "indirect" Roman rule, it was
sold at Rome to the highest bidders from among the equestrian businessmen.

Such a policy of tax collection had several results. First, the process produced a situation that developed into a practice in which the Ptolemaic administration cooperated with wealthy and aristocratic families in the various districts. Furthermore, tax farming pretty much required, or at least allowed, the tax farmers not only to inflate the tax requirements to please the Ptolemies but also to collect above and beyond the official requirements in order to line their own pockets. As a result, there developed an increased burden of taxation upon the local population. But this was not the only ramification of tax farming. The auctioning process itself created competition and animosity between various wealthy and aristocratic families desirous of the posts. Moreover, the animosity and ill feelings of the heavily taxed population were directed not only toward the Ptolemaic government but also toward those natives who were tax farmers and thus considered to be arms and instruments of the foreign oppressors. So ultimately, tax farming contributed to the factionalization within the Temple state and most likely all of Jewish Palestine.

Family Struggles for Dominance

Struggles for political and economic power among major Judean families within the Second Temple era community or communities either in or having ties to the Temple state can be seen during Ptolemaic times. The Zenon papyri make frequent reference to Tobias, a Transjordanian Yahwistic sheik who headed a military colony in Ammanitis. He may have been a descendant of Tobiah the Ammonite of Nehemiah's day (see Neh. 6:17–19; 13:4–9). Tobias was strongly pro-Ptolemaic and served, with a garrison of Macedonian and Yahwistic, including Judean, troops, as one of the defenders of Ptolemaic territory against the Arabs. Tobias frequently sent gifts of various sorts to both the Ptolemaic monarch and his finance minister (see Text 2).

Josephus has preserved a long narrative about the descendants of this Tobias (*Ant.* XII.154–241). Joseph, one of the Tobiads and a nephew of the high priest Onias II, had taken up residence in Jerusalem. When Onias II failed to pay the Ptolemies "the tribute of twenty talents of silver which his fathers had paid to the kings out of their own revenues" (for the office of high priesthood? *Ant.* XII.158), Joseph led local opposition against the high priest. The latter may have been tardy in making payment to the Ptolemies, anticipating a Seleucid takeover of Palestine, which seemed almost certain until the surprise Egyptian victory over Antiochus III at Raphia in 217 B.C.E. Joseph succeeded, at a public assembly, in having himself made the official representative of the Jews at the Ptolemaic court, replacing Onias II in this capacity. In addition, after borrowing money from friends in Samaria, he outbid all of his competitors and secured the office of tax

TEXT 2:
LETTERS OF TOBIAS

Tobias to Appollonios, greeting. As you wrote to me to send [gifts for the king in the] month of [Xandikos], I have sent on the tenth of Xandikos [Aineias] our agent bringing two horses, six dogs, one wild mule bred from an ass, two white Arab donkeys, two wild mules' foals, one wild ass's foal. They are all tame. I have also sent you the letter which I have written to the king about the gifts, together with a copy for your information. Farewell. Year 29, Xandikos 10.

To King Ptolemy from Tobias, greeting, I have sent you two horses, six dogs, one wild mule bred from an ass, two white Arab donkeys, two wild mules' foals and one wild ass's foal. Farewell. (Address) To Apollonios. (Docket) Tobias, about the items sent to the king, and the copy of his letter to the king. Year 29, Artemision 16, at Alexandria.

Tobias to Apollonios, [greeting]. If you and all your affairs are flourishing, and everything else is [as you wish it], many thanks to the gods. I too have been well, and have thought of you at all times, as was right.

I have sent to you Aineias bringing a [eunuch] and four boys, houseslaves and a good stock, two of whom are uncircumcised. I append descriptions of the boys for your information. Farewell. Year 29, Xandikos 10.

Haimos. About 10
Dark skin. Curly hair.
Black eyes. Rather big jaws
with moles on the right jaw.
Uncircumcised.
Audomos. About 10.
Black eyes. Curly hair.
Nose flat. Protruding lips.
Scar near the right eyebrow.
Circumcised.

Atikos. About 8
Light skin. Curly hair.
Nose somewhat flat,
Black eyes, scar below
the right. Uncircumcised.
Okaimos. About 7.
Round face. Nose flat.
Gray eyes. Fiery complexion.
Long straight hair. Scar on
Forehead above the right
  eyebrow.
Circumcised.

(Address) To Appollonios. (Docket) Tobias, about a eunuch and four boys he has sent to him (Apollonios). Year 29, Artemision 16, at Alexandria. (*GHD* 97–98) collector for all of Syria and Phoenicia. With a contingent of Ptolemaic troops, brutal tactics, and probably no little avarice, Joseph showed himself an efficient administrative official.

Joseph's activity had several consequences for the Temple state. His challenge of the high priest Onias II led to a division of power and authority between the Tobiad and Oniad families. Joseph used his office and influence to accumulate great wealth and purchase influence. "Having thus collected great sums of money and made great profits from farming the taxes, he used his wealth to make permanent the power which he now had" *(Ant.* XII.184). His work demonstrated that wealth and power could be acquired through adventuresome undertakings in power politics and by breaking with routine procedures. Finally, his work and the wealth resulting from the flow of money he channeled into Jerusalem brought the city more into the mainstream of Ptolemaic and Hellenistic life. In evaluating Joseph's life, Josephus's source, in flattering fashion, reports that he "had been an excellent and high-minded man and had brought the Jewish people from poverty and a state of weakness to more splendid opportunities of life during the twenty-two years when he controlled the taxes" *(Ant.* XII.224).

The Adoption of Greek Customs

The adoption of Greek culture and lifestyle permeated many aspects of life in Judah and Jerusalem as well as other places in Palestine and wherever else Yahwists lived. Hellenistic bureaucrats, soldiers, and traders made contact with virtually all levels of Yahwistic society in the Temple state during Ptolemaic times. In addition, Greek cities and military colonies were sufficiently widespread in Ptolemaic times to radiate the influence of Greek culture even to those regions where it might not be expected. Several Greek cities were located in Transjordan and along the Phoenician coast, where Greek culture was enthusiastically welcomed. The way in which power was exercised in the military colonies can be exemplified by the Ptolemaic threat made to the uncooperative Onias II. "The king sent an envoy to Jerusalem to denounce Onias for not rendering the tribute, and threatened that, if he did not receive it, he would parcel out their land and send his soldiers to settle on it" *(Ant.* XII.159).

The adoption of Greek culture by Yahwists in Judean society as a whole, including the Temple state, is attested in various ways. It can be seen in the use of Greek for personal names, correspondence, and business contracts, as well as the appearance of numerous Greek loan words in Hebrew. But it is also attested to by the involvement of segments of Jerusalemite society in the larger Ptolemaic world. This involvement, when practiced to the fullest extent, included among other things the practice of *epispasm*. This was a painful operation to reverse circumcision that would allow participation in the activities in the gymnasium. It can also be seen in the appearance in the political and social milieu of such individuals as Tobias and Joseph. These men were sometimes willing to achieve their goals without scruples, moral convictions, or fidelity to allegedly traditional ways. So they set themselves up to be, and they often were, used by the foreign rulers to advance their own ends.

The aristocratic and wealthy families in Judah and Jerusalem would have been most exposed to Greek customs. Moreover, they would have been most able to separate themselves from their customs and practices while still remaining Yahwists. Additionally, they would have been the most capable of turning good relationships with Greek-speaking non-Yahwists or even those Yahwists who were not part of, or did not have affinities with, the *Ethnos* of the Jews into wealth and power.

The Period of Seleucid Dominance

The closing years of the third century witnessed the demise of Ptolemaic control over Palestine. Egypt at the time was ruled by Ptolemy V (204–180 B.C.E.; he was still a minor, having been born about 210 B.C.E.). The Seleucid monarch was Antiochus III, surnamed the Great (223–187 B.C.E.), an energetic and competent ruler. Antiochus was "a man who both conceived great projects and possessed courage and capability to execute his designs" (so Polybius V.34).

Antiochus III and the Jewish People

Shortly after assuming the kingship, Antiochus (III) the Great almost had Palestine in his grasp before his forces suffered a humiliating defeat at Raphia (217 B.C.E.). For the first time, the Ptolemies used significant numbers of native Egyptians as troops, a move that, Polybius reports, "although acceptable for the present involved a miscalculation for the future. For they [the Egyptians] were elated by the success of Raphia and could no longer endure to take orders, but looked for a figure to lead them as they believed they were now able to fend for themselves" (Polybius V.107.1–3; *HW* 371). Struggle over control of the territory was renewed in 201 B.C.E., after Antiochus had secured his Asian frontier to the border of India and while Egypt was torn by internal strife (Polybius XI.34). The Seleucid army quickly overran the region. Scopas, the Greek commander-in-chief of the Egyptian forces, gallantly counterattacked, reconquered much of southern Syria and Palestine, and stationed a garrison in Jerusalem. Josephus, quoting Polybius, reports that "Scopas, the general of Ptolemy, set out for the upper country and during the winter subdued the Jewish nation" (*Ant.* XII.135; see also Daniel 11:14). Jerome, commenting on Daniel 11.14, states: "During the conflict between Antiochus the Great and the generals of Ptolemy, Judaea, which lay between them, was rent into contrary factions, the one favoring Antiochus, and the other favoring Ptolemy." He further reports that after his initially successful counterattack, Scopas "took the aristocrats of Ptolemy's party back to Egypt." Civil strife, if not civil war, between pro-Ptolemaic and pro-Seleucid factions must have torn at the fabric of Jewish life. This situation probably provides the context for understanding Josephus's statement about the strife within the Tobiad family: "The elder brothers [pro-Seleucid?] made war on Hyrcanus [pro-Ptolemaic?] . . . and the population was divided into two camps. And the majority fought on the side of the elder brothers, as did the high priest Simon [II]" (*Ant.* XII.228).

At Panion, near the source of the Jordan River, Antiochus III defeated Scopas in 200 B.C.E. Two years later Jerusalem was taken by the Seleucids, who were supported by many Judeans "who went over to him [Antiochus] and admitted him to their city and made abundant provision for his entire army and his elephants; and they readily joined his forces in besieging the garrison which had been left by Scopas in the citadel (the *acra*) of Jerusalem" (*Ant.* XII.133).

Peace was concluded between Ptolemy V and Antiochus III in 195 B.C.E., one year after the Isthmian Proclamation and the concomitant Isthmian Doctrine made by the Roman general, Flamininus, representing the will of the Roman Senate. This doctrine was the manifestation of the Roman senatorial policy whereby any eastern nation that had hellenized segments within it became a Roman protectorate. Although the Ptolemies had long since acknowledged Roman suzerainty, the Seleucids had not yet done so. Hence a state of affairs developed in which a Seleucid who rejected the implications of the Isthmian Doctrine was now in control of Palestine. The Ptolemaic ruler had aligned himself to the Seleucids by marriage. Ptolemy V took in marriage Cleopatra, the daughter of Antiochus.

Antiochus III took a rather lenient posture toward his subject people. Consequently, it is not surprising that he rewarded his Jewish sympathizers and supporters with numerous concessions. Josephus reports on a number of privileges that he granted the Temple state, for example (see Text 3). Josephus may have paraphrased Antiochus's orders to his military commander Ptolemy, who had previously been an Egyptian official. But there is no reason to doubt that he has faithfully reproduced their content insofar as his understanding of what constituted the Yahwistic community in the Temple state permitted. In addition to economic assistance and

TEXT 3:
ANTIOCHUS THE GREAT'S
SO-CALLED EDICT OF PRIVILEGES

King Antiochus to Ptolemy, greeting. Inasmuch as the Jews, from
the very moment when we entered their country, showed their eagerness to serve us and, when we came to their city, gave us a splendid
reception and met us with their senate (*gerousia*) and furnished an
abundance of provisions to our soldiers and elephants, and also
helped us to expel the Egyptian garrison in the citadel, we have seen
fit on our part to requite them for these acts and to restore their city
which has been destroyed by the hazards of war, and to repeople it by
bringing back to it those who have been dispersed abroad. In the first
place we have decided, on account of their piety, to furnish them for
their sacrifices an allowance of sacrificial animals, wine, oil and frank-
incense . . . fine flour . . . wheat . . . and salt. And it is my will that these
things be made over to them as I have ordered, and that the work on
the temple be completed, including the porticoes and any other part
that it may be necessary to build. The timbers, moreover, shall be
brought from Judaea itself and from other nations and Lebanon without the imposition of a toll-charge. The like shall be done with the
other materials needed for making the restoration of the temple more
splendid. And all the members of the nation (*ethnos*) shall have a form
of government in accordance with the laws of their country, and the
senate, the priests, the scribes of the temple, and the temple-singers
shall be relieved from the poll-tax and the crown-tax and the salt-tax
which they pay. And, in order that the city may the more quickly be in-
habited, I grant both to the present inhabitants and to those who may
return before the month of Hyperberetaios exemption from taxes for
three years. We shall also relieve them in future from the third part of
their tribute, so that their losses may be made good. And as for those
who were carried off from the city and are slaves, we herewith set them
free, both them and the children born to them, and order their property to be restored to them. (*Ant.* XII.138–44)

concessions, Antiochus's move was an attempt at reparation for a militarily devastated area. This is particularly substantiated by the decree granting the entire community the right to exist as an autonomous priestly *ethnos*, or Temple state, with "a form of government in accordance with the laws of their country."

Antiochus would have viewed that state as subject to himself, even after he had granted it the right to exist as an autonomous priestly *ethnos*, since autonomy did not then mean what it means to us today. During the Hellenistic era, a state could be autonomous and still subject to yet another state, nation, or monarchy, and this was a common geopolitical structure. Moreover, there is no justification for assuming that the "laws of their country" were to be equated with the Mosaic law, be that "law" the written or the unwritten Torah. The anachronistic perspective equating the two would certainly have been considered a true understanding of earlier circumstances by the time in which Josephus was writing. So for Josephus as for the early Rabbinates, Antiochus's grant that the Temple state would be able to use the "laws of their country" for governance would have been interpreted anachronistically as if it were explicit permission to live by some form of the Mosaic Torah and derivative customs and practices.

Likewise, in Josephus's day, the factionalization of both the social and the worshiping Yahwistic community may no longer have been remembered as such. Rather, as we would expect of someone who had lived through the great civil war between different factions of Jews that is generally treated as the first Jewish Revolt against Rome, and who lived to see what that did to his country, this would be viewed from an idealized perspective as a time in which there was unity to the extent that there was one community and one worshiping body of Yahwists in the Temple state. Moreover, both the community and the worshiping body were considered one and the same entity, as is suggested by early rabbinic writings. It is meaningful that these writings take up the attitude of the redactors of 1 and 2 Maccabees respectively. So from this perspective, but only this perspective, those who were not part of that entity were few in number and clearly heretical or even apostate.

Even by the time of 2 Maccabees, the grant of the right to live as a priestly *ethnos* having autonomy was not construed as what it really was: a boon unilaterally given by a suzerain in accordance with established policy. Rather, according to 2 Maccabees, these "royal concessions to the Jews" were the product of negotiation between the *Ethnos* of the Jews and the Seleucids. Therefore, they represented some special and unique type of bequest to the Temple state. If 2 Maccabees is correct—which we doubt because it was not unusual for a Hellenistic monarch to allow a state to be autonomous and live under its paternal laws—such negotiations would have been under the direction of the Oniad high priest Simon II. But if this "grant" were, as is most likely, merely a ramification of Seleucid policy, reflecting customary governance of those under Seleucid control, then clearly Simon II would have been the one to gain by this newly resolved status. But those in the Temple state would have viewed this as a reestablishment of the status it had formerly held under the Persians. So those subject to Simon II's rule as high priest, particularly those who favored the Oniad family, would have attributed the gain of the "restoration" of the Temple state as such to him. In a glowing laudation of Simon, the author of Ecclesiasticus spoke of Simon II as the one

> Who in his life repaired the house,
>   and in his time fortified the temple.
> He laid the foundations for the high double walls,
>   the high retaining walls for the temple enclosure.
> In his days a cistern for water was quarried out,
>   a reservoir like the sea in circumference.
> He considered how to save his people from ruin,
>   and fortified the city to withstand a siege.
>   (Ecclus. 50:1–4)

Simon's energetic leadership demonstrates that the high priest at the time was both the head of the cult and the ruler of the hierarchic state. In other words, both traditional civil and religious authority were in his hand. He was the equivalent of a monarch unto himself. It is not surprising, granted these circumstances, that Simon II was a moving force behind the policy of openness to the Seleucids.

The reasons for the pro-Seleucid policy of Simon II and his supporters were probably numerous: (1) The religious community in Judah and Jerusalem had had strong ties with the Yahwistic Diaspora in the East throughout the Babylonian and Persian periods. Conditions for such relations—pilgrimages, financial contracts, and common language—were more favorable under Seleucid control where both communities were under a common overlordship. (2) Greater autonomy was possible under the Seleucids, who granted considerable freedom in their multinational empire, than under the Ptolemies. (3) The Judean community—primarily rural and agriculturally oriented—was more similar to the mass culture of the Seleucid Empire than to the highly commercial character of the Ptolemaic state. (4) Perhaps recognizing the inevitability of Seleucid control over Palestine, Simon II saw the opportunity of negotiating afresh the relationships between subject power and overlord.

According to Josephus, a second proclamation was issued by Antiochus III in addition to the so-called Edict of Privileges (*Ant.* XII.145–46). This proclamation prohibited any foreigner from entering the enclosure of the Jerusalem Temple. It also prohibited the transportation into the city of unclean flesh (horses, mules, asses, leopards, and so forth) forbidden to the Jews, and the breeding of such animals and the transport of their hides in the city. It established a fine of three thousand drachmas of silver for violation of these prohibitions.

These concessions were more favorable to the priestly aristocracy than to any other group. They granted special privileges to the priests, allowed for the sacred law (obviously as the priests construed it) to serve as a primary legal authority, and restricted trade in Jerusalem to curtail free mercantile operations. (Throughout the Hellenistic and subsequently the Roman world, the control of trade and "trade-guilds," like that of other professions and their respective professional associations, was always in the hands of the suzerain.) This restriction probably was a blow to the interests of the Tobiads, even those who were pro-Seleucid. The concessions indicate that once again the high priest, now represented in the person of Simon II, had become the primary political representative of the religious community before the court of the foreign overlord.

The ancient texts make no reference to the concessions and commitments made by the Jews to the Seleucids. These certainly would have included a recognition of Seleucid authority in the area and a pledge of cooperation in matters economic and military.

Antiochus III and the Romans

Antiochus III's aggressive expansion of his kingdom led him into occasional political alliances with Egypt and cooperative military actions with Macedonia. But eventually he was manipulated by the Aetolians. The latter were trying to stir up a war with Rome (Livy XXXV.12) and to draw Antiochus into their war effort. So it was made to seem as if the Aetolians "had hoped that Antiochus would take possession of Europe" after the Roman armies had left it (Livy XXXV.12.2). Although it is not clear if this is what they really wanted, we do not know if Livy's representation represents Roman ideology or Aetolian guile. This, together with Antiochus's desire to expand his sphere of influence if not his actual kingdom, led him into conflict with the Romans. This conflict may well have been inevitable since once they had defeated Hannibal at Zama Regia in 202 B.C.E., the Romans deemed world domination to be their "manifest destiny." Accordingly, they were conducting their own business at the same time as they were guiding eastern Mediterranean affairs so as to bring this about.

The Roman attitude regarding Rome's manifest destiny was fostered by various Roman client kings, who used it to their own advantage. For that reason, these kings tried to manipulate the Romans into going to war with Antiochus (so, for example, Livy XXXV.13.6–10 describes some machinations on the part of Eumenes of Pergamum). Most likely, the client kings did not have so much love for their Roman overlords that they were trying to get Rome to implement what Rome itself believed to be its manifest destiny. Rather, their actions were grounded in their own personal benefit, whereby their own kingdoms would be extended or at least protected should Rome gain suzerainty over the entire East.

The Seleucid Antiochus, on the other hand, played his own game. He gave his daughter Cleopatra in marriage to Ptolemy V of Egypt, in the winter of 194–193 B.C.E. (Livy XXXV.13.4). Perhaps he hoped that the next Egyptian ruler would be his grandson and thus favorably disposed to the Seleucid power. Perhaps he wished Rome to see that, by virtue of this alliance, he was not a threat to Egypt, which already had an established relationship with Rome. He may not have understood that the Romans interpreted the "crowns" and other gifts Egypt gave to them annually as acknowledgment of Roman hegemony. On the other hand, Antiochus's marriage of his daughter to the Egyptian monarch may have reflected some desire to come to a favorable accord with Rome, which was already Egypt's patron. Perhaps he thought that this marriage would effect that accord and yet allow him to maintain his *status quo ante.* There is no reason to believe that Antiochus did not want to establish favorable relations with Rome. He did not yet realize that Rome was a direct threat to him, and he believed the Romans would limit their "aggression" if he pursued a reasonable foreign policy with them. Moreover, he still thought of himself as Rome's equal. As such, he thought that he could drive the Romans out of mainland Greece by a forceful show of arms, and he also believed that he could harbor, with impunity, Rome's "eternal" enemy, Hannibal.

If his actions reflected political machinations that went beyond a desire to exert dominion in mainland Greece, then perhaps he did not attempt to intrude himself in that arena as a dupe of the Aetolians. But rather, he really believed, particularly with Hannibal "egging him on," that he could bring the Romans to some accord whereby they could divide the world between themselves. Unfortunately, this must remain a hypothetical construct since neither Polybius nor Livy (our major extant sources), who show his actions in Greece as being ill-conceived, suggests that this was his intent.

Whatever he really desired, Antiochus III "hedged his bets." His expressed interest in the mainland was not as adamant as it might seem. For example, he had previously entered into an agreement over the division and control of the Aegean region with Philip V, king of Macedon, during the Second Macedonian War (the war that the Romans waged against Philip and his allies). Philip, who was now allied with and subject to the

Romans, had aroused their anger by supporting Hannibal during the Second Punic War (218–202 B.C.E.). This was a time during which Hannibal was at his best and may well have beaten Rome. So Antiochus III was not only a former ally of Philip but a willing "player" in the feuds between the various political and military alliances that had existed in mainland Greece for some time, albeit forming and reforming themselves in different configurations. We stress that Philip was now subject to the Romans and owed his kingship to them once he had been defeated at Cynocephalae. The Romans, however, would not have forgotten that Philip had previously supported Hannibal, no matter how geopolitically advantageous it was for them to put that memory in abeyance for the time being. Nor would they ignore the fact that Antiochus, who had had dealings with Philip, and who was attempting to invade mainland Greece, now harbored Hannibal.

The sequence of the various, clearly interrelated wars is of importance in understanding the full implications of the war Antiochus III waged against the Romans. Following their victory over the Carthaginian forces, the Romans soon became involved in the war against Philip (the Second Macedonian War). This war really developed as a result of competition and vying for power between two major alliances of Greeks that had formed in mainland Greece. Viewed simplistically, as both Polybius and Livy wished the reader to understand the course of events, the Romans had been drawn into it because they honored their alliances with the Aetolians, who were later to become their enemies. The *causa belli* (as opposed to the *casus belli*) was not even ostensibly political but religious. The ideological presentation of the origins of the Second Macedonian War represents the *causa belli* as the execution of two young Acarnanians, who had violated the Eleusinian Mysteries at Athens. It treats the war as quickly accelerating to the point in which it involved all the mainland Greek city-states.

Whatever the expressed basis for the war, we assume it was economically, politically, and territorially based, and its *casus belli* was the same need for expansion that had caused the various Greek city-states to send out colonies toward the end of the Greek "Dark Ages." Whatever the expressed reason for the Roman entry into that war, we believe it was in support of their manifest destiny, which according to both Polybius (I.3.6–7, 9–10; V.104.3; XV.10.2, 5 et al.) and Livy (XXX.32.2) was already held by the Romans by the end of the Hannibal War (Second Punic War). This is certainly so if both Livy and Polybius are correct in their assessment of the speech that Hannibal and Scipio (P. Cornelius Scipio Africanus) allegedly gave to their respective armies just before Zama Regia in 202 B.C.E. Whatever the real geopolitical machinations and desires behind what the

Romans were doing, they entered the Second Macedonian War in support and at the request of their allies. What is most important is that they already viewed those allies as being under their protection in Greece. When they won this war, not only did they "liberate" Greece from Philip's control but also, in 197–196 B.C.E., they restricted him to his Macedonian territory.

Rome was not the only "foreign" nation to become embroiled in the conflict. Antiochus III had also become involved in the events related to the war, albeit after it had been concluded. He had been enticed into the still "bubbling cauldron" of affairs in postwar (that is, the Second Macedonian War) mainland Greece as a result of the machinations of the Aetolian League. This was a political-military alignment comprising some of the Greek city-states, which sought help from Antiochus against their Roman "liberators." This soon brought about a new and seemingly different war between Rome and the Greeks, which the Romans thought of as the War against Antiochus.

Antiochus III, the Seleucid monarch, responded to the leaders of the Aetolian League and invaded the Greek mainland in 192 B.C.E. He was soon forced back into Asia, where he was subsequently decisively defeated by the Romans at the Battle of Magnesia in 190 B.C.E. In the subsequent Peace of Apamaea (188 B.C.E.), severe terms were imposed upon the Seleucids (see *HW* 265–67). They were forced to give up all of western Asia Minor, to surrender most of their naval fleet and elephants, to send hostages to Rome, to cease recruiting troops from the Aegean lands, and to pay, over a several-year period, an enormous war indemnity—in fact, when correlated in terms of changing monetary values, the largest war indemnity ever imposed in recorded history from the past up till today. From the Roman perspective, one of the most important facets of this, although not included in the articles of peace, was that Antiochus would have to put Hannibal to death. Whether the demand for Hannibal was propaganda so as to forewarn others who might go to war against Rome of the consequences of that action, or whether it was merely something that was set forth so as to satisfy the Roman public, who thought of Hannibal as the "bogey man," who could and would come again, or whether this was merely vengeance is of no importance. It does not even matter if the Roman Senate understood that this was a trivial point, being meaningless in terms of their new geopolitical standing, and if consequently it was demanding Hannibal's execution for propagandistic ends, or if the Senate really believed that it was important to Rome's as well as its own (senatorial) hegemony.

Under the peace articles the Romans granted Antiochus no official action was taken to regulate Ptolemaic and Seleucid relationships. The Romans would not have considered such a stipulation necessary since they thought of themselves as being the hegemon of both nations, as was shown by Popilius's actions during the siege of Alexandria during the next decade. At about this same time, the eastern provinces of Armenia, Parthia, and Bactria rebelled and proclaimed their independence from Seleucid control.

Antiochus III died a year later, while looting a wealthy temple in the old territory of Elam. Hostile propaganda has it that he was seeking funds for his Roman indemnity, but because the indemnity was to be paid in installments, the pressure to pay was not as great as the totality of the reparation would make it seem. So, although it sounds reasonable at first to assume that Antiochus was seeking funds for reparations, he may have had other reasons for the raid on the temple. There is no need to hypothesize some unique event here, particularly since this was not the first temple whose treasury Antiochus had raided. However, his motivation cannot be determined, and it is likely that we will never know why he acted as he did. In any case, the story about his death is no more to be believed than any other story in which an "evil" monarch dies a gruesome death because he harmed some deity.

Tensions in the Judean Community

The high-priestly successor to Simon II was his son Onias III, and the royal successor to Antiochus III was his eldest son Seleucus IV (187–175 B.C.E.). Neither of these men was a dynamic leader. Little is known about the state of relationships between the Judean community and the Seleucid kingdom during the early reign of Seleucus IV. Second Maccabees 3:3 states that "Seleucus, the king of Asia, defrayed from his own revenues all the expenses connected with the service of the sacrifices," although Dan. 11:20 speaks of his sending "an exactor of tribute through the glory of the kingdom."

Internal struggles for power and factional conflicts within the Judean Temple state soon caused direct involvement of the Seleucids in the affairs of Jerusalem. International politics provides one lens through which these struggles may be viewed. In their broadest context, they may be seen as a clash between pro-Seleucid and pro-Ptolemaic factions. In time-honored fashion, the Temple state community—significantly located on the land bridge joining Asia and Africa—was caught in the middle of Near Eastern politics and was forced to respond to external pressures in the hope of making the most of a bad situation.

From a more internal perspective, the clashes may be seen as the struggle of dominant and powerful Yahwistic families for dominance. Ultimately, four important families vied for superiority: the Tobiads, the Oniads, the Simonites, and the Hasmonaeans (Maccabeans). At stake was not only the leadership and authority over the community but also the power to control the financial and tribute-collecting apparatus with its attendant economic gains and privileges. There are four literary sources, not to be aligned with the perspective of the respective families, for reconstructing the history of these struggles, which eventually led to the Hasmonaean triumph:

1. Daniel 11:20–39 contains an outline of the main events but is written as pseudo-prophecy in cryptic language and with apocalyptic coloring.

2. The book of 1 Maccabees, written near the end of the second century B.C.E., contains a reasonably full history of the Maccabean struggles. Unfortunately it contains no detailed exposition of the events before the rise of the Hasmonaeans; rather, it views the conflicts in almost purely religious perspectives and is a document propagandizing for the Hasmonaean family (perhaps so called after an ancestor of Judas Maccabeus and his brothers).

3. The book of 2 Maccabees provides a summary of a five-volume work composed by an otherwise unknown Jason of Cyrene (2 Macc. 2:19–32). While this work provides the fullest treatment of the pre-Hasmonaean situation, it ends before the death of Judas. Moreover, it is characterized by strong theological and supernaturalistic interests, probably added to Jason's narrative by the unknown summarizer.

4. Josephus, in his *Antiquities* and *War*, provides a history of this period but is primarily dependent upon 1 Maccabees and provides little supplementary information.

Foreshadowing the later and more intense conflict in the Jerusalem community was the so-called Heliodorus affair (2 Macc. 3:1–4:6; see Dan. 11:20). The authority and the administration of Onias III were challenged by a certain Simon, the captain or chief administrator of the Temple (for the office, see Jer. 20:1; 2 Chron. 24:11). Second Maccabees 3:4 describes him as a member of the tribe of Benjamin, of which the first king, Saul, had also been a member. This affiliation may have been an ideological fiction used by the writer of 2 Maccabees or his sources to discredit Simon. We must remember that, in the Temple state, the ideology relating to the rule of the Davidic line was basic to its worldview. So the allegation that Simon was a Benjaminite, that is, a member of the tribe of the first and rejected king Saul, would have been a rallying point for those who would treat this tribal allegation as a threat to the established order. Consequently it is particularly important that subsequent references to Simon's brothers, however, imply that the Simonites were a priestly family and therefore not from the nonpriestly tribe of Benjamin. (Old Latin and Armenian texts of 2 Macc. 3:4 associate Simon with the priestly order of Bilgah; see 1 Chron. 24:14.)

Conflict between the Oniads and the Simonites erupted when Simon and Onias argued over the administration of the city market. It may be that Simon sought the office of administrator, although if so, it was to no avail.

Failing to acquire what must have been a second prominent and profitable position, Simon entered into a conspiracy with Apollonius, the Seleucid administrator of Coele-Syria and Phoenicia. Its intent was to accuse Onias of hoarding untold sums of money in the Jerusalem Temple. Onias was denounced before Seleucus IV, who sent Heliodorus to Jerusalem to confiscate the funds. Second Maccabees contains a legendary account of how, by divine intervention, the Seleucid representative was prevented from entering the Temple and taking the funds. After Heliodorus left Jerusalem, Simon sought to blame Onias for the entire episode, continued to stir up trouble, and even had his agents commit murder on his behalf. When matters approached the level of civil war, Onias set out to make a personal appearance before the king—a journey from which he never returned. Clearly, Simon, perhaps in collusion with the pro-Seleucid branch of the Tobiad family, was seeking to wrestle some of the economic and political power from the hands of the Oniads. Also, in all likelihood some members of the Oniad family, including the high priest, had developed or were contemplating a more pro-Ptolemaic attitude.

On deposit in the Temple were funds belonging to the pro-Ptolemaic Hyrcanus, the youngest son of Joseph the nephew of Onias II. If we can trust Josephus, and if Joseph and Hyrcanus really existed, then this youngest member of the Tobiad family had assumed control of the ancestral estate in Transjordan (present-day *Araq, el-Emir*), established an independent sphere of rule, greatly strengthened his residential fortress (*Ant.* XII. 229–34), and may have built a temple in his compound. His money on deposit in Jerusalem suggests that Hyrcanus was able to utilize the banking facilities of the Temple, particularly since there were certainly grounds to Simon's charge that Onias was guilty of being "a plotter against Seleucid government"— that is, of cooperation with pro-Ptolemaic factions (2 Macc. 4:2).

Antiochus IV Epiphanes

Onias III was never able to argue his case before Seleucus. The latter was assassinated by his minister Heliodorus. Seleucus was succeeded on the throne by his brother Antiochus IV Epiphanes (175–164 B.C.E.). The latter, upon returning from his stay as a hostage in Rome where he was well treated and had involved himself in Roman party politics, with the assistance of the Attalids of Pergamum (*HW* 268–69), usurped the crown from his nephews (see Dan. 11:21). This could not have come about without the connivance of certain factions at Rome, who clearly wanted to see a change of ruler in the Seleucid kingdom, possibly to offset the developing Parthian threat. It was characteristic of the Romans to give limited support to (client) kings who would protect the borders of what Rome considered its territorial domain. At the same time, Rome would use whatever means possible to weaken those kings to prevent them from viewing themselves as too powerful and therefore as not needing Rome. (Rome's treatment of Rhodes is illustrative of what happened to those who became "uppity.") So, once Antiochus IV was in power, the Romans did nothing to alter his status as hegemon over his empire, although they clearly limited his external expansion. His relationship to Rome was such that the Romans may have understood that they could control him.

Antiochus IV proved to be an aggressive ruler who shared both the imperialistic ambitions and the frustrations of his father. His aspirations, however, were tempered by numerous problems. The remaining eastern provinces were becoming more independent from Seleucid control, and the Parthians were becoming a serious military threat. In the West, the Romans had long since implemented their designs on the eastern Mediterranean coast and were orchestrating events in their favor. Antiochus IV must have feared that it was only a matter of time before there would be another decisive confrontation with the Romans to whom he had become subordinated. (Whether or not he liked it, they were now his de facto hegemon, both by virtue of the Isthmian Doctrine and by the "peace" granted his father at Apamaea.) What he did not understand was that the Romans preferred to gain their dominion peaceably or by intimidation and would rather not go to war. But if confronted, they would do whatever was necessary to maintain their posture and dominion. As the incident with Popilius Laenas demonstrated (Livy XLV.12.3–6; Polybius XXIX.27), Antiochus IV would come to learn this. Clearly this confrontation was inevitable if he should not abide by the peace terms granted at Apamaea. Internally, the kingdom's financial conditions were in poor shape. The new monarch—who did not initially have the unanimous support of his subjects—was pressed to accept and confiscate funds over and above those raised through taxation and tribute.

It is difficult to know whether the Seleucid king's character and personality may have contributed to some of the problems experienced during his reign. Ancient historians were somewhat baffled by his behavior and could, at times, speak of him not as Antiochus Theos Epiphanes ("Antiochus the God Manifest") but as Antiochus Epimanes ("Antiochus the Mad Dog"). Polybius's description of the ruler and his behavior can be seen in Text 4.

Jason as High Priest

While Onias was seeking a hearing at the Seleucid court in Antioch, his brother Jeshua, who also bore the Greek name Jason, served as deputy in the high priesthood (see 2 Macc. 4:29). With the accession of Antiochus IV,

TEXT 4:
POLYBIUS'S DESCRIPTION OF ANTIOCHUS IV

Sometimes he would slip away from the palace, unnoticed by his servants, appearing in the city at one time here, at another time there, sauntering along in the company of one or two others. Very frequently he could be seen in the workshops of the silversmiths and goldsmiths, where he would chat with the moulders and other workmen and seek to impress them with his love of art. Then he would condescend to engage in familiar conversation with any of the common people he happened to meet, and carouse with strangers of the lowest rank whom he stumbled upon by chance. On learning, however, that somewhere young people were holding a drinking-bout, he would march in unannounced with horn and bagpipe, so that most of them, being frightened by this strange sight, would take to flight. Quite often he would exchange his royal robes for a toga, go to the forum and apply as a candidate for an office. He would then seize some people by the hand and embrace others, asking them to give him their vote, sometimes as if for the office of aedile and sometimes as if for that of tribune. If he succeeded in obtaining the office and was seated according to Roman custom in an ivory chair, he would take note of the contracts signed in the forum and give his decisions in a serious and conscientious manner. Reasonable folk, therefore, did not know what to make of him. Some regarded him as a simple and modest man, while others said that he was mad. He acted in a similar fashion when he distributed gifts. To some he gave dice made of bone, to others dates, whilst another group received gold. When he happened to meet someone whom he had never seen before, he would bestow upon him unexpected presents. With regard to the sacrifices which he ordered to be offered in the cities and the honours to be shown to the gods, he outshone all other kings. As evidence we may point to the temple of Zeus at Athens and the statues around the altar at Delos. He used to frequent the public baths when they were quite full of ordinary citizens, and had vessels with precious perfumes brought to him. When somebody once said to him, "You kings are fortunate to have such ointments of exquisite fragrance," he went the next day, without saying anything to the man, to the place where he bathed, and had a large vessel of the most precious ointment, called *stacte*, poured over his head; whereupon everyone rose and rushed forward to receive a share of this aromatic perfume. But because of the slippery state of the floor, many fell over, amid shouts of laughter, the king himself joining in the mirth. (*History* XXVI.1; see *HW* 269–71)

Jason moved to secure the high priesthood for himself. For the position he offered the new king "three hundred and sixty talents of silver [as annual tribute?] and, from another source of revenue, eighty talents" (2 Macc. 4:8). Antiochus IV was confronted with the option of affirming Onias in the office—but there was question about his loyalty—or of recognizing Jason in the position. The latter, as we have noted, offered sizable funds. The royal appointment of chief priests and even the sale of such offices at public auction seem to have been rather widespread in cities throughout the Seleucid Empire (see *HW* 129–30; *GHD* 216–17).

In addition to the high-priestly office, Jason requested, after offering an additional 150 talents, that he be granted the right (1) to establish a gymnasium in Jerusalem; (2) to create an *ephebeion,* or youth corps, to utilize and be educated in the facility, and (3) to enroll the men of Jerusalem as citizens of Antioch, that is, either to create an independent Hellenistic *polis* (city-state) within Jerusalem or, more likely, to turn Jerusalem into a Hellenistic *polis* (2 Macc. 4:9). Antiochus IV accepted all Jason's offers, and he seems to have granted all his requests.

Jason's effort to transform the Temple state community along Hellenistic lines—or to establish an independent Greek city-state within the boundaries of, but nevertheless apart from, the Temple state—and thus move those factions in Jerusalem that had not yet become hellenized into the mainstream of Hellenistic life (1 Macc. 1:11) not only required the introduction of new institutions into that faction of the community whose life had not yet been brought into conformity with Hellenistic culture and style but also made necessary some "constitutional" type of reform. In sharply critical language, the unsympathetic author of 2 Maccabees reports: "When the king assented and Jason came to office, he at once shifted his countrymen over to the Greek way of life. He set aside the existing royal concessions to the Jews" (2 Macc. 4:10–11). A gymnasium (from the Greek word *gymnos,* meaning "naked") was constructed at the bottom of the citadel in the vicinity of the Temple.

The gymnasium and the *ephebeion* were two characteristic institutions in Greek life and education, and education was one of the distinguishing "Greek forms of prestige" (2 Macc. 4:15). Both books of Maccabees emphasize the enormous attraction that athletics had for Jerusalemite youth, who wore their broad-brimmed hats, a customary part of ephebic attire. The gymnasium seems to have replaced the Temple as the center of Jerusalem's social life. Second Maccabees 4:13–15 notes that even the priests hastened to leave the Temple services to participate in the games in the *palaestra,* the "wrestling grounds." Some Yahwistic youths underwent operations to remove the marks of circumcision (1 Macc. 1:15) so they would be indistinguishable from non-Judeans in athletic contests. (We know from the poetry of Martial, a Roman poet of the Early Empire, that it was also possible to disguise circumcision without an operation. It is impossible to ascertain if this was in practice during the second century B.C.E.)

Jerusalem as a Greek City

"To enroll the men of Jerusalem as citizens of Antioch" in Jerusalem (2 Macc. 4:9) would have been the major and most significant task in establishing Jerusalem as a Hellenistic city. The enrollment involved the determination of the citizenry of the city—who would make up the *demos* of the *polis*. Not everyone was automatically a citizen in a Hellenistic-age Greek *polis*, and Jason and his supporters had acquired the authority to determine which inhabitants would be granted rights and privileges as citizens. Such constitutional changes meant that the "old" royal concessions, granted by Antiochus III, which spoke of "all the members of the nation" (*Ant.* XII.142) and the general thrust of the "Mosaic law" (whatever that really was and however it had been interpreted), with its definition of community members (again however that was defined and interpreted), had to be rescinded (2 Macc. 4:11). Religious conservatives (in the strict sense of the term), Ptolemaic sympathizers, and others out of favor with Jason (perhaps members of the Jerusalem branch of the Tobiad family and their supporters?) or his theo-political precepts, could be disenfranchised. Hence they could at least be partially excluded from the economic benefits of city status. They could also be excluded from membership on the political governing council (*gerousia*) and participation in the educational program of the gymnasium and *ephebeion*.

Several factors are noteworthy in the texts that discuss Jason's "Hellenistic reform" and his attempt to build a bridge between Judah and Jerusalem, and the larger Hellenistic world of the Seleucid Empire:

1. The initiatives for the transformation of Jerusalem into Antioch-in-Jerusalem came from the Jewish community itself.
2. No reference is made to any overt opposition to Jason's moves. Instead, note is taken of the many who supported him (1 Macc. 1:11), support that continued for several years. It is true that when Jason sent 300 drachmas to pay for a sacrifice to the god Hercules at the quadrennial games held at Tyre, the Jewish emissaries had qualms about this and requested that the funds be used instead for the construction of triremes (2 Macc. 4:18–20).
3. None of the texts accuse Jason of altering the cultic Yahwism practiced in the Jerusalem Temple or with prohibiting the normal practices of Judaism.
4. When Antiochus IV later made a personal visit to Jerusalem (in

172 B.C.E.?), "he was welcomed magnificently by Jason and the *polis*, and ushered in with a blaze of torches and with shouts" (2 Macc. 4:21–22). Such a text gives no hint of any strong communal antagonism toward either Jason or Antiochus.

CHART II. The Later Hellenistic Period

Ptolemaic Rulers	*Major Events*	*Seleucid Rulers*
180–145 Ptolemy VI Philometor		175–164 Antiochus IV Epiphanes
	Seleucid forces occupied Jerusalem and turned the city into a military colony (167)	
	Syrian cult introduced into Jerusalem Temple (December 167)	
	Several Maccabean victories (167–164)	
	Death of Antiochus IV (164)	
		164–162 Antiochus V Eupator
	Rededication of the Jerusalem Temple (164)	
	Partition of the Ptolemaic kingdom between Ptolemy VI and Ptolemy VIII	
	Execution of Menelaus (162)	
	Appointment of Alcimus as high priest (early 162)	
	Judas functioned as high priest (162–160)	
		162–150 Demetrius I Soter
	Alcimus reconfirmed as high priest (162)	
	Death of Judas (160)	
	Reassertion of Seleucid authority in Palestine	
	Death of Alcimus (159)	

Interregnum in high-
    priestly post (159–152)

                                152–145 Alexander
                                    Balas (a pretender)

Jonathan appointed high
    priest (152)
Demetrius II killed in
    battle (150)
Jonathan made military and
    civil leader of Judea (150)

145 Ptolemy VII Neos Philopator   146–140 Demetrius II
                                    Nicator

(170)–116 Ptolemy VIII Euergetes II   145–142 Antiochus VI
                                    Epiphanes (a pre-
                                    tender)

Simon appointed governor
    of the coastal plain (145)
Death of Jonathan (143/42)
Simon confirmed as high
    priest by Demetrius II
Antiochus VI killed by Trypho
Independence of the Jews (142)

                                  142–139 Trypho (a
                                    pretender)

Capture of the Akra in
    Jerusalem (141)
Parthians annexed
    Babylonia (141)

                                  139–129 Antiochus
                                    VII Sidetes

Antiochus VII reaffirms
    Judean independence (139)
John Hyrcanus succeeded
    Simon (135)
Antiochus VII killed in war
    against Parthians (129)

                                  129–126 Demetrius II
                                    Nicator

                                126–125 Seleucus V

Ptolemaic Rulers	Major Events	Seleucid Rulers
116–80 Ptolemy IX Soter II		125–113 Antiochus VIII Grypus
114–88 Ptolemy X Alexander		116–95 Antiochus IX Cyzicenus
		111–96 Antiochus VIII Grypus
	Aristobulus I succeeded Hyrcanus (104) Establishment of Hasmonaean monarchy Alexander Jannaeus succeeds Aristobulus (103)	
		After 96, numerous claimants, to the throne
	Demetrius III invaded Hasmonaean territory (88) Tigranes, king of Armenia, took possession of the Seleucid kingdom (83–69)	
80 Ptolemy XI Alesander II		
80–51 Ptolemy XII Neos Dionysos		
	Queen Alexandra Salome succeeded Jannaeus (76) At Alexandra's death, her sons Hyrcanus II and Aristobulus II divided the rule (67) Civil war between the brothers Roman intervention (63)	

Menelaus as High Priest

Three years after Jason's assumption of the high-priestly office, a new turn of events took place. Menelaus, who was the brother (and successor?) of Simon who previously held the office of Temple administrator, while carrying Jason's payment to Antioch outbid the latter for the office of high priest, offering 300 talents more for the post (2 Macc. 4:23–24). Menelaus, whatever his status with regard to a priestly background, did not belong, like the Oniad Jason, to the hereditary family from which the high priests had recently come. The family of Simon, to which Menelaus belonged, although a significant one in Jerusalem, was probably able to make its move because of the support of the Tobiads. The Tobiad support of Menelaus would have been based on the fact that Jason had not taken a friendly attitude toward this group and perhaps had disenfranchised them in his reorganization of Jerusalem society. The Tobiads had probably encouraged Simon in the earlier charges leveled against Onias III in their efforts to oust the Oniads, but Jason had acted in such a way as to outmaneuver them. Josephus reports that, early in the reign of Antiochus IV, "Onias [Jason?], one of the chief priests, gaining the upper hand [in the dissension which arose among the Jewish nobles], expelled the sons of Tobias from the city" (*War* I.31). Menelaus was able to claim the office of high priest only with the support of Antiochus IV, the assistance of the Tobiads, and civil war. "The populace was divided between the two, the Tobiads being on the side of Menelaus, while the majority of the people supported Jason" (*Ant.* XII.239).

Jason was forced out of the city and "driven as a fugitive into the land of Ammon" (2 Macc. 4:25–26), perhaps seeking refuge in the domain of Hyrcanus. Aided by his brother, Lysimachus, Menelaus pilfered sacred vessels and treasures from the Temple to cover his financial responsibility to the Seleucids and to bribe high officials (2 Macc. 4:27–32). Andronicus, deputy of Antiochus IV, was bribed to do away with Onias III, who had sought sanctuary at Daphne near Antioch (2 Macc. 4:33). When the absent Antiochus IV returned to the capital, he received Jewish appeals protesting the murder of Onias III and immediately took actions to have his murderer publicly humiliated and subsequently executed (2 Macc. 4:35–38). In the meantime, Lysimachus, serving as Menelaus's deputy during an absence of the latter from Jerusalem, continued the practice of absconding with Temple vessels. Confronted with a major uprising of the people, Lysimachus sent three thousand armed men (the *demos* of the *polis?*) against the crowds but was himself killed in the ensuing conflict (2 Macc. 4:39–42). On the basis of an appeal by the Jewish *gerousia*, Menelaus was called to account by Antiochus IV for these outrageous acts and the turmoil created. However, he was able, by bribing important governmental officials, to retain his position, and even to have some of his accusers put to death (2 Macc. 4:43–50).

Antiochus IV Epiphanes
and the Jewish Struggles

The struggle between Jason and Menelaus eventually brought Antiochus IV fully into the internal Judean conflicts produced by the struggle for power among the several competing families. The exact chronology of the events associated with Antiochus's intervention remains somewhat uncertain. It is not clear if the Seleucid monarch made one or two visits to Jerusalem. Like-wise, we do not know how Jason's final attempt to regain power is to be cor-related with Antiochus's two Egyptian campaigns (compare Dan. 11:29–31; 1 Macc. 1:20–23; 2 Macc. 5:1–22; *Ant.* XII.239–50; *War* I.31–33).

On his first invasion of Egypt, Antiochus IV, responding to renewed Ptolemaic activity, posed as the supporter of his nephew Ptolemy VI against the latter's brother Ptolemy VIII. In his second movement into the country, Antiochus IV seems to have been bent on annexing Egypt. After taking Memphis, he issued coins and an edict as king of the country. He was, however, unable to capture Alexandria. On this second invasion, An-tiochus IV was confronted by a Roman legate without *imperium,* that is, without legal "power" to command, Popilius Laenas, who ordered him to end his war against Egypt and leave the country immediately (Livy XLV.12.3–6; Polybius XXIX.27; *HW* 271–73). Many scholars, misunder-standing the full impact of Popilius's actions, incorrectly regard him as a consul. This is a logical error precisely because as consul he would have had *imperium.* In effect, Rome's authority was such that by this time a Roman legate had enough authority, simply by being a Roman representative, to successfully order Antiochus IV to withdraw from his campaign against Egypt, even though Rome was not outwardly a participant in the affair. So the reaction from Antiochus IV was an acknowledgment of Rome's protec-torate of Egypt, and at the same time it was an acceptance of his own subor-dination to Rome. Likewise, Popilius's treatment of Antiochus IV (Polybius XXIX.27.1–7) "was intended as a demonstration of the power which the republic now exercised over the kings of the East" (*CAH* 7/1, p. 99).

During these invasions of Egypt, "a false rumor arose that Antiochus was dead." Consequently, "Jason took no less than a thousand men and suddenly made an assault upon the city [Jerusalem]" (2 Macc. 5:5). Jason achieved some initial success, gained control of the city, forced Menelaus to take refuge in the citadel, slaughtered many of his countrymen, but was eventually forced to withdraw. Jason, in flight, finally made his way to Egypt and later to Sparta, where he died (2 Macc. 5: 6–10). It was probably at this time that Hyrcanus committed suicide (*Ant.* XII.236).

Antiochus IV, learning that "Judea was in revolt" (2 Macc. 5:11), left Egypt and came to Jerusalem to restore tranquillity. The city had to be taken by storm; Seleucid troops carried out a terrible massacre; many Judeans were sold into slavery; and the king, assisted by Menelaus (2 Macc. 5:15), confiscated some of the wealth of the Temple (1 Macc. 1:21–22). Although this is generally construed as necessitated by the king's need for money to pay the Roman war indemnity, it might simply reflect the eastern belief that when you conquered a nation (and this included those who were already within a ruler's suzerainty, but who had revolted), you took the god(s) of that nation as well as anything or even everything that belonged to him/them captive. Unfortunately, given the extant data, we cannot know the truth of this matter.

Antiochus IV, who had earlier been willing to call Menelaus to account for his actions, was now, confronted with the deeds of Jason and his followers, left with no choice but to support Menelaus wholeheartedly. Suspecting further trouble, Antiochus IV left a certain Philip as governor in Jerusalem and a certain Andronicus in charge over the Samaritan community with its temple on Mount Gerizim. Menelaus was restored to authority as high priest and "lorded it over his fellow citizens worse than the others did" (2 Macc. 5:22–23). Sometime later (two years later according to 1 Macc. 1:29), Antiochus IV had to send the military commander Apollonius with a force of twenty-two thousand troops to quell renewed troubles in Jerusalem. He gained access to the city "deceitfully" (1 Macc. 1:30), apparently entering while the community was observing the Sabbath (2 Macc. 5:24–25). Repressive action was taken against the population: many were killed, the city was partially destroyed, and women, children, and cattle were seized (1 Macc. 1:31–32; 2 Macc. 5:26). Most significant, however, was Apollonius's refortification or construction of a new citadel (*akra*) in what is called "the city of David" (1 Macc. 1:33; see 14:36) and his stationing of a foreign colony of troops there. The latter meant a radical reorientation of the city's security and in fact a military occupation. The settlement of foreign troops in a city and the conversion of a city into a military colony were acts of major consequence in the Hellenistic period (see Ptolemy's threat against Onias II in *Ant.* XII.159), since these involved the confiscation and redistribution of property and the imposition of an outside military authority.

CHAPTER 2

The Hasmonaeans

Internal turmoil was characteristic of life in the Jerusalem community following the appointment of Menelaus as high priest. Rivalry and strife did not lack for participants. The traditional Oniad sympathizers, that is, the supporters of Jason, and pro-Ptolemaic proponents were opposed to Menelaus. Likewise, they were opposed to what must have seemed to be a new phase of Seleucid involvement in Judean affairs. Part of the anti-Menelaus opposition was probably led by the Hasmonaeans, themselves from a priestly, but not high-priestly class. Four families were now struggling for control of Judah and Jerusalem: the Tobiads, the Oniads, the Simonites, and the Hasmonaeans.

The Background of
Judas Maccabeus and His Family

The reader of 2 Maccabees is first introduced to the Hasmonaeans in the narrative about Apollonius's assault on Jerusalem: "Judas Maccabeus, with about nine others, got away to the wilderness" (2 Macc. 5:27). Second Maccabees, unlike the more pro-Hasmonaean 1 Maccabees, has nothing to say about Mattathias, the legendary patriarch of the Hasmonaean family. It makes no reference to the Hasmonaean revolt having its inception in revolutionary actions in Modein. Neither 1 nor 2 Maccabees really makes clear the class or the sectarian struggle involved in the revolt (see 1 Macc. 2:1–70). So they do not explicitly state that the Hasmonaeans were aristocrats. Likewise, they do not explicitly state that those people, called the *Ethnos* of the Jews, who followed them do not seem to have been of the same class. As depicted in 1 and 2 Maccabees and in Josephus's works, the latter seem to be what we now categorize as "true believers." Most likely they were from those (lower) classes that had nothing to gain from Seleucid rule. Additionally there were "pietists," who may, but need not, have been of the lower classes. They may, but need not, have been part of the *Ethnos* of the Jews.

Second Maccabees presents the origins of the Hasmonaean forces as well as of the revolt in a radically different light from 1 Maccabees. If we follow the account in 2 Maccabees, which probably represents a more historically correct narrative than that of 1 Maccabees, two conclusions follow:

1. The Hasmonaean involvement in the struggles in Jerusalem preceded the occupation of Jerusalem by Seleucid troops. First Maccabees 2:66 takes an interesting stance when it describes Judas as "a mighty warrior from his youth." Interestingly enough, we know that under Ptolemaic rule, which admittedly had ended in 200 B.C.E., mercenaries from Coele-Syria were to be found in the Egyptian forces. Likewise, under Seleucid rule, mercenaries from Coele-Syria were to be found in the Seleucid forces. It is impossible to ascertain from 1 Maccabees 2:66 if Judas had actually served as some type of mercenary, although he certainly had some knowledge of military tactics. This statement may actually have been meant to present Judas as a second David. This is a particularly apt allusion since David like Judas was a terrorist leader in his early career. What matters is that the events since 168 clearly show that Antiochus's actions were not directed against Jews in general, despite the later Hasmonaean propaganda. Rather, they were directed against those who opposed the Seleucid monarch. Because of this opposition the king did two things. He made the practice of the cult in what the Hasmonaeans and the *Ethnos* of the Jews would have considered its traditional form illegal, and he placed a foreign military colony in the citadel. We cannot determine whether the *Ethnos* of the Jews continued to exist as an entity unto itself, or even as an entity of any sort, and if so what form it took in these circumstances.

2. The view of 1 Maccabees 1:41–2:64, that the origins of the Hasmonaean revolt are to be seen in purely religious perspectives, is a greatly oversimplified version of events. Thus the idealized presentation in 1 Maccabees of the role Mattathias played in the revolt represents an *ex post facto* glorification of the movement. Clearly it was intended for propaganda purposes. It does not take into consideration the geopolitical, theopolitical, or economic forces at play.

Despite the fact that 2 Maccabees may be said to be more historically correct than 1 Maccabees on this matter, we must not assume that 1 Maccabees is primarily theologically grounded whereas 2 Maccabees is primarily historically grounded. There is something of both in each of the works. Even though 2 Maccabees has a very different perspective regarding the development of the Hasmonaean revolt from that found in 1 Maccabees, 2 Maccabees still presents the actions of Judas and his followers as a religious holy war. Second Maccabees depicts this war as having been fought so as to liberate the Jews, as if the *Ethnos* of the Jews represented all of Israel, from foreign oppression and to secure the privileges of religious freedom.

Clearly, religious issues played a significant role in the revolt from any Jewish, and even historical, perspective. But this should not be stressed to the point of overlooking the ideological perspective of 2 Maccabees, which in the writer's day was not even anachronistic. On the one hand, it was an expression of wish fulfillment. But on the other, it was an ideologically based fiction. In either case, it must have emanated from the by then well-established Hasmonaean monarchs so as to shore up their self-defined, spear-won right to rule the Temple state. This was treated as a theo-political rather than a spear-won right, however, insofar as it properly correlated appointment to the high priesthood with rule of the state. So what matters even in 2 Maccabees is the need to justify Hasmonaean appointment to the high priesthood although the family was not a high-priestly family.

Second Maccabees was written about 125 B.C.E. Its author was adaptively summarizing (the technical term for this is periochizing [from the Greek usage] or epitomizing [from the Latin usage]) the works of Jason of Cyrene, who wrote either about 161 B.C.E. or 142 B.C.E. Nevertheless, we need not assume that the perspective of the writer of 2 Maccabees was the same as that in Jason of Cyrene's work. Even if the same material were presented by both, 2 Maccabees may still have slanted its own narrative so as to support the already successfully concluded Hasmonaean enterprise as rightful from a legal perspective, and God-warranted from a theological one. We must not deem 2 Maccabees dishonest on this account. A periochizor/epitomizor in antiquity could and frequently did significantly alter even the data as well as the historical and/or literary perspective in his "revision" of what he had received. This attempt to be "politically correct" was accepted methodology in antiquity.

Little is known of the background of the Hasmonaean family. It belonged to the priestly course of Jehoiarib. Judging from biblical texts, this priestly subdivision had grown in prominence in late postexilic times. The order does not appear in the lists of Ezra (2:36–39) and Nehemiah (7:39–42), but by the time the list of priests in 1 Chronicles (9:10–13) was composed, the order occupied second position. In the priestly list of 1 Chronicles 24 it has moved to first rank. (The shape of 1 Chronicles 24 may thus be the result of Hasmonaean redaction of the material.) The Hasmonaean family had roots in Jerusalem (1 Macc. 2:1; *Ant.* XII.265) but owned an estate in Modein, a town about seventeen miles northwest of Jerusalem, located administratively outside the traditional Persian-Hellenistic province of Judah/Judea. The family therefore possessed, in Modein and its environs, a base of power where local strength could be developed in a reasonably independent fashion. The basis of the family's strength was to be found there or even in the portions of Judah that were not as urbanized as Jerusalem, rather than in Jerusalem proper.

Antiochus IV and Life
and Worship in Jerusalem

Seleucid actions in Judah and Jerusalem following Apollonius's seizure of the city (probably in early 167 B.C.E.) form the context within which to view the rise of the Hasmonaeans and to understand the nature of their support. On the one hand, the Hasmonaeans entered the picture when political conditions had reached a new stage of development. The strength of the Oniads and the Tobiads had dissipated. The Simonites, represented by Menelaus, were officially in authority. The fact that the presence of Seleucid troops in the city and a military occupation were required to keep Menelaus in power must have alienated significant segments of the society. This illustrates how fragile Menelaus's control really was.

Menelaus and others in the Temple state community cooperated with, or at least acquiesced in, Seleucid activity. This is particularly meaningful to our understanding that not every Yahwist viewed the Seleucid monarch's actions as antipathetic to Yahwism. Since this cooperation involved the transformation of the Temple in Jerusalem into a cult place for the occupying forces as well as for those who would worship Yahweh, it means that some Yahwists were not as exclusivistic as the Hasmonaeans alleged themselves to be and the *Ethnos* of the Jews actually was.

Tradition later condemned Menelaus for cooperating with Antiochus IV and accused him of being a traitor to his people: "Menelaus was to blame for all the trouble" (2 Macc. 13:4). Josephus, in narrating the episode of Menelaus's execution, has a Seleucid general claim that Menelaus "had been the cause of the mischief by persuading the king's [Antiochus V's] father [Antiochus IV] to compel the Jews to abandon their fathers' religion" (*Ant.* XII.384; see Dan. 11:30, 32, 34). In many ways, once he had gained power, Menelaus is reminiscent of King Manasseh, who in the seventh century had of necessity to be the instrument of a foreign authority if he was to remain in office.

The Hasmonaean revolutionaries and their followers considered the changes in the Temple cult to be by far the most heinous action of Antiochus IV. With a Syrian garrison stationed in the Akra, which itself seems to have been given the status of a Greek city-state (*polis*), the facilities of the Jerusalem Temple were transformed to serve the religious needs of the soldiers who were members of the military colony. Additionally, those soldiers had been given property, although we do not know that that property was confiscated from the locals (see Dan. 11:39; *Ant.* XII.147–53, 159). This was customary in the establishment of a military colony, and occasionally so in the establishment of a city-state as well. Since the Seleucid monarch, as overlord, actually had the property rights to what was

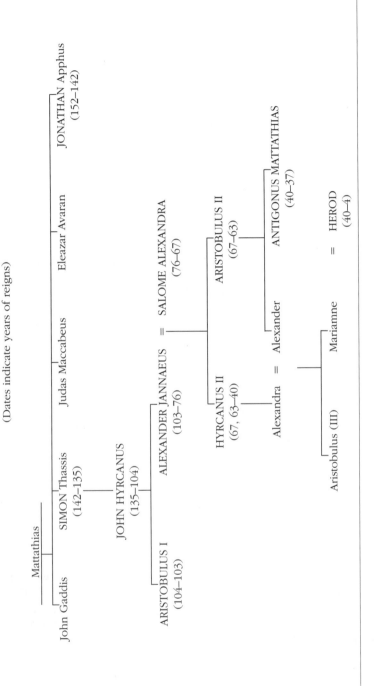

CHART III. Partial Genealogy of the Hasmonaeans
(Dates indicate years of reigns)

Mattathias

John Gaddis

SIMON Thassis
(142–135)

Judas Maccabeus

Eleazar Avaran

JONATHAN Apphus
(152–142)

JOHN HYRCANUS
(135–104)

ARISTOBULUS I
(104–103)

ALEXANDER JANNAEUS
(103–76)

= SALOME ALEXANDRA
(76–67)

HYRCANUS II
(67, 63–40)

ARISTOBULUS II
(67–63)

Alexandra = Alexander

ANTIGONUS MATTATHIAS
(40–37)

Aristobulus (III)

Mariamne = HEROD
(40–4)

ostensibly and in practice the private property of individuals, he could confiscate private property legally. This situation occurred because civil law and monarchical law overlapped. Monarchical law extended throughout the king's realm, while civil law was mostly local. When they were in conflict, the rights of the Seleucid king (monarchical law) rather than those of the individual (civil law) took precedence.

Our sources do not make it clear as to whether a military establishment or a city-state was established or whether both were established simultaneously. The two were quite different from each other, and they would not have been perceived as the same thing to someone who understood Hellenistic conventions at the time. The demarcation between them, however, could have been confused by those who did not understand those conventions. This may have been true of the followers of Judas Maccabeus, but not Judas himself, who seems to have been a consummate politician. It would hardly be recognized by someone writing at a later time when the delineations were no longer meaningful. So, for example, neither 1 nor 2 Maccabees nor Josephus could be expected to recognize the distinction even when they relied on sources that may have done so. In any case, several features of the developments in Jerusalem are noteworthy:

1. The Temple was dedicated to Olympian Zeus (see Dan. 11:37–39). Perhaps Olympian Zeus was in some way identified with Yahweh, the traditional Hebrew deity. There was frequently a blending of deities in the Hellenistic age. The Samaritans, to avoid the charges against and the treatment given the Judeans from the Temple state, requested that the temple on Mount Gerizim be dedicated to Zeus Hellenios (2 Macc. 6:2) or Zeus Xenios (according to Josephus; *Ant.* XII.257–64). Second Maccabees 6:2, again from the viewpoint of the writer's day and ideology, simply assumes that the renaming of the sanctuary was part of the Seleucid activity against the practice of Judaism. We hear nothing about any major alteration of cult and customs in the temple on Mount Gerizim. Shechem had not been turned into a military colony and thus there was no need to alter worship activity in the temple to accommodate foreign forces.

2. A secondary altar—"the abomination of desolation" (Dan. 11:31) or "desolating sacrilege" (1 Macc. 1:54)—was constructed upon the altar of burnt offerings in the Temple courtyard. It was on this altar and similar ones outside Jerusalem that swine were said to have been offered (1 Macc. 1:44–47; *Ant.* XII.253) after the cessation of the traditional, daily *tamid* sacrifices (Dan. 11:31). Elements in this description, however, may be ideological fictions, since 2 Maccabees contains no reference to this secondary altar and its associated cult.

3. The worship of Dionysus became a matter of concern. Dionysus is sometimes viewed as a vegetation and dying-rising deity but more likely

was a popular "great" god. His formal worship was manifested in cultic rituals that are relatively unknown because they were part of what we call a "mystery" religion. Some limited portions of the cult of Dionysus, however, would have been open to outside observation. And it may be on the basis of those nonsecret aspects that "outsiders," such as the author/redactor of 2 Macc. 6:3–5 or the Censor at Rome, where it was also introduced and officially rejected because of the violence and orgiastic rites with which it was allegedly associated (Livy XXXIX.8–19), would interpret the religion as evincing strong orgiastic activities. Although they might not have realized it, this development represents an invalid interpretation of the mysteries if we can trust what little is said about them in Euripides' *Bacchae*. Nevertheless, this could represent a real, popular, cultic aspect during the Hellenistic era.

According to 2 Macc. 6:3–5, Dionysiac worship was made a part of the new cult, and Jews "were compelled to walk in a procession in honor of Dionysus, wearing wreaths of ivy" (2 Macc. 6:7). According to some later traditions, the worship of the goddess Athena was also introduced. By the Classical period Athena was not only worshiped as a great, but also as a virgin, goddess—her prehistoric role as mother goddess having long since been forgotten. In her newfound form, she became part of a triad of deities, father, (virgin) mother, and son—a widespread pattern in the Near East. These three gods had probably already been assimilated to their Syrian counterparts, Baal Shamem (the supreme male deity), the goddess Anat, and Dushara (the god of wine).

4. Special celebrations were held on the monthly commemoration of the king's birthday. (For similar celebrations elsewhere, see the Canopus Decree [*GHD* 222] and Text 7 [page 91].) Such celebrations do not necessarily suggest that Antiochus IV was worshiped as a god (2 Macc. 6:7), although he may well have been.

Along with the utilization of the Temple in Jerusalem as a Syrian cult place, Antiochus IV took action to suppress the opponents of his policies and of Menelaus, his own appointed head of the community. Such a program of oppression undoubtedly involved some actions to suppress certain Jewish religious practices and customs. The tradition, however, subsequently treats this as if all Jewish religious practices and customs had been interdicted.

A number of reasons make it doubtful that there was an official edict forbidding and outlawing "Jewish" religion and practices per se, that is, Yahwism with or without sectarian distinctions. (1) Only 1 Maccabees, the most pro-Hasmonaean of our sources, speaks of any official decree and then in terms that do not suggest the author is quoting from any document (1 Macc. 1:41–51). (2) Second Maccabees, which presents the most dramatic portrayal of Jewish suffering for the faith (2 Macc. 6:10–7:42), does not mention any decree outlawing Jewish religion (but see 2 Macc. 6:8). (3) In its description of Antiochus's actions, the book of Daniel makes no reference to any such edict (Dan. 7:21; 8:9–12, 24–25; 9:27; 11:21–35). (4) Menelaus would hardly have cooperated with a move to suppress the Yahwistic cult in the Temple since the priesthood and the Temple were economically dependent upon such activity.

It appears, nonetheless, quite clear that Seleucid practices and Menelaus's actions involved harsh suppression of opposition to state control, and thus to the superimposition of monarchical law over civil law. This was interpreted as demanding the persecution of those who were guilty of no more than being Jews who practiced a specific type of Yahwism, and who also refused to compromise their strict adherence to their own understanding of what they deemed the Torah's stipulations. If we can trust the "documents" in 2 Maccabees to be genuine—some documents in 1 and 2 Maccabees are in fact genuine, but we cannot be sure about all of them—we can see this suggested by the later Seleucid decrees that indicate that there had been an earlier repression of Judaism (see 2 Macc. 11:24–25, 30–31), or at least of some specific sectarian practices. According to 2 Maccabees, an Athenian, Geron, was sent to Jerusalem "to compel the Jews to forsake the laws of their fathers and cease to live by the laws of God" (6.1). But the "laws of their fathers" and the "laws of God" must not be construed to have been the same for all the different groups within Judaism.

No doubt Antiochus could have argued a logical case for his actions. Again, we must not forget that monarchic law and civil law operated side by side even when they contradicted each other. When a conflict between the two did occur, monarchic law took precedence. So the right of certain sects of Jews in the Temple state to live according to what they termed their ancestral laws, which themselves may not have been the same for each of the communities even within the Temple state, may have already been rescinded by Jason and the city reorganized as a Greek city-state, or it may simply have become subordinated to the monarchic law that was itself operative when the city-state was "founded." On the other hand, a new type of civil law, which was characteristic of the Greek city-state, became operative by virtue of the charter whereby Antioch-in-Jerusalem came into existence. This too, however, was concomitant with monarchic law.

Since it was customary for the king or even the mother city-state that chartered a new city-state or colony to become its patron or protector, Antiochus must be seen as the protector, that is, the patron, of the Greek city-state, Antioch-in-Jerusalem, established by and named after him. The city was located within his realm, and most important, in a sensitive zone on the southern flank of his empire. This is particularly important since Coele-Syria had always served as a "buffer" between Egypt and Syria. This is why both Ptolemaic and Seleucid powers had sought to control it during the

Hellenistic era. In the same way Egypt and the two major Mesopotamian empires (Assyria and Babylon, respectively) had consistently striven to control it—albeit more Israel than Judah—during the Divided Monarchy that came into being after Solomon's death. So when Antiochus IV sought to crush the rebel opponents by whatever means possible, he was taking appropriate action to protect himself from what he perceived as a threat. It would not have mattered if the rebels were pro- or anti-Ptolemaic. All that really mattered was that they were not pro-Seleucid, and therefore they had the potential to become pro-Ptolemaic. And we can see why those who were pro-Ptolemaic were dangerous to, or at least considered dangerous by, the Seleucid monarch. There was yet another factor: Rome. The Romans had held real, not merely ideologically predicated, hegemony over Egypt from at least 201 B.C.E. (Livy XXX1.2.1–4) and over the Seleucid kingdom from 190 B.C.E. In contrast, they had held an ideologically predicated hegemony over the entire world from 196 B.C.E. onward. They strove to make this real from that point onward, using their guise of being the protector of Greek liberty *(patrocinium libertatis Graecorum)*. Although Antiochus IV would have had to acknowledge this in his dealings with Rome, he need not have done so with those subordinate to him unless it suited Rome's interests to force him to do so. As we shall see, Judas's future interactions with the Romans make this a viable reason for Antiochus to be afraid of what the rebels would do in the geopolitical arena. From any perspective, then, even prior to their organization as armed forces under Hasmonaean leadership, the opposition to him posed a danger to Antiochus.

One way of attempting to crush the rebel opponents was to strike at what they (not Antiochus) would have construed as the conservative basis of their strength—the appeal to "the traditional ways" and the "law of Moses." These were the same factors that Antiochus and yet others would have construed as "radical" rather than conservative. Again, we stress that neither the "traditional ways" nor the "law of Moses" had to have been identical for everybody. Even if Antiochus himself were not aware of this delineation, his "friends" (a technical term for his advisors and cabinet) would have so informed him. If Antiochus were the sometimes unstable character that some ancients described (see page 51, Text 4), then his actions could also be seen as the expression of the frustrated ambitions of the would-be imperialist striking out at recalcitrant opposition, the symbolic embodiment of his shattered dreams. But even this must be questioned since, in antiquity, those monarchs who were hated while alive were frequently vilified in various ways, including depicting them as crazy, after they died. And, most important, the rebels do not seem to have been a significant factor in the policies of the Temple state until after the successful revolt. We must remember that what was allegedly a revolt against the Seleucid monarch was more realistically a civil war in which those who were not in power opposed those who owed their position of power to that monarch.

Hasmonaean Struggles against the Seleucids

With the settlement of a military garrison in Jerusalem, the city was turned into what the Hasmonaean followers would consider to be a "dwelling of strangers." This together with the oppression of those Jews who continued to follow the traditions of the law as they understood it seems to have shifted the conflict from the capital city to the rural districts. According to 1 and 2 Maccabees, mass flight to the wilderness, mountainous regions, and rural areas allegedly took place (1 Macc. 1:38; 2:29–30; 2 Macc. 5:27). It is more likely, however, that the majority of the Hasmonaean followers came from the rural areas in the first place as 2 Macc. 8:1 seems to suggest.

Not surprisingly, the Hasmonaeans set up headquarters in the wooded areas of the Gophna Hills, a few miles northeast of Modein. This location provided the opportunity for the Hasmonaeans to recruit their followers: "Judas, who was also called Maccabeus [= 'the hammer' or 'the hammerheaded'], and his companions secretly entered the villages and summoned their kinsmen and enlisted those who had continued in the Jewish faith, and so they gathered about six thousand men" (2 Macc. 8:1).

The Hasmonaean army (2 Macc. 8:5) under the leadership of Judas and his four brothers—Simon, Jonathan, John, and Eleazar—was soon joined by other religious enthusiasts and freedom fighters from the villages and their environs. "There united with them a company of Hasideans [= 'devout ones'], mighty warriors of Israel, every one who offered himself willingly for the law. And all who became fugitives to escape their troubles joined them and reinforced them" (1 Macc. 2:42–43; see 2 Macc. 14:6).

Who the Hasideans were remains uncertain, although there has been much speculation about their identity. The description in 1 Maccabees does not seem to categorize them as a distinctive sect. Most important, 1 Maccabees cryptically tells us that, in addition to the devout ones, those who joined the Hasmonaean rebels were the poor and the members of the lowest social classes. Although the implications seem to be that the troubles that caused them to become fugitives were religious, 1 Maccabees does not make a case for this. More likely their troubles were based on socioeconomic factors.

The first phase of the Hasmonaean movement was directed against fellow countrymen, particularly against pro-Seleucid elements and fellow

Judeans who were unwilling to join the cause. Fear and compulsion made neutrality difficult. Allegedly apostate Jews—and they were apostate from the perspective of the followers of if not the Hasmonaeans themselves—were killed wherever they fell into the hands of the Hasmonaeans. Villages were burned. What were construed as "pagan" altars were pulled down—again, Yahwistic altars that did not fit into the rebels' sectarian perspective may well have been categorized as pagan. Force was used to achieve compliance with the law of circumcision, and many were forced to flee to the Gentiles for safety (1 Macc. 2:44–48; 2 Macc. 8:6; *Ant.* XII.278).

> He [Judas] searched out and pursued the lawless;
>> he burned those who troubled his people.
> Lawless men shrank back for fear of him;
>> all the evildoers were confounded;
>> and deliverance prospered by his hand.
> . . . .
> He went through the cities of Judah;
>> he destroyed the ungodly out of the land;
>> thus he turned away wrath from Israel.
>> (1 Macc. 3:5–6, 8)

On one level, therefore, the Hasmonaean struggle was an adventure in civil war, beginning with terrorist uprisings but concluding with heavy armed conflict. The Hasmonaeans and their followers not only used terrorist attacks and armed warfare, but they practiced psychological warfare as well. They categorized their opponents as few in number and identified them with the lawless. By defining their Yahwistic opponents as lawless they classified them not only with evildoers or criminals but also with those who were theologically lawless because they had rejected the Mosaic law.

The Hasmonaeans certainly did not have unanimous, and as is likely not even the majority, support of their compatriots. So it is important that many Jews even later continued to fight against the Hasmonaeans (1 Macc. 3:13–15; 6:18–21; *Ant.* XII.288–89, 299). On the other hand, among Hasmonaean supporters were some who were hardly what we would consider "normative" or "orthodox" (2 Macc. 12:40). There were also others who were merely opportunists open to being bribed (2 Macc. 10:18–22).

Hasmonaean strategy seems to have anticipated military conflict with Seleucid forces. This made what was happening seem to be more of a revolt against the Seleucid overlord than a civil war in which different groups of Jews were vying for political or even theo-political power. The Hasmonaeans quickly focused on gaining possession of "strategic positions" (2 Macc. 8:6), dominating the main communication routes, and thus blockading Jerusalem and the Akra through guerrilla warfare. Judas seems to have been successful in dominating the main roads linking Jerusalem with Seleucid centers in the coastal plain and with the city of Samaria.

The Hasmonaeans were aided by events external to their struggle. Because Antiochus IV was preoccupied with the Parthians far to the east, and had engaged many of his forces on that front, the Hasmonaeans were able to win decisive battles against Syrian forces sent to suppress the uprising. Because of disagreements between 1 and 2 Maccabees, the exact sequence of these battles cannot be determined. However, Judas is credited with defeating forces under Apollonius (1 Macc. 3:10–12), Seron (1 Macc. 3:13–26), and Nicanor and Gorgias (1 Macc. 3:38–4:27; 2 Macc. 8:8–29).

Attempts to Settle the Conflict

After the initial victories of the Hasmonaeans, diplomatic steps were taken by the Seleucids in an effort to restore tranquillity in the area. Four of the documents related to these efforts are now found in 2 Maccabees 11 but in a literary context that places them in the period after the death of Antiochus IV. The internal evidence of the texts, however, suggests that probably all but one of these come from the last years of the reign of Antiochus IV. On the basis of these documents, it is possible to reconstruct the following course of events.

The earliest of these documents is found in 2 Macc. 11:27–33. This is a letter from Antiochus IV to the Judean *gerousia* (senate) and people. As a result of diplomatic negotiation carried out by Menelaus on behalf of the people, Antiochus took two actions early in 164 B.C.E. (the letter is dated about the beginning of March, although the date given may have been accidentally copied from one of the following letters). First, the king granted amnesty to those Judeans who would return to their homes peacefully by a certain date. Second, the decree officially rescinded Antiochus's earlier policy of persecution and restored "full permission for the Judeans to enjoy their own food and laws, just as formerly." This represented cessation of the Seleucid suppression of the practices that were considered characteristically Jewish. Apparently most of the Jews in the Temple state, although not the main Hasmonaean party, accepted the proclamation of this decree as the official end of Seleucid persecution, if we can trust the validity of the ideological basis of what was celebrated in later times (see *Megillat Ta'anit*, 28 Adar; *MPAT* 187).

Antiochus's action did not end the civil war between the Hasmonaeans and the followers of Menelaus. As a result, the general Lysias was sent to suppress the rebels. Second Maccabees 11:11–15 seems to provide an account of this expedition. Lysias and his forces were defeated by the Hasmonaeans. The Seleucid general then entered into direct negotiations with the Hasmonaeans. Second Maccabees 11:13–15 reports this in the following way:

> So he [Lysias] sent to them [the Hasmonaeans] and persuaded them to settle everything on just terms, promising that he would persuade the king, constraining him to be their friend. Maccabeus, having regard for the common good, agreed to all that Lysias urged.

Thus Lysias settled those matters under his authority. Second Maccabees 11:16–21 contains his letter to "the people (crowd) of the Jews"—the Hasmonaeans and their sympathizers. This letter shows that Lysias (1) made concessions to the Hasmonaeans (obviously acting in the name of the Seleucid monarch); (2) communicated some disputed matters to the king for further negotiation; (3) promised to intercede with the king on behalf of the Hasmonaean party if they maintained good will toward the government; and (4) made arrangements for continued communication between himself and the Hasmonaeans.

Roman ambassadors on their way to Antioch were informed of the negotiations with the Hasmonaeans. They consented to the arrangements established by Lysias as their magisterial position gave them the right to do, and promised to intercede with the king on behalf of the Hasmonaeans once they received word from them concerning matters. The Roman ambassadors were in fact acting in exact accordance with Rome's ideology whereby Rome was the protector of Greek liberty as well as Antiochus's suzerain. So they were warranting that Rome's protectorate extended to the Seleucid king as well as to the Hasmonaean rebels. In the case of the latter, this was ironic, because it was Antiochus's establishment of the Greek city-state in the citadel at Jerusalem that justified the Roman treatment of the rebels as under its protection.

The letter in 2 Macc. 11:34–38 is the ambassadors' statement addressed to "the people *(demos)* of the Jews" (which may well be the Hasmonaean party, but again construing them as if they had been hellenized), although the monthly date given in v. 38 may be wrong since it is identical to that in v. 33. The Romans had asserted their influence throughout the eastern Mediterranean since the last quarter of the third century. It is impossible to determine how involved they had already become in Palestinian affairs before the outbreak of the Hasmonaean struggles, but this does not mean that they had not been involved, particularly in light of the Isthmian Doctrine. Because of the location of Jewish Palestine on the land bridge that was so important for trade and so on, their involvement may have been more significant than is generally acknowledged. Roman support of the Hasmonaean party, which involved support of a totally unofficial group, could only have given encouragement to the rebels and have fitted Roman policy of weakening other powers that were or might become their opponents, in this case the Seleucids. In some ways the Roman action was in accord with the type of foreign policy Rome had exercised in its dealings with various city-states everywhere: Rome supported the pro-Roman party.

There was a conundrum in this case, since the pro-Roman party was generally the aristocratic or even the most aristocratic party, and this cannot be said of the Hasmonaean party. This is easily resolved, however, when we realize that the Hasmonaean family was aristocratic even though its followers may not have been. To all intents and purposes, the Romans both at this time and henceforth interacted with the Hasmonaeans and/or their representatives, not with their followers

Negotiations with Antiochus IV were not brought to a conclusion because the Seleucid king was killed in battle in the East late in November or early in December of 164 B.C.E. (see *HW* 236–37). With the death of Antiochus IV, his minor son succeeded him as Antiochus V. The new king immediately sent a letter to Lysias which reaffirmed his father's earlier declaration ending the persecution. His declaration, and the latest of the four documents in 2 Maccabees 11, like those of many new rulers throughout history, also granted new concessions with the intent of establishing good relations at the inauguration of his reign. The following is the content of the new king's official letter:

> King Antiochus to his brother Lysias, greeting. Now that our father has gone on to the gods [died], we desire that the subjects of the kingdom be undisturbed in caring for their own affairs. We have heard that the Jews do not consent to our father's change to Greek customs but prefer their own way of living and ask that their own customs be allowed them. Accordingly, since we choose that this nation also be free from disturbance, our decision is that their temple be restored to them and that they live according to the customs of their ancestors. You will do well, therefore, to send word to them and give them pledges of friendship, so that they may know our policy and be of good cheer and go on happily in the conduct of their own affairs. (2 Macc. 11:22–26)

Although the king no doubt intended to surrender Temple control to Menelaus and the recognized and official Jewish authorities, Judas and his supporters had by this time already seized the Temple area. Whether this occurred before the death of Antiochus IV (see 1 Macc. 4:52; 6:16) or afterward (see 2 Macc. 9:1–10:9) cannot be determined with certainty.

Apparently the practice of the Seleucid cult in the Temple had been short-lived, since the Hasmonaeans allegedly found "the sanctuary desolate, the altar profaned, and the gates burned. In the courts they saw bushes sprung up as in a thicket, or as on one of the mountains. They saw also the chambers of the priests in ruins" (1 Macc. 4:38).

This description, however, may have been more propagandistic than factual. In any case, under Judas's supervision, the Temple was purified, the altar for the Seleucid cult was demolished, the old but profaned Temple altar was dismantled and another constructed, Temple vessels and sacred precincts were prepared and consecrated. On the twenty-fifth of the Jewish month of Chislev (in December 164 B.C.E.) the Jewish sacrificial cult was reinstituted (1 Macc. 4:42–58; 2 Macc. 10:1–7) in the Jerusalemite Temple. The occasion became the basis for the later festival known as Hanukkah (1 Macc. 4:59; 2 Macc. 10:8). The Hasmonaeans, probably in the period immediately following the purge of the Temple, developed a rationale for the new celebration (see 2 Macc. 1:10; 2:18). Judas was depicted as the "successor" to Nehemiah, who, it was argued, had restored the original fire upon the rebuilt Jerusalemite altar and founded a library housing the sacred books.

The Political Ambitions
of the Hasmonaeans

The inner dynamic of the Hasmonaean movement with its political goals and family ambitions was not thwarted by the "good tidings which came to the Jews that they need not turn from the law" (*Megillat Ta'anit*). In a number of decisive actions, the Hasmonaeans took the offensive.

1. The Temple Mount was fortified with high walls and strong and garrisoned towers, and the strategic southern city of Beth-zur was fortified (1 Macc. 4:60–61).

2. Raids were made throughout the region of Transjordan, into Galilee and Idumea, and against Greek cities along the coast (1 Macc. 5; 2 Macc. 10:10–38). Many of these attacks were against cities where Jewish populations were threatened; others appear to have been plundering razzias; some helped consolidate Hasmonaean authority in the area. Judeans from Galilee (1 Macc. 5:21–23) and Gilead (1 Macc. 5:45–54) were brought back to Judea for their safety and no doubt to increase the size of Judas's military.

3. Judas besieged the Akra, hoping to destroy its Syrian forces and pro-Seleucid Judeans (2 Macc. 6:18–20; *Ant.* XII.362–64). Members of the Syrian military colony stationed in the citadel along with pro-Seleucid Judeans ("ungodly Israelites") appealed to the king for help. They reported recent

Hasmonaean activity and charged Judas and his followers with unrestrained killing and the illegal seizure of property (2 Macc. 6:18–27).

Recognizing that the Hasmonaeans were unwilling to live within the rights granted in spite of earlier agreements (2 Macc. 11:15), Antiochus V and Lysias raised an army and marched into Judea (1 Macc. 6:28–31). Menelaus, no doubt hoping to regain possession of the Temple, offered his support to the invading Syrians. But following Lysias's advice, the young king sent the Jewish high priest to Beroea to be executed (2 Macc. 3:3–8; *Ant.* XII.383–85).

The Seleucid troops attacked from the south, encamped against Beth-zur, and forced the Hasmonaeans to raise the siege against the Jerusalem citadel. The Hasmonaean forces fared badly: Beth-zur was occupied by the Syrians, and the Temple Mount was besieged (1 Macc. 6:32–54; see 2 Macc. 13:9–22, which turns the defeat into a victory!). Those defending the Temple suffered not only from the Syrian assault but also from a scarcity of food occasioned by the sabbatical year (1 Macc. 6:49, 53–54). News of political turmoil at home forced the withdrawal of the Seleucids. A certain Philip who had been designated as vice-regent by the dying Antiochus IV in place of Lysias, who had paid no regard to the king's final edict, had returned to Antioch and was rallying support. Lysias and Antiochus V immediately negotiated peace terms that allowed the citizens of the Temple state to "live by their laws as they did before" (1 Macc. 16:55–61). This perhaps denotes the general restoration of the privileges earlier granted by Antiochus III. Antiochus V "yielded and swore to observe all their rights, settled with them and offered sacrifice, honored the sanctuary and showed generosity to the holy place" (2 Macc. 13:23). Before departing, however, the Syrians demolished the defense walls encircling the Temple Mount (1 Macc. 6:62).

Nothing is said of Judas's participation in this phase of negotiations with the Seleucids. Neither 1 nor 2 Maccabees places him in Jerusalem at the time of the siege. Josephus says he had fled to the toparchy of Gophna, some ten miles north of Jerusalem (*War* I.45; contrast *Ant.* XII.375, 382). Second Maccabees mentions Judas's meeting with the king only after negotiations were over (13:24). Who were the "Jews" with whom negotiations were held and a peace treaty agreed upon? No certainty can be attained, but it appears not to have been with the main Hasmonaean party. This is strange indeed! But it would not be surprising if the Seleucid monarch realized or at least suspected that the Hasmonaeans had been conspiring with Rome against him. (We iterate that the letter in 2 Macc. 11:34–38 is the ambassadors' statement addressed to "the people (*demos*) of the Jews," and this type of conspiring is just what the Roman legate's interference on behalf of the Jews may have suggested.)

Negotiations may have been with the Jerusalem *gerousia*, those recognized by the Seleucids as authorities in the Jewish community, as well as some of the other dissident parties. Perhaps at this time Alcimus was appointed as high priest (see 2 Macc. 14:3). Onias IV, having been passed over for the office, fled to Egypt, where he later constructed a Yahwistic temple in Leontopolis (see *Ant.* XII.387–88; XIII.62–73; contrast *War* I.33).

Judas's Last Days

Judas and the Hasmonaean supporters apparently refused to accept Alcimus as the new head of the Jewish community. Nevertheless some previously anti-Seleucid elements seem to have done so or at least to have welcomed the opportunity to negotiate with him (1 Macc. 7:13–14). Instead, the Hasmonaeans intensified the civil war (1 Macc. 7:5–11; 2 Macc. 14:3–10) and set up a rival counter government. The latter carried on direct negotiations with the Romans "to establish friendship and alliance" (1 Maccabees 8; *Ant.* XII.415–19). Judas assumed the functions of high priest (*Ant.* XII.414, 419, 434). Neither 1 nor 2 Maccabees clearly mentions Judas's role as high priest (but see 2 Macc. 14:26). Perhaps there was some question about its theological validity, and both 1 and 2 Maccabees were skirting the problem. So it is meaningful that the Jewish *gerousia* does not seem to have supported him in this role. But the Seleucid king did not seem to recognize him as high priest either. So it would seem as if he had no impeccably legitimate claim to the office. Josephus reports that "the people [the Hasmonaean troops?] gave the high priesthood to Judas," that is, recognized him as holder of the office, although the historian places his three-year rule after the death of Alcimus (*Ant.* XII.414).

What is most important, however, is that the Romans apparently recognized him as high priest, just as they recognized almost but not all of the Hasmonaean high priests from thence. Once Rome had become hegemon over the East, even when it was by its own definition, it had a "say" in the appointment of the respective rulers. So from the time of the Isthmian Doctrine (196 B.C.E.) onward, or perhaps more realistically from the defeat of Antiochus III at Magnesia (190) onward, the kings, rulers, and high priests of eastern nations subject to Rome's hegemony were confirmed in office by the Roman Senate. Moreover, the Romans viewed this right to confirm as an effortless manifestation of their power over client states. Josephus understood this, and was not being anachronistic when he consistently tells us that Rome confirmed the appointments of high priests in Judah and Jerusalem.

Despite the newly established roles of Syria and Rome after Magnesia and Apamaea, Antiochus V's lack of recognition of Judas as high priest and the Roman granting of recognition may have represented some power play between the two great powers. Under that circumstance, recognition or nonrecognition would have had no relationship to the theological legitimacy of Judas's accession to that office. In any case, Judas apparently held the office of high priest for three years (*Ant.* XII.434), the period from Menelaus's deposition (in the 150th Seleucid year = 162 B.C.E.; 1 Macc. 6:20) until his death (in the 152d Seleucid year = 160 B.C.E.).

As reported in the extant works, Alcimus was unable to exercise any effective governmental control over the community prior to the death of Judas. He was confirmed in office by Demetrius I (162–150 B.C.E.), a son of Seleucus IV and brother of Antiochus IV. Demetrius had escaped from Rome, with the connivance of a certain faction or even factions of the Roman aristocracy. That he had been held at Rome as a hostage was not unusual. It was good foreign policy to assure the tenure of those client kings Rome wanted to remain in office. It also usually sufficed to ensure the continued compliance of those whose children or relatives were being held hostage. This means that Demetrius became the client of some Roman aristocrat or aristocratic family, whose faction helped him "to escape" from Rome and return to Syria to seek what he deemed to be his throne. So when he succeeded to the throne after the murder of Antiochus V and Lysias (1 Macc. 7:1–7), there was no strong opposition from the Senate. It is to be suspected that the latter, or at least some faction of the latter, may have desired just that event, no matter what lip service they otherwise gave.

The representation that even with strong Seleucid support, including troops, Alcimus was ultimately forced to leave Judea and return to Antioch for additional help (1 Macc. 7:5–11, 19–25; 2 Macc. 14:3–10) may then be somewhat other than what it is made to seem. On the one hand, we are told in both 1 and 2 Maccabees (1 Macc. 7:26; 2 Macc. 14:11–14) that the Seleucid court dispatched Nicanor to set up Alcimus as high priest and put down the Hasmonaean party. We do not know why Nicanor did not do as ordered, but it is possible that he had not yet given his allegiance to Demetrius. In any case, he seems at least temporarily to have sided with Judas, even entering, according to Alcimus's charge, a covenant recognizing Judas as high priest (1 Macc. 7:27–29; 2 Macc. 14:18–27).

This is most interesting in light of the Roman Senate's support of the Hasmonaeans as attested to by its having granted Judas and the *Ethnos* of the Jews an *amicitia* (friendship = a diplomatic agreement), and its having confirmed him as high priest. What is more difficult to explain is that, according to 1 and 2 Maccabees, Nicanor was ordered to take up arms against Judas, whom he had been supporting, and he complied, with the result that he was slain in the ensuing battle (1 Macc. 7:30–49; 2 Macc. 14:28–15:36). But we must ask two questions. First, why did he comply? Second, did his compliance represent a change in allegiance on the part of Nicanor, who now showed his allegiance to his new liege lord? Lacking documentation from a Syrian perspective, we can do no more than speculate, but the fact that he died in this battle is itself suspicious.

Demetrius, however, did not allow the rebels to enjoy their victory. He reacted to Nicanor's defeat by sending a large retaliatory force to Judea, under Bacchides and accompanied by Alcimus, and in the subsequent battle Judas, with a force of only eight hundred loyal followers, was defeated and killed (1 Macc. 9:1–18). The size of Judas's forces suggests that much of his power base had eroded after the granting of concessions by the Seleucids and the appointment of Alcimus.

The Rule of Jonathan

After the death of Judas, the future appeared bleak for the Hasmonaean forces. The official administration under Alcimus and the pro-Syrian Jews regained dominance in the region and thereby control of the Temple and governmental apparatus. Hasmonaean supporters were sought out and executed (1 Macc. 9:23–27). Judas's brother Jonathan assumed leadership of the group but was compelled to flee to the wilderness and unpopulated areas where, like David of old, he temporarily operated as chieftain of what amounted to a guerrilla band, successfully maneuvering to stay out of Seleucid hands (1 Macc. 9:28–49).

The Syrian general Bacchides took several actions hoping to consolidate Syrian supremacy in the area and to stabilize conditions in Judea: (1) Several strategic cities were fortified or strengthened (including the Akra in Jerusalem), garrisoned with Seleucid troops, and provisioned with supplies (1 Macc. 9:50–52); (2) hostages were seized and placed under guard in the Akra (1 Macc. 9:53); (3) after Alcimus died, while architectural changes of an uncertain nature were being made in the Temple precincts, no successor was officially appointed (1 Macc. 9:54–56; *Ant.* XX.237).

After the withdrawal of Bacchides, the Hasmonaeans were able to reassert themselves and to pose a threat to those whom Bacchides had "put in charge of the country" (1 Macc. 9:25). The Seleucid general returned to the area, at the invitation of Jewish authorities, but failed to realize his goal, the capture of Jonathan (1 Macc. 9:58–68). The visit resulted instead in Bacchides' reprisal against some of his Jewish supporters (1 Macc. 9:69). On the initiative of Jonathan, a general truce was arrived at between the Hasmonaeans and the Seleucids (1 Macc. 9:70–73). The terms of the treaty provided for cessation of hostilities, exchange of prisoners, and apparently the right of Jonathan to exercise some governmental authority with head-quarters in Michmash, a few miles north of Jerusalem. The Hasmonaeans were not yet capable of achieving their political objective—absolute authority in Jerusalem—but they had acquired a major diplomatic concession from the Seleucids.

After about five years, on which the sources are silent, internal political struggles over the Seleucid throne delivered to the Hasmonaeans what their efforts had not achieved on the military battlefield. From this time on, no king was very secure on the Seleucid throne, which rested on a rapidly decomposing empire. Alexander Balas (152–145 B.C.E.), a pretender claiming to be the son of Antiochus Epiphanes and enjoying the support of not only numerous eastern Mediterranean kings who detested Demetrius but also the Roman Senate, or again that faction of it which found something to be desired in a puppet or client king favorable to itself rather than to some other faction of the Senate, laid title to the kingship in the seacoast town of Ptolemais (1 Macc. 10:1–2; see *HW* 280–81).

The contenders vied with one another for the support of Jonathan, offering him concession after concession. Demetrius granted Jonathan the right to raise and equip a standing army and the privilege of being the liberator of the hostages held in the Akra (1 Macc. 10:3–6). Jonathan's public reading of Demetrius's concessions in Jerusalem, however, produced alarm both among the general population and the men in the Akra. Undoubtedly many of the Jews, and not just the pro-Seleucid faction, had grave doubts about the Hasmonaeans and were far from giving them their full support (1 Macc. 10:7–8; see 10:61–11:25 and 14:44–45). Jonathan's newly acquired privileges were personal grants to an ambitious individual, not rights bestowed upon the Jewish community as a whole; nor was the office of Jonathan clearly defined. Jonathan took up residence in Jerusalem and began the city's refortification (1 Macc. 10:10–11). Except for the Akra and Beth-zur, the strongholds established by Bacchides were surrendered to the Hasmonaeans (1 Macc. 10:12–14).

Not to be outdone, the Seleucid pretender to the throne, Alexander Balas, in exchange for friendship and military support, appointed Jonathan as high priest, an office with some defined rights and responsibilities. He also appointed him the king's friend, thus making him a member of the royal court (1 Macc. 10:15–20) and council of advisors. Although not from the high-priestly families, nor an Oniad, Jonathan assumed the office at the Feast of Tabernacles, probably in 152 B.C.E., thus ending a seven-year interregnum in the post.

Gambling for support, Demetrius sought to bypass the Hasmonaean party and Jonathan, who now had gone over to Alexander, by appealing directly to the Jewish people. In a special letter, addressed directly to the Jewish nation, he made no reference whatsoever to Jonathan, whom Demetrius probably correctly understood as a Hellenistic type of despot without full support of the community. In exchange for their support, Demetrius promised the reduction or elimination of many taxes and tributes, the existence of Jerusalem as a holy and tax-free city, the surrender of the Akra, the release of all captive Judeans throughout the empire, the freedom to observe all religious celebrations, the right of Judeans to join the royal forces, the annexation of some Samarian territory as well as the city of Ptolemais, special financial privileges for the Temple, and revenues for rebuilding and restoring the Temple, Jerusalem, and other cities (1 Macc. 10:22–45). Circumstances never provided occasion to test the seriousness of Demetrius's concessions. The Jews reacted with incredulity and Demetrius, shortly thereafter, died in battle with Alexander (1 Macc. 10:46–50).

Throughout the rest of his tenure as high priest (until 143/2 B.C.E.), Jonathan shrewdly took advantage of the continuing conflict over the Seleucid throne and became increasingly involved in the struggles, an involvement that eventually led to his death. After the wedding of Alexander Balas to Cleopatra, daughter of the Egyptian ruler Ptolemy VI (180–145 B.C.E.), in 150 B.C.E., Jonathan was invited to the festivities at Ptolemais (1 Macc. 10:51–59) and lavished both kings and their friends with "silver and gold and many gifts" (1 Macc. 10:60). Unfortunately, the text does not reveal the source of Jonathan's wealth, but it does report that "a group of pestilent men from Israel, lawless men" (= non-Hasmonaean supporters) unsuccessfully sought to present charges before Alexander against Jonathan (1 Macc. 10:61). On the occasion, Jonathan was made general and governor of Judea (= military and civil leader; 1 Macc. 10:62–66).

A few years later, when Demetrius II (146–140; 129–125 B.C.E.) challenged Alexander for the throne, Jonathan fought gallantly on Alexander's behalf and in the process temporarily seized the coastal city of Joppa, acquired great booty from the cities of Azotus and Ascalon, and was presented the city of Ekron as a gift (1 Macc. 10:67–89). Ptolemy VI for unknown reasons sided with Demetrius II, forced his son-in-law Alexander to flee to Arabia, where he was murdered, and he himself took the crown as king of Asia only to die from battle wounds three days after Alexander's death (1 Macc. 11:1–19; *Ant.* XIII.103–19). During the turmoil of this unexpected change of events Jonathan besieged the Akra but was unsuccessful. Again "silver and gold and clothing and numerous other gifts" tempered the wrath of the Seleucid king, as did Jonathan's lifting of the siege and the promise to pay three hundred talents. After Jonathan's benevolence, Demetrius II refused to hear Jonathan's accusers but confirmed him in his previous posts and granted additional concessions to the Jewish people, clearly recognizing their right to possession of the territory of Judea as well as three additional districts annexed from Samaria (1 Macc. 11:20–37).

Under the new Seleucid monarch, Jonathan rapidly found himself to be an important "cog in the wheel" of Seleucid conspiratorial machinery. Demetrius II, relying upon mercenary troops, dismissed his regular forces, reduced or eliminated their pay, and, in the absence of adequate veterans' benefits, was confronted with a major military revolt (see *HW* 281–82). Being promised that the king would withdraw his troops from the Akra, Jonathan sent three thousand troops to Antioch and rescued the king from his own subjects only to have Demetrius renege on his promise (1 Macc. 11:38–53; *Ant.* XIII.129–30, 133–43). Demetrius was subsequently confronted with organized revolt led by Diodotus Trypho (see *HW* 282–83), who placed the infant son of Alexander Balas and Cleopatra on the throne as Antiochus VI (145–142). Jonathan allied himself with Trypho and Antiochus VI, who reconfirmed him as high priest and as king's friend and appointed his brother Simon as governor of the coastal plain between Phoenicia and Egypt (1 Macc. 11:54-59). In the civil war between the two Seleucid contenders, Jonathan exercised an enormous power, rallying dissident Syrian troops to his cause, ranging over the territory from Gaza in the southwest to Damascus in the northeast, and occasionally clashing with Demetrius's forces (1 Macc. 11:60–74; 12:24–32). Jonathan had either been granted far greater territorial authority by Antiochus VI than he had enjoyed under the previous rulers (see 1 Macc. 10:65; 11:34) or else, more probably, he took advantage of the crisis of power and exercised an ambitious and independent authority on his own in the area.

Within the province of Judea, the Hasmonaeans moved to consolidate further their rule and rid the territory of direct Seleucid control. Beth-zur was taken (1 Macc. 11:65–66), fortresses were constructed, the defenses of Jerusalem were strengthened, and a barrier was built to isolate the Akra from the rest of the city (1 Macc. 2:35–38). Diplomatic moves on the international scene were made to establish friendship and alliances. Ambassadors and letters were sent to Rome, Sparta, and elsewhere (1 Macc. 12:11–23; *Ant.* XIII.163–70; XII.225–26). The introduction to the Spartan letter, which refers to "Jonathan the high priest, the senate (*gerousia*) of the nation, the priests, and the rest of the Jewish people" (1 Macc. 12:6), demonstrates that the Hasmonaeans were now in effective control of all Jewish institutions in the Temple state and had removed their opposition from all posts of importance.

Fearing the rising power of the Hasmonaeans, who could field a formidable force of forty thousand, Trypho moved to capture Jonathan through a ruse—after showering him with gifts and appealing to self-interest by promising him Ptolemais and other strongholds. Jonathan was seized after entering Ptolemais with only a token force. Negotiations conducted by his brother Simon, after his hasty completion of Jerusalem's fortification, and even payments and the delivery of Jonathan's sons as hostages to Trypho were to no avail. Simon, however, was successful in thwarting the invasion of Judea by Trypho. The latter put Jonathan and apparently his sons to death in Transjordan after his plans to invade Judea were further frustrated by an unusually heavy snowfall. Jonathan's bones were later reinterred at Modein, where Simon built for his family a massive memorial, characterized by the features of Greek victory monuments, to commemorate Hasmonaean victories on land and (anticipated) sea (1 Macc. 2:39; 3:30; 14:5).

The Rule of Simon

Simon reestablished relationships with Demetrius II. The latter was now confronted with the claim to kingship by Trypho (142–139 B.C.E.), who had ordered the murder of the young Antiochus VI. Demetrius responded by confirming Simon as the high priest. He had apparently already been so proclaimed by the people, that is, the Hasmonaean forces and supporters (see *Ant.* XIII.213; 1 Macc. 4:35, 38). Demetrius also granted a general amnesty, ended the collection of taxes in Jerusalem, and reaffirmed all previous privileges and grants (1 Macc. 3:31–40).

First Maccabees 13:41–42 notes that the Judeans marked this diminishment of Seleucid power in Judea by dating their documents and contracts by the year of Simon's reign—a means of noting the beginning of a new era and of repudiating Seleucid authority, since legal practice required the name of the reigning king to appear in all documents.

Simon moved quickly to capture the city of Gazara (Gezer). This removed an adjacent and hostile enclave with a Syrian garrison (see 1 Macc. 9:52; 14:34; 15:28) that interfered with Hasmonaean access to the seacoast (see 1 Macc. 4:5). Simon expelled the inhabitants of the city, turned it into a military colony, and settled it with loyal Yahwists under the leadership of his son John Hyrcanus (1 Macc. 13:43–48, 53). In so doing, he followed the pattern employed earlier by Antiochus IV in the latter's takeover and occupation of Jerusalem.

The infamous Akra in Jerusalem was finally starved into submission. After they "cleansed the citadel from its pollutions," the Jews entered the Akra with great pomp and festivities and Simon decreed that this date (probably in June 141 B.C.E.) should be commemorated in an annual celebration (1 Macc. 13:49–52; see *Megillat Ta'anit,* 23 Iyyar; *MPAT* 185).

Numerous prerogatives were bestowed upon Simon by his supporters.

These are noted in a document found in 1 Macc. 14:27–45, which purports to be a copy of an official inscription on bronze tablets publicly displayed in the Temple (1 Macc. 4:27, 48–49). The document contains a declaration proclaimed "in the great assembly of the priests and the people and the rulers of the nation and the elders of the country " (1 Macc. 14:28). Much of the proclamation is simply praise of Jonathan and Simon, but it does contain the rights granted to Simon by "the Jews and their priests": (1) Simon was to be leader and high priest forever, that is, he and his family were to rule in perpetuity; (2) he was to be governor with appointive power in all governmental areas; (3) he was to have full authority over the sanctuary; (4) his word was to be obeyed by all; (5) all contracts in the country were to be written in his name; and (6) he was to be clothed in purple and wear gold (1 Macc. 4:41–43).

Although the pro-Hasmonaean author of 1 Maccabees presented Simon as savior of his nation and prince of peace and in almost lyrical fashion depicted him as the fulfillment of prophecy (1 Macc. 14:4–15), it is quite clear that, even in his day, not all of his surviving countrymen were Hasmonaean supporters. In addition to the rights granted to Simon, the document not only implies opposition to the Hasmonaeans even within the Temple state—in its overkill of praise for Jonathan and Simon it "protests too much" and hedges the rights granted with the statement "until a trustworthy prophet shall arise"—but also clearly takes such opposition into consideration: (1) it prohibited people or priests from nullifying or opposing what Simon said; (2) it prohibited the convening of an assembly in the country without his permission; (3) it denied anyone the right to be clothed in purple or put on a gold buckle; and (4) it stipulated that the death penalty could be imposed on anyone acting contrary to or nullifying the rights granted to Simon (1 Macc. 14:44–45).

In addition, the Roman letter, addressed to various "kings and countries," that commended the administration of Simon and affirmed and encouraged peaceful relationships with the Jewish people recommended that "if any pestilent men have fled to you from their country, hand them over to Simon the high priest, that he may punish them according to their law" (1 Macc. 24; 15:15–24). The Romans were reestablishing the *amicitia* with Simon, as it was their custom to renew treaties, diplomatic agreements, and any type of accord whenever a new king, ruler, or monarch came into power. In other words, the Romans were confirming Simon as the rightful client ruler of Judah and Jerusalem.

The same decree that granted rights and privileges to Simon and his descendants thus greatly curtailed the rights and privileges of others and clearly presupposed strong anti-Hasmonaean sentiments in the Temple state society. Who were these potential or actual opponents of the

Hasmonaeans? Had not a quarter of a century of Hasmonaean suppression and slaughter of its opposition eliminated all opponents? Who were those that might have been unwilling to join the liberation chorus singing the praises of this newly gained freedom?

Parties and Groups
in Hasmonaean Times

Throughout the books of 1 and 2 Maccabees, constant references are made to the opponents and nonsupporters of the Maccabees. These are ordinarily referred to with generalizing and denunciatory epithets such as "the lawless" (1 Macc. 3:5; 9:23), "troublers of the people" (1 Macc. 7:22), "the ungodly" (1 Macc. 9:73), and so forth. Since the Hasmonaean revolt and the events that led up to it involved a power struggle among four major families—the Oniads, the Tobiads, the Simonites, and the Hasmonaeans—it is safe to assume that the members and supporters of the first three families were opponents and rivals of the Hasmonaeans. Only the Oniad family survived the struggle with any strength, however, and then only in Egyptian exile. Supporters of continued Seleucid control and involvement in Temple state Judean life would have comprised one element among the anti-Hasmonaean groups. Throughout the Hasmonaean struggles, many Jews in the Temple state continued to support the Seleucid government. Simon and two of his sons were murdered by his son-in-law Ptolemy, who along with his followers expected to pull off a coup with Seleucid support (1 Macc. 16:11–22). They must have been counting on at least some general acceptance of their plans among the population at large.

Evidence presented by Josephus and Pliny, incidental references in the books of Maccabees, and the Dead Sea Scrolls indicate that various parties or schools of thought existed or came into being during the Hasmonaean period. (Josephus calls these groups *haereseis* [the term later translated as "sects"] or "philosophies.") The texts refer to "seekers after righteousness and justice," Hasideans, Pharisees, Sadducees, Essenes, and "members of the new covenant." The origins of these groups, their beliefs and practices, their relationships to one another, their attitudes toward the Hasmonaeans, and whether some deserve the designation of party or sect are still matters of historical uncertainty and scholarly conjecture.

"Seekers after Righteousness"

First Maccabees 2:29–38 refers to a group "who were seeking righteousness and justice," actually never clearly named, that fled to the wilderness in the early days of the struggle with the Seleucids. A thousand of this group were killed on the Sabbath without offering resistance because of the day's holiness. Members of this group—and there is no reason to assume that all were killed—were certainly religiously motivated quietists. This quietist-passive attitude is reflected in the book of Daniel, whose author, writing probably in late 164 B.C.E., considered armed rebellion against the Seleucids (that is, the Hasmonaean revolt) to be only "a little help" (Dan. 1:34) and recommended passive submission to the point of martyrdom but held out the hope of future resurrection (Dan. 12:1–3).

The Hasidim

The Hasideans (Hasidim = "Pious Ones" or "Devout Ones") are first mentioned in 1 Macc. 2:42, where they are described as a group or company of "mighty warriors." They joined the Hasmonaeans and participated in their "war" against those who were deemed apostate Yahwists (1 Macc. 2:43–48). Later, they appear along with or as part of a group of scribes who sought peace with the high priest Alcimus and the Seleucid commander Bacchides, saying, "A priest of the line of Aaron has come with the army, and he will not harm us," although some (scribes? Hasideans?) were disappointed in their confidence when sixty of them were later slaughtered (1 Macc. 7:12–18). Second Maccabees refers to the Hasideans only once, during the time of Alcimus, who accused them, under their leader Judas Maccabeus, of "keeping up war and stirring up sedition," and not letting "the kingdom attain tranquillity" (14:6).

The Hasideans were therefore depicted as if they were militant pietists, who were willing to fight in armed resistance for the right to practice the Yahwistic religion as they understood it, that is, according to their own ideological interpretation. If this is historically valid, they were probably not so much a sect as a movement, a movement that was broader even than the number of those willing to support the Hasmonaean endeavors in their earliest phase.

Pharisees, Sadducees, and Essenes

Josephus referred to three groups—Pharisees, Sadducees, and Essenes—as existing during the time of Jonathan (*Ant.* XIII.171–73). The situation was probably more complex than he, or his source, imagined. Josephus, or a source he used for the period, simply noted the three parties that continued to exist into his own day. The manner in which Josephus abruptly refers to these three groups—between his description of Jonathan's letter to the Lacedaemonians (Spartans) and Jonathan's further wars against Demetrius II—and the fact that they play no role in his narrative suggest that they appeared in a source he was using and that the groups were organized as definable entities at the time of Jonathan. Josephus says very little about these groups at this point in history, only discussing their understanding of Fate (Providence) and its relationships to human events and achievements. The Essenes are said to see everything as the product of Fate, the Sadducees to do away with Fate altogether, and the Pharisees to assign some events to Fate and others to human initiative. If we transpose this general description into a political key, the Essenes would appear as passive quietists, the Sadducees as political realists, and the Pharisees as somewhere in between.

Elsewhere Josephus describes the basic difference between the Pharisees and Sadducees as follows:

> The Pharisees had passed on to the people certain regulations handed down by former generations and not recorded in the Laws of Moses, for which reason they are rejected by the Sadducean group, who hold that only those regulations should be considered valid which were written down (in Scripture), and that those which had been handed down by the fathers need not be observed. And concerning these matters the two parties came to have controversies and serious differences. (*Ant.* XIII.297–98)

The Pharisees were thus advocates of a twofold law, the written Torah and a particular version of oral, unwritten legal precepts. They stood therefore in the line of Ezra and Nehemiah, who had sought to apply, extend, modify, and supplement the Torah to cover ever-changing human situations. The Sadducees also obviously had their own methods and mode of reading and applying Scripture, since the interpretation of any authoritative text requires a method of exegesis and an understanding of how texts are to be read and applied and what is considered of lesser and greater importance. It is impossible to know whether the Pharisees, who allegedly were the traditionalists, were necessarily more or less conservative than the Sadducees. One could argue that the Sadducees, by appealing to the explicit text of the Scriptures (the Torah), were reformers seeking to counter the traditional and explicative lore of the Pharisees.

Josephus's description of the Essenes (*Ant.* XVIII.18–22; *War* II.119–61; see Philo, *Every Good Man Is Free*, 75–91) presents them as an ascetic sect that was scattered throughout the country. They possessed their own distinctive practices and beliefs and lived rather isolated from the rest of Judaism.

The Qumran Community

The so-called Dead Sea Scrolls, discovered in 1947 and the years following in the vicinity of Wady Qumran on the northwestern shore of the Dead Sea, reveal the life and faith of a sectarian group that has many affinities with

TEXT 5:
THE ORIGINS OF THE
QUMRAN COMMUNITY

And now, listen, all those who know justice, and understand the actions of God; for he has a dispute with all flesh and will carry out judgment on all those who spurn him. For when they were unfaithful in forsaking him, he hid his face from Israel and from his sanctuary and delivered them up to the sword. However, when he remembered the covenant of the very first, he saved a remnant for Israel and did not deliver them up to destruction. And at the moment of wrath, three hundred and ninety years after having delivered them up into the hands of Nebuchadnezzar, king of Babylon, he visited them and caused to sprout from Israel and from Aaron a shoot of the planting, in order to possess his land and to become fat with the good things of his soil. And they realised their sin and knew that they were guilty men; but they were like blind persons and like those who grope for the path over twenty years. And God appraised their deeds, because they sought him with a perfect heart and raised up for them a Teacher of Righteousness, in order to direct them in the path of his heart. And he made known to the last generations what he had done for the last generation, the congregation of traitors. These are the ones who stray from the path. This is the time about which it has been written: (Hos 4:16) "Like a stray heifer so has Israel strayed," when "the scoffer" arose, who scattered the waters of lies over Israel and made them veer off into a wilderness without path, flattening the everlasting heights, diverging from tracks of justice and removing the boundary with which the very first had marked their inheritance, so that the curses of his covenant would adhere to them, to deliver them up to the sword carrying out the vengeance of the covenant. For they sought easy interpretations, chose illusions, scrutinised loopholes, chose the handsome neck, acquitted the guilty and sentenced the just, violated the covenant, broke the precept, colluded together against the life of the just man, their soul abominated all those who walk in perfection, they hunted them down with the sword and provoked the dispute of the people. And kindled was the wrath of God against his congregations, laying waste all its great number, for his deeds were unclean in front of him. (*Damascus Document* I.1–II.1; from *DSST* 33) the Essenes as these are described by Josephus and Philo. If the Essenes were a movement that came into being in the late third century B.C.E. and produced such works as *1 Enoch* and *Jubilees*, then the Qumran community may be seen as a sect within the larger Essene movement. From the Qumran texts, which refer to their leader and opponents with various epithets, it is clear that the community was strongly critical of the status of religious life in Jerusalem and of its leaders, especially the Hasmonaeans. Because of the cryptic nature of the textual references, any attempt to speak about the history of the group, however, must be based on numerous hypotheses.

The Qumran community dated its origin to a time 390 years after Israel was "given into the hand of king Nebuchadnezzar of Babylon" (*Damascus Document* I.5–8a; see Text 5). Since Jerusalem was taken in 586 B.C.E., the community claimed to have come into being just after the beginning of the second century. This was a time contemporary to when the Jewish community came under Seleucid control. In fact, it also came into being at the time when Flamininus, the Roman general who was responsible for the conquest of Philip of Macedon and the successful conclusion of the Second Macedonian War, issued his Isthmian Proclamation (196 B.C.E.), which became part of what may be construed as Rome's Isthmian Doctrine, reflecting Rome's own perspective of its own manifest destiny. The reason for the group's split with the Jerusalem Temple community is never explicitly spelled out, but the new role of Rome in the affairs of a hellenized Jerusalem, in addition to the more local issue of the religious and cultic calendar to be followed, played a significant role. 196 B.C.E. may be the year to which *Damascus Document* I.5–8 refers. (1) From 196 B.C.E. onward, Roman support of hellenized people, be they natives or ethnically of Greek or Greco-Macedonian stock, was a danger to those who preferred to remain isolationists, and who did not want to be subject to any foreign suzerain. (2) The sectarian Qumran group followed a solar calendar of 364 days in a year, with a division of the year into four periods of 91 days each. This same calendar is reflected in the books of *1 Enoch* and *Jubilees* (see Text 6). Under such a system, the festivals would always have fallen on the same days of the week. The calendar followed in the Jerusalem Temple was lunar, and the festivals fell at fixed times vis-à-vis the moon, not on fixed days of the week. But these calendrical differences need not have been solely a matter of theological differences. They may have reflected geopolitical ones as well.

In all probability, during Ptolemaic control of Palestine, a solar calendar was utilized by the Jewish community or at least was a matter of controversy. So it is significant that the same sort of interests in calendrical matters is to be found in the Canopus Decree of 238 B.C.E. This decree, proclaimed by the Egyptian priesthood, sought to regulate certain religious celebrations, reinforce the importance of the solar calendar, and

TEXT 6:
THE SOLAR CALENDAR

On the new moon of the first month, and on the new moon of the fourth month, and on the new moon of the seventh month, and on the new moon of the tenth are the days of remembrance, and the days of the seasons in the four divisions of the year. These are written and ordained as a testimony for ever. And Noah ordained them for himself as feasts for the generations for ever, so that they have become thereby a memorial unto him. And on the new moon of the first month he was bidden to make for himself an ark, and on that (day) the earth became dry and he opened the ark and saw the earth. And on the new moon of the fourth month all the mouths of the depths of the abyss beneath were closed. And on the new moon of the seventh month all the mouths of the abysses of the earth were opened, and the waters began to descend into them. And on the new moon of the tenth month the tops of the mountains were seen, and Noah was glad. And on this account he ordained them for himself as feasts for a memorial for ever, and thus are they ordained. And they placed them on the heavenly tablets, each had thirteen weeks; from one to another (passed) their memorial, from the first to the second, and from the second to the third, and from the third to the fourth. And all the days of the commandment will be two and fifty weeks of days, and (these will make) the entire year complete. Thus it is engraven and ordained on the heavenly tablets. And there is no neglecting (this commandment) for a single year or from year to year. And command thou the children of Israel that they observe the years according to this reckoning—three hundred and sixty-four days, and (these) will constitute a complete year, and they will not disturb its time from its days and from its feasts; for everything will fall out in them according to their testimony, and they will not leave out any day nor disturb any feasts. But if they do neglect and do not observe them according to His commandment, then they will disturb all their seasons, and the years will be dislodged from this (order), [and they will disturb the seasons and the years will be dislodged] and they will neglect their ordinances. And all the children of Israel will forget, and will not find the path of the years, and will forget the new moons, and seasons, and sabbaths, and they will go wrong as to all the order of the years. For I know and from henceforth will I declare it unto

thee, and it is not of my own devising; for the book (lies) written before me, and on the heavenly tablets the division of days is ordained,
lest they forget the feasts of the covenant and walk according to the
feasts of the Gentiles after their error and after their ignorance. For
there will be those who will assuredly make observations of the
moon—how (it) disturbs the seasons and comes in from year to year
ten days too soon. For this reason the years will come upon them
when they will disturb (the order), and make an abominable (day)
the day of testimony, and an unclean day a feast day, and they will
confound all the days, the holy with the unclean, and the unclean day
with the holy; for they will go wrong as to the months and sabbaths
and feasts and jubilees. For this reason I command and testify to thee
that thou mayst testify to them; for after thy death thy children will
disturb (them), so that they will not make the year three hundred and
sixty-four days only, and for this reason they will go wrong as to the
new moons and seasons and sabbaths and festivals, and they will eat
all kinds of blood with all kinds of flesh. (*Jubilees* 6:23–38; from *Apocrypha and Pseudepigrapha of the Old Testament*, ed. R. H. Charles [Lon-
don: Oxford University Press, 1913], 2.22–23)

make provisions for leap years (see Text 7). The Seleucids followed a lunar
calendar, as did the Jews of the Temple state from the second century onward. A lunar calendar has about 354 days in a year. It must be adjusted to
the solar year by the addition of a month about every third year. Because
of this variability in the calendar, the festivals fall on different days from
year to year.

If a solar calendar had been employed in the Jerusalem Temple during
Ptolemaic times, then the lunar calendar may have been introduced into
the cult by Simon II during the "honeymoon" period enjoyed by the Jewish community with Antiochus III. Since a dominant characteristic of the
Qumran community was its concern with calendrical issues—the proper
times and seasons—the adoption of such a lunar calendar would have
been a serious factor in precipitating the break-off of the group from the
authoritative powers and the cult in Jerusalem.

The Qumran community described itself as "groping for the way" for
twenty years, after which God raised up a leader for the group, the Teacher
of Righteousness, a priest, who taught the community the true inspired
way of understanding Scripture so as to see their history and beliefs fore-
told in sacred writ (*Habbukuk Commentary* VII.4–5; *DSST* 200). The com-

TEXT 7:
THE SOLAR CALENDAR
IN THE CANOPUS DECREE

In the ninth year of the reign of Ptolemy, son of Ptolemy and Arsinoe the Brother-and-Sister Gods, the priest of Alexander and the Brother-and-Sister Gods and the Benefactor Gods being Apollonidas son of Moschion and the canephore of Arsinoe Philadelphos being Menekrateia daughter of Philammon, on the seventh of the month Apellaios, the seventeenth of the Egyptians' (month) Tybi: decree: the chief-priests and the prophets and those who enter the shrine for the adorning of the gods and the feather-bearers and the sacred scribes and the other priests who come together from the temples in the country for the fifth of (the month) Dios, on which day is celebrated the birthday of the king, and for the 25th of the same month, on which day he received the kingdom from his father, (all these) having assembled together on this day in the temple of the Benefactor Gods in Canopus spoke: . . . And whereas feasts of the Benefactor Gods are celebrated each month in the temples in accordance with the previously written decree, the first (day) and the ninth and the twenty-fifth, and feasts and public festivals are celebrated each year in honor of the other greatest gods, (be it resolved) for there to be held each year a public festival in the temples and throughout the whole country in honor of King Ptolemy and Queen Berenike, the Benefactor Gods, on the day on which the star of Isis rises, which is reckoned in the sacred writings to be the new year, and which now in the ninth year is observed on the first day of the month Pauni, at which time both the little Boubastia and the great Boubastia are celebrated and the gathering of the crops and the rise of the river takes place; but if, further, it happens that the rising of the star changes to another day in four years, for the festival not to be moved but to be held on the first of Pauni all the same, on which (day) it was originally held in the ninth year, and to celebrate it for five days with the wearing of garlands and with sacrifices and libations and what else that is fitting; and, in order also that the seasons may always do as they should, in accordance with the now existing order of the universe, and that it may not happen that some of the public feasts held in the winter are ever held in the summer, the star changing by one day every four years, and that others of those now held in the summer are held in the winter in future times as has happened in the past and as would be happening now, if the arrangement of the year remained of 360 days plus the five days later brought into usage (be it resolved) for a one-day feast of the Benefactor Gods to be added every four years to the five additional days before the new year, in order that all may know that the former defect in the arrangement of the seasons and the year and in the beliefs about the whole ordering of the heavens has come to be corrected and made good by the Benefactor Gods. (*GHD* 222–25)

munity went into exile in Damascus probably at the outbreak of civil war in the 170s, where under the Teacher they formed the new covenant of true believers (*Damascus Document* IV.3; VI.2–11; XIX.33–34; *DSST* 35, 36–37, 46). (The sect of the Therapeutae in Egypt, known from Philo's account [*The Contemplative Life*, 80], may have been a similar splinter group within the larger Essene movement that chose to take refuge in Egypt.)

The Qumran community spoke of many of their opponents and of the Jewish leaders with whom they did not agree, but identification is difficult since references are always in epithets, such as "the Man of Lies" and "the Wicked Priest." The most prominent opponent of the community was the Wicked Priest, "whom God delivered into the hands of his enemies" who "took vengeance upon his body of flesh" (*Habbakuk Commentary* IX.1–12; *DSST* 200–201). This is perhaps a veiled reference to the Hasmonaean Jonathan, who was seized, held captive, and eventually killed by the Seleucid general Trypho (1 Macc. 12:46–13:23). The Wicked Priest is said to have "pursued the Teacher of Righteousness to the house of his exile that he might confuse him with his venomous fury. And at the time appointed for rest, the Day of Atonement [according to the Qumran calendar], he appeared before them to confuse them, and to cause them to stumble" (*Habukkuk Commentary* XI.4–8; *DSST* 201–2). This encounter, in which the Wicked Priest sought to kill the Teacher of Righteousness, probably took place during the group's exile in Damascus. First Maccabees notes that Jonathan, whom the community probably described as the Wicked Priest, was in Damascus on two occasions, at the height of his power and ambition (1 Macc. 11:62; 12:32).

The community probably had no better relationship with, or opinion of, Simon than they had of Jonathan, since both were "instruments of violence" (*4Q Testimonia*; *DSST* 138). The right of extradition referred to in the Roman letter supporting Simon's reign would suggest that he was not favorably disposed to "pestilent men" (= non-Hasmonaean supporters) who had fled the country (1 Macc. 15:21). The community probably remained in exile in Damascus during the days of Jonathan and Simon, returning to Judea and settling at Qumran, as the archaeological evidence at the site suggests, during the early days of Simon's successor when Hasmonaean authority had been greatly weakened.

The Hasmonaean Dynasty

Simon was the last of the three Hasmonaean brothers to rule. Two of the first generation had fallen in battle. (Eleazar had died in battle when a Seleucid elephant fell on him [1 Macc. 6:43–46] and John on a mission to the Nabateans was killed by a marauding band from Medeba [1 Macc. 9:35–36].) The successors to the original Hasmonaeans consolidated and expanded the territorial rule of the dynasty. Their kingdom eventually rivaled that of ancient Israel at its height. In the process, the Hasmonaeans became increasingly unpopular with their own people.

John Hyrcanus

Following Simon's murder by his son-in-law Ptolemy and his supporters, Simon's son John Hyrcanus (135–104 B.C.E.) assumed his father's position. Two sons of Simon, as well as Hyrcanus's mother, were either killed along with Simon (1 Macc. 6:16) or subsequently after a long period of maltreatment during which time they were used as hostages to stall Hyrcanus's attack (so Josephus, *Ant.* XIII.228–35). Simon's son-in-law eventually fled the country seeking refuge with the king of the city of Philadelphia.

John Hyrcanus was soon confronted with Seleucid efforts to reassert Syrian authority in the area. Antiochus VII (139–129 B.C.E.) had earlier sought the return of Joppa, Gazara, and the Akra in Jerusalem, as well as indemnity and tribute from Simon (1 Macc. 5:25–36). Simon and his forces, however, had been sufficiently strong to repulse a Seleucid invasion, but Hyrcanus was not so successful. Antiochus VII now ravaged Judea. Even Jerusalem was subjected to a lengthy siege during which conditions became so bad that Hyrcanus expelled the aged and those incapable of fighting so as not to deplete the city's food supply. Finally Hyrcanus was forced to capitulate and come to terms: five hundred talents had to be paid, hostages given over, tribute agreed to, and arms surrendered. In addition, Antiochus pulled down the walls (or battlements) of the city (*Ant.* XIII.236–48). As part of the peace settlement, Hyrcanus seems to have been compelled to contribute troops for Seleucid wars, since the Jewish high priest accompanied Antiochus on his Parthian campaign, during which the Seleucid monarch was killed and replaced on the throne by Demetrius II, who was released by the Parthians after having been held prisoner for ten years (*Ant.* XIII.250–53). Subsequent contention over the Seleucid throne allowed Hyrcanus to reassert Jewish independence: "He . . . revolted against the Macedonians, and no longer furnished them any aid either as a subject or as a friend" (*Ant.* XIII.273; but see XIV.247, which could refer to further conflict in the early days of Antiochus IX [116–95 B.C.E.]).

John Hyrcanus was soon able to extend the borders of the Hasmonaean state. Cities in Transjordan were taken as well as towns in the district of Samaria. Shechem was overrun and the Samaritan temple on Mount Gerizim destroyed (*Ant.* XIII.254–56). Late in his career, the city of Samaria itself was razed after a year's siege: "Not being content with that alone, he effaced it entirely and left it to be swept away by the mountain-torrents, for he dug beneath it until it fell into the beds of the torrents, and so removed all signs of its ever having been a city" (*Ant.* XIII.275–81). Idumea, to the south of Judea, was conquered and its citizens forcibly converted: "He permitted them to remain in their country so long as they had themselves circumcised and were willing to observe the laws of the Jews" (*Ant.* XIII.257–58). Friendly relationships were retained with the Romans, who diplomatically supported the Judeans in the struggles with Antiochus VII (*Ant.* XIII.259–66) and perhaps Antiochus IX (*Ant.* XIV.247).

Significant internal developments under John Hyrcanus included:

1. Hyrcanus became the first Hasmonaean to employ foreign mercenary troops. The tomb of David was looted of much of its wealth to pay for the mercenary forces as well as to bribe Antiochus VII (*Ant.* XIII.249; VII.393; *War* 61).

2. When trouble with the Seleucids subsided, Hyrcanus was free to suppress his own people. Josephus reports that he possessed "leisure to exploit Judea undisturbed, with the result that he amassed a limitless sum of money" (*Ant.* XIII.273). The Qumran community reflects such a situation in its condemnation of the Jerusalem high priests for their love of riches and their desire to "accumulate riches and loot from plundering the peoples" (*Habakkuk Commentary* IX.3–5; *DSST* 201). In the *War,* Josephus states that the prosperous fortunes of John Hyrcanus and his sons "provoked a sedition among his envious countrymen, large numbers of whom held meetings to oppose them and continued to agitate [see 1 Macc. 14:44–45], until the smouldering flames burst out in open war and the rebels were defeated" (*War* I.67).

3. Hyrcanus broke with the Pharisees and sided with the Sadducees (*Ant.* XIII.288–98). According to Josephus, Hyrcanus had been a follower of the Pharisees, as were probably all of the early Hasmonaeans, and was greatly loved by them. When the Pharisees as a group or one of their mem-

bers suggested that Hyrcanus give up the high priesthood and content himself with political authority and went on to insinuate that Hyrcanus's mother had not met the sexual purity required for a high priest's wife (see Lev. 21:13–14), he is said to have deserted the Pharisees and supported the Sadducean party, abrogating Pharisaic regulations (their oral law). The widespread popular support of the Pharisees apparently led to outbreaks that had to be squelched by Hyrcanus (*Ant.* XIII.299).

When John Hyrcanus died, he left behind a secure state with ever-expanding borders. Josephus eulogized him as one who had excellently directed the government: "Truly a blessed individual and one who left no ground for complaint against fortune as regards himself. He was the only man to unite in his person three of the highest privileges: the supreme command of the nation, the high priesthood, and the gift of prophecy" (*War* I.68; *Ant.* XIII.299–300).

Aristobulus I

John Hyrcanus intended that political power should pass to his wife upon his death, which would have met the demands of the Pharisees for the separation of religious and civil authority. His eldest son, Aristobulus I (104–103 B.C.E.), however, seized power and imprisoned his mother and three of his brothers. His mother was allowed to die from starvation while incarcerated (*Ant.* XIII.301–2). Only one brother, Antigonus, was initially treated with any favor. He, however, quickly fell victim to his brother's jealous insecurity when a court intrigue, apparently orchestrated by the queen, who feared that the healthy and vigorous Antigonus would seize power from her ailing husband, led to his entrapment and murder (*Ant.* XIII.303–13).

In spite of the internal strife that characterized the one-year reign of Aristobulus I, who bore the designation "Philhellene" (friend of the Greeks), two significant events transpired during his short reign:

1. The Hasmonaean high-priestly rule became a monarchy: "Aristobulus saw fit to transform the government into a kingdom, which he judged the best form, and he was the first to put a diadem on his head" (*Ant.* XIII.301). No statement is given concerning popular and pious reaction to this assumption of the kingship by a non-Davidic figure, but there certainly must have been some disaffection.

2. He, or probably his brother Antigonus, defeated the Itureans settled between Phoenician territory on the west and Damascus on the east and forced them "if they wished to remain in their country, to be circumcised and to live in accordance with the laws of the Jews" (*Ant.* XIII.318). This probably means that it was Aristobulus who brought Upper Galilee under Hasmonaean control and produced the further judaization of the region.

Alexander Jannaeus

When the ailing Aristobulus died of an illness aggravated by "remorse for the murder of his brother . . . his mind being so troubled by his guilty deed that his inward parts were corrupted by intense pain, and he vomited blood" (*Ant.* XII.314), the queen, Salome Alexandra, released his surviving brothers from prison. Josephus reports that the queen appointed Alexander Jannaeus (103–76 B.C.E.) as king, and his narrative suggests but does not state explicitly that she married him (*Ant.* XIII.320; see Lev. 21:13–14; Ezek. 44:22). Two tendencies were characteristic of Jannaeus's reign: external expansion and internal turmoil.

1. The extension of Jewish borders did not progress without occasional setbacks for Jannaeus. His reign witnessed successful encounters with, as well as defeats from, the Nabateans, the Egyptians, and the Syrians. At the time, both Ptolemaic and Seleucid power and effectiveness were severely weakened by internecine and fratricidal struggles in both ruling houses. For a time, Judea became a battleground between Ptolemy Lathyros, ruler in Cyprus—a region that, like Coele-Syria, Egypt considered vital to her defense—and his mother Cleopatra III, whose forces were under the command of the Judeans Hilkiah and Hananiah, the sons of Onias IV. Ironically, it was the Oniad Hananiah whose intervention prevented Cleopatra from invading and annexing Judea from the Hasmonaeans (*Ant.* XIII.284–87, 352–55).

Jannaeus was able to gain control of all the Palestinian seacoast south of Mount Carmel with the exception of Ascalon (see Map 2). His attempt to take the important seaport city of Ptolemais ended in failure (*Ant.* XII. 324–29). In addition, Jannaeus, primarily late in his reign, conquered territory in Transjordan from the Nabateans and subdued several independent Greek cities in the area. Under him, four districts of Palestine—Judea, Samaria, Galilee, and Transjordan—were under Hasmonaean control. All of these regions were "converted" to Judaism. A city like Pella was "demolished because the inhabitants would not agree to adopt the national customs of the Jews" (*Ant.* XIII.397). This political situation had its economic advantages, since it gave the Judeans dominance over the commerce passing through Palestine, and possession of the coastal cities allowed for Jewish participation in maritime trade.

2. Internally, the reign of Jannaeus aroused enormous, hostile opposition, which the king was able to suppress only through the employment of his Pisidian and Cilician mercenaries and of which he was freed only when his main opponents, eight thousand strong, fled into exile. Josephus's narrative suggests that there were three stages in the people's opposition to Jannaeus.

In the first stage, popular opposition expressed itself at an observance

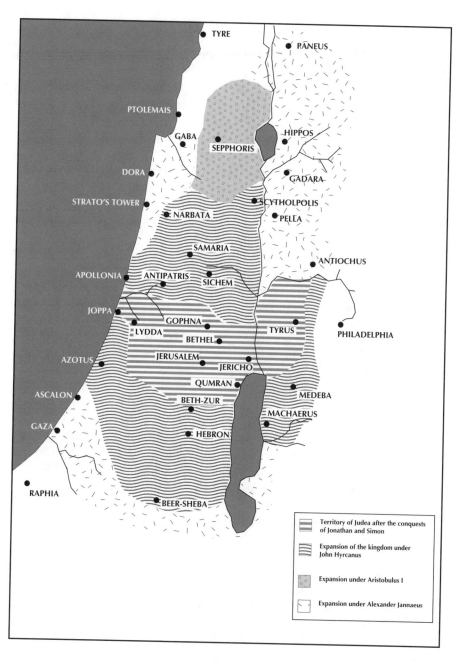

MAP 2.
THE HASMONAEAN KINGDOM
AT ITS GREATEST EXTENT

of the Feast of Tabernacles, "for it was on these festive occasions that sedition is most apt to break out" (*War* I.88). The king, at the altar, was pelted with lemons and greeted with shouts declaring "that he was descended from captives [see Lev. 21:14] and was unfit to hold office." Jannaeus responded by slaughtering six thousand of his countrymen and by constructing a barrier around the inner sacred precincts to prevent any close access by the people (*Ant.* XIII.372–73).

In the second stage, after Jannaeus was humiliated in battle by the Nabatean king Obedas, general civil war broke out. "When the nation attacked him upon this misfortune, he made war on it and within six years slew no fewer than fifty thousand Jews. And so when he urged them to make an end of their hostility toward him, they only hated him the more on account of what had happened. And when he asked what he ought to do and what they wanted of him, they all cried out, 'to die'" (*Ant.*XIII.374–76).

In the third stage, in about 88 B.C.E. some of the Jews appealed to Demetrius III of Damascus, a Seleucid rival, for assistance against Jannaeus. The anomalous armies, with Jews in the Seleucid ranks and with Jannaeus relying upon foreign mercenaries for the defense of his homeland, met in battle near Shechem. The Hasmonaean army was defeated, the mercenaries killed, and Jannaeus put to flight (*Ant.* XIII.377–79). Josephus reports that this melancholy scene aroused the pity of some of the Jewish populace, whose temporary support of Jannaeus led to Demetrius's withdrawal. Jews, however, continued to fight Jews. Jannaeus, when victory was in his hands, vented his fury against the leaders of his opposition: "He brought them back to Jerusalem; and there he did a thing that was as cruel as could be: while he feasted with his concubines in a conspicuous place, he ordered eight hundred of the Jews to be crucified, and slaughtered their children and wives before the eyes of the still living wretches" (*Ant.* XIII.380).

Unfortunately, Josephus does not provide any clear information about the reasons for the internal turmoil during Jannaeus's reign. A number of factors seem to have been significant.

1. The transformation of the Jewish state into a monarchy gave the ruler greater opportunity to exercise autocratic power. Many of Jannaeus's coins refer to him as king. Some also refer to the "Congregation of the Jews," but coins minted late in his reign merely contain the inscription "King Alexander" (in Greek and Aramaic). Undoubtedly, his rule was characterized by even greater despotism than that of his predecessors, differing little if at all from that of numerous other Hellenistic age tyrants.

2. His wars of expansion and the employment of mercenary forces probably produced excessive economic burdens for his subjects. The conquered territory provided benefit primarily for the ruler, who claimed it under the rules of conquest for himself and his high associates.

3. In addition to these political and economic factors, religious issues apparently also played a role. The rift between the Hasmonaeans and the Pharisees, which had begun under John Hyrcanus, seems only to have widened under Jannaeus. According to Josephus, the ever-conquesting king, in spite of a three-year illness brought on by excessive drinking, died on a campaign, but not before warning his queen:

> She should yield a certain amount of power to the Pharisees. . . . These men, he assured her, had so much influence with their fel-low-Jews that they could injure those whom they hated and help those to whom they were friendly; for they had the complete con-fidence of the masses when they spoke harshly of any person, even when they did so out of envy; and he himself, he added, had come into conflict with the nation because these men had been badly treated by him. (*Ant.* XIII.398–404)

This deathbed report, although probably fictitious overall, points to Phar-isaic opposition as a significant feature in the internal imbroglio of Jan-naeus's reign.

Queen Alexandra

Upon the death of Jannaeus, the kingdom was bequeathed to the queen, Salome Alexandra (76–67 B.C.E.), who assumed the role of sovereign and appointed her son, Hyrcanus II, who was a Pharisaic supporter, as high priest. During her rule, the Pharisees became the dominant authority in the state. The Pharisees,

> gradually taking advantage of an ingenuous woman, became at length the real administrators of the state, at liberty to banish and to recall, to loose and to bind, whom they would. In short, the en-joyments of royal authority were theirs; its expense and burdens fell to Alexandra. (*War* I.111; compare *Ant.* XIII.405–6)

Acquiring enormous power in the queen's administration, the Pharisees used political and murderous tactics to gain revenge on their enemies and to establish their authority through coercion. They put to death a close ad-visor of Jannaeus, "proceeded to kill whomsoever they would," "recalled exiles, and freed prisoners, and, in a word, in no way differed from ab-solute rulers" (*War* I.111–14; *Ant.* XIII.408–9). The queen seems to have re-tained significant power in military and international affairs, where she "by continual recruiting doubled her army, besides collecting a consider-able body of foreign troops; so that she not only strengthened her own na-tion, but became a formidable foe to foreign potentates" (*War* I.112).

Civil War Again

Some of the "friends" of Jannaeus—former dignitaries at court and members of the military nobility—appealed along with the queen's son Aristobulus (II) for respite from Pharisaic reprisals and were stationed as military commanders throughout the land (*War* I.114; *Ant.* XIII.214–17). Building upon this base of support and with his mother terminally ill, Aristobulus moved to seize the kingdom. "In barely fifteen days he had occupied twenty-two fortresses, and obtaining resources from these, he gathered an army from Lebanon, Trachonitis and the local princes" (*Ant.* XIII.427). When Hyrcanus II succeeded to the rulership upon the death of his mother, civil war was inevitable. The brothers' forces met in battle near Jericho, but most of Hyrcanus's troops deserted to Aristobulus. Hyrcanus and his remaining supporters fled to Jerusalem, where Aristobulus's wife and children were held captive. Hostilities ended when Hyrcanus agreed to surrender the crown and high-priestly office to his brother and to "live without taking part in public affairs, and be undisturbed in the enjoyment of the possessions that he then had" (*Ant.* XIV.4–7).

The unambitious Hyrcanus II, however, soon fell under the influence of Antipater, governor of the Jewish district of Idumea, whose ambition was sufficient for the two (*Ant.* XIV.8–10). Antipater persuaded Hyrcanus that he should seek to regain the throne and convinced Aretas III, the Nabatean king, to support the endeavor (*Ant.* XIV.11–17). Aretas, assured that victory would secure restoration of Nabatean territory seized by Jannaeus (*Ant.* XIV.18), marched against Aristobulus, who, after many of his supporters deserted to Hyrcanus, took refuge in the Temple (*Ant.* XIV.19–21). With the native population in great dissension, with the reigning monarch besieged in the Temple by a foreign ruler, and with brother fighting against brother, the Romans moved to exercise a direct hand in the affairs of this Jewish client kingdom.

CHAPTER 3

The Herodian Period

In 67 B.C.E., the Roman general Pompey had just completed a successful campaign in Spain. The Roman Senate, having been convinced by Marcus Tullius Cicero and the Optimate Party to do so, assigned Pompey the province (*provincia*) of the eastern Mediterranean region (by passing the Manilian Law), with the major task of subduing the pirates that preyed upon Rome's grain trade. It fell within his assigned province (*provincia* = assignment of duties) to conclude the Roman war with Mithridates of Pontus and Tigranes of Armenia and to bring stability to the area. In the latter capacity he presided over the early phase of the Roman *dominatio* in (= explicit suzerainty over) Judea. For the next two centuries, Roman and Judean relations would take many forms, ranging from limited Jewish "political independence" as a client kingdom under Roman suzerainty to direct Roman rule.

Although we generally think of a province as a territorially defined entity, the Romans construed it primarily as a magistrate's assigned duty, and at first only as such. As the Republic became more involved in nondomestic affairs, the concept of the province contracted in some instances to denote a territorially defined entity to which a magistrate who was not a consul or of consular rank had been assigned or which a consul or magistrate of consular rank drew by lot. When Rome had begun to accrue foreign territory that could not be incorporated or that the Romans were unwilling to incorporate within the state itself albeit with a set of rights different from those held by Roman citizens, it established these territories as provinces.

Pompey's province was assigned, under the Manilian Law, with "unlimited power" (*imperium infinitum*) or "rather great power" (*imperium maius*), which means that Pompey could do pretty much whatever he wanted to do *as long as he was in office*. This was not an unusual attribute for a *provincia*, that is, a magisterial assignment. An assignment with unlimited power, however, does not mean that the magistrate, particularly one of senatorial rank, had total freedom of action without consequences. He could be charged with any crimes committed in office, once he left office and he no longer held *imperium*. In particular, he could be prosecuted for treason under various laws, including Sulla's *lex de maiestate* (*EDRL Lex Cornelia*), a law that categorized misconduct of a promagistrate while in his *provincia* as harming the "majesty" of the Roman Republic; but, additionally, he could be prosecuted for *perduellio* (treason) or for *repetundae* (extortion and other illegal forms of self-enrichment by officials of senatorial rank) or for both (*EDRL perduellio* and *repetundae*), which were under the provenience of the *quaestio perpetua* (the unending court). Unfortunately, as Cicero noted, crimes against the provincials continued despite the laws (*de officiis* II.75).

Pompey's Conquest of Judea

While occupied in Armenia, Pompey sent Scaurus, one of his lieutenants, into Syria to occupy the capital and to prepare for his arrival. Having secured Damascus, Scaurus was informed of affairs in Judea and headed south to do what was necessary to settle affairs in the client kingdom, although Josephus treats this as if it were to take advantage of "a godsent opportunity" (*War* I.127) that allowed the Romans once again to play the role of savior.

Josephus may in fact be correct, but it is not likely. The events leading up to Pompey's taking of Jerusalem, or the taking of the city itself, were hardly likely to have been the result of what would seem to be an opportune act of aggression by a general in the field. The Romans intervened in foreign affairs, especially those of their client kings, if and only if they had to do so. Even when requested to intervene by the kings themselves, they frequently declined to act. Intervention in and of itself was costly and often brought about the burden of having to deploy troops, which had become an extremely expensive thing to do once the post-Marian paid professional army replaced the drafted citizen forces that had made Rome great. Even prior to the development of the paid army early in the first century B.C.E., the Romans did not want to send their (drafted) citizen army to any war that was not necessary, for various reasons, as both Polybius and Livy have shown *ad nauseam* for the periods covered in the extant portions of their works (which unfortunately do not take us beyond the mid-second century B.C.E.).

Moreover, Jerusalem was not relevant to Pompey's plans or agenda, and he had more pressing matters to take care of. So he sent Scaurus to settle the civil war there, and he did not himself go at that time. There is little doubt that when ultimately he had to go to Judea and take Jerusalem himself, Pompey might well have thought of this as being more trouble than

CHART IV. The Early Roman Era (65–40 B.C.E.)

Roman Affairs	*Major Events*	*Roman Administrators in Syria-Palestine*
	Rome annexed Seleucid territory (64)	65–62 Aemilius Scaurus
	Jewish delegations met with Romans and Pompey (64–63)	
	Pompey captured the Jerusalem Temple after a three-month siege (63)	
60 First triumvirate of Pompey, Crassus, and Caesar	Pompey marched in triumph in Rome accompanied by Aristobulus II and other Jews (61)	61–60 Marcius Philippus 59–58 Lentulus Marcellinus
58–50 Caesar in Gaul	Alexander sought to seize power in Palestine (57)	57–55 Gabinius
	Aristobulus and Antigonus escaped from Rome and led Palestinian uprising (56)	
	Alexander led second attempt to gain power (55)	
53 Parthians defeated and killed Crassus	Crassus looted Jerusalem Temple	54–53 Licinius Crassus
51 Parthians advanced to Antioch	Jewish uprising led by Peitholaus	53–51 Cassius Longinus 51–50 Bibulus
49 Caesar crossed the Rubicon; Pompey fled Rome	Aristobulus poisoned Alexander beheaded at Antioch on order of Pompey	50–49 Veiento 49–48 Metellus Scipio
48 Battle of Pharsalus; death of Pompey in Egypt	Hyrcanus and Antipater changed alliance to Caesar's party (48)	
	Antipater aided Mithridates of Pergamum in his support of Caesar in Egypt (47)	47–46 Sextus Caesar
47 Caesar in Syria	Hyrcanus and Antipater rewarded by Caesar (47)	
	Herod and Phasael appointed as governors	
	The Hezekiah affair in Galilee	

Roman Affairs	Major Events	Roman Administrators in Syria-Palestine
46 Caesar in Africa	Antipater aided Sextus in his struggles	46–44 Caecilius Bassus
44 Caesar murdered in Rome		44–42 Cassius Longinus
43 Second triumvirate of Lepidus, Mark Antony, and Octavian	Cassius raised funds for his cause throughout Syria and Judea (43) Antipater poisoned by Malichus, a strong supporter of Hyrcanus (43) Malichus killed in Tyre on	
42 Battle of Philippi; Antony and Octavian defeated Cassius and Brutus, who commited suicide	orders of Herod (42) Revolt of Helix and Malichus's brother in Jerusalem and Judah Antigonus, son of Aristobulus, led uprising in Galilee Herod became engaged to Hasmonaean princess Mariamne Herod submitted to Antony; he and Phasael confirmed in power Antony repressed anti-Herod Jews	41–40 Decidius Saxa
40 Antony in Egypt; invasion of Parthians	Antigonus proclaimed king in Jerusalem; Herod fled; Phasael committed suicide; Hyrcanus was mutilated.	

the venture was worth. Jerusalem, although not Judea itself, was of no great strategic importance to Rome's "border" defenses in the East. These were better served by cities other than Jerusalem even in Palestine. But Pompey's mandate in the East was to secure or restore the border defenses, part of which abutted Judea.

Scaurus on behalf of Pompey had thus intervened in the affairs of the Hasmonaean state for two reasons, one unimportant and one very important. Pompey's aid had been requested by the warring brothers—the unimportant reason. The important reason was that it was crucial to Rome's geopolitics to keep the "land bridge" that included Judea safe for Roman armies, should they need to pass through, and for trade, and to guard the frontier of Rome's empire where it abutted Judea.

Envoys from Aristobulus and Hyrcanus, armed with claims for their patrons and laden with gifts to buttress the arguments, greeted Scaurus, vying for his support. Josephus, perhaps influenced by charges to be brought later against both Scaurus and Gabinius by Aristobulus at Antioch, seems to have overlooked the long-established "propriety" (actually "necessity") of bringing gifts to Rome or to the Romans even in the field, especially when asking for favorable treatment. Consequently, he treats both Aristobulus and Hyrcanus as bringing bribes to Scaurus. He does not make it clear whether it was Aristobulus's shrewd act of bringing the larger gift (according to *War* I.128) or simply a distrust of Hyrcanus's capabilities (according to *Ant.* XIV.30–31) that led the Romans to side with Aristobulus and to force Aretas and the Nabateans to lift the siege of Jerusalem. More likely, Scaurus was more concerned about the "alliance between" Aretas and Hyrcanus in pursuit of Jerusalem than he was persuaded by either the size of Aristobulus's gift or by some distrust of Hyrcanus's capabilities. But Josephus does not pursue this avenue of thought. In any case, Scaurus returned to Damascus. Afterward, Aristobulus attacked the withdrawing Nabateans and Hyrcanus, their Jewish ally. Near Jericho, Aristobulus was successful in a battle that produced the death of Phallion, the brother of Antipater (*War* I.129–30; *Ant.* XIV. 32–33).

When Pompey arrived to winter in Antioch (64 B.C.E.), he was met by envoys from Hyrcanus II and Aristobulus II. The latter accused Pompey's lieutenants, Scaurus and Gabinius, of demanding and receiving bribe money from him. This was an unexpected charge that, whether or not it was true, must have alienated Pompey's subordinates from Aristobulus's cause (*Ant.* XIV.37). And there are problems involved. On the one hand, it is unlikely that the charge was true because those who accepted bribes could have been punished for such action once their own assignments had concluded. (In 64 B.C.E., all Rome would still remember that in 70 B.C.E., once his magistracy was over, Veres was tried for extortion of Sicily, the province of which he had been governor. He only escaped conviction on this capital charge by virtue of his flight and exile from Rome.) On the other hand, there is no reason to assume that Aristobulus was stupid, and he must have understood that such a charge would alienate Pompey from him. Even if Aristobulus knew that there could be repercussions at Rome, he had no assurance that Pompey would punish men in his service. By this time, the army owed its loyalty to its general, and only secondarily to Rome. The history of Marius and Sulla showed that a loyal and paid army would or at least could follow its general, even bringing about revolution in Rome itself. Pompey could not have been expected to alienate those officers who were loyal to him unless he himself feared repercussions once he no longer held *imperium*. This problem then remains unresolvable.

In the spring, Pompey came to Damascus, again to be met by envoys from Syria, Egypt, and Judea, bearing gifts (*Ant*. XIV.34–36). Three deputations came from the Jews. One was from Aristobulus II and bore a gift valued at five hundred talents, probably taken from the Temple, and Pompey treated it as a gift to Rome. Josephus notes that he himself had seen Aristobulus's gift in the temple of Jupiter Capitolinus (*Ant*. XIV.36), which means that Aristobulus's gift was properly treated as the property of the Senate and people of Rome. Aristobulus argued that only he possessed the character of a ruler (*Ant*. XIV.34–36). Another envoy represented Hyrcanus II, who claimed the seniority rights of the firstborn and accused Aristobulus of raiding neighboring areas and of engaging in piracy at sea, as well as unwarranted violence against his own subjects (*War* II.131–32; *Ant*. XIV.42–44). This would have been a particularly heinous charge since Pompey had been given a mandate to eradicate piracy at sea that had plagued the Mediterranean for some time. The piracy charge, therefore, may have been of greater significance in the determination that Pompey made regarding rulership of Judea than either the primogeniture, the raiding of neighboring areas, or the violence against his own subjects. A third came from the Jewish "nation" opposed to both men, "saying that it was the custom of their country to obey the priests of the God who was venerated by them, but that these two, who were descended from the priests, were seeking to change their form of government in order that they might become a nation of slaves" (*Ant*. XIV.41).

Some of Aristobulus's emissaries were "young swaggers, who offensively displayed their purple robes, long hair, metal ornaments and other finery, which they wore as if they were marching in festive procession instead of pleading their causes" (*Ant*. XIV.45). Aristobulus put in an appearance "arrayed in the most regal style imaginable. But feeling it beneath his dignity to play the courtier, and scorning to further his ends by a servility that humiliated his magnificence, he, on reaching the city of Dium, took himself off" (*War* I.132).

The fact that Hyrcanus, Aristobulus, and "the Jews" brought their grievances for adjudication to Pompey when he was at Damascus itself shows that they understood that Pompey had the right to settle their differences. Pompey, being as much a politician as a general, and having a sure knowledge of Roman law, as Cicero acknowledges, would have been well aware of what he could and should do in matters concerning a client kingdom. So, it is not surprising that he gave them an audience (*Ant*.14.41). The Hasmonaean scions and the Jews, acting as Roman clients, went to their patron state's representative to arbitrate their disputed rule. Pompey listened to them but postponed making a decision, saying he wanted to see first how things were with the Nabateans (*Ant.* XIV.46–48). And, as Roman clients, the Hasmonaeans were obliged to wait for his decision before acting. So when Aristobulus did not wait for Pompey to make his decision about Judea, he was in open rebellion against Rome.

When Pompey arrived in Judea, he found that Aristobulus had taken refuge in the fortress of Alexandrium and that his forces had occupied other strongholds. A game of cat and mouse ensued between Aristobulus and Pompey before the latter finally forced Aristobulus to issue handwritten orders to his garrison commanders to surrender the fortresses they held. "He obeyed, but retired resentfully to Jerusalem and set about preparing for war" (*Ant.* XIV.48–53; *War* I.133–37).

Aristobulus's resolve for war was ephemeral but that of his supporters was not. He came to Pompey "promising to give him money and admit him into Jerusalem, [and] begged him to stop the war and do as he liked peaceably" (*Ant.* XIV.54–57). Aristobulus's followers in Jerusalem made it impossible to fulfill either promise (*War* I.138–41; *Ant.* XIV.54–57). Confronted with such obstinacy, the Romans marched against the city, demanding its surrender.

The population of Jerusalem was rapidly torn by dissension. The supporters of Aristobulus, "insisting on a battle and the rescue of the king" (*War* I.142), finally being outnumbered, retreated to the Temple fortress and cut the bridge connecting it with the city. The partisans of Hyrcanus opened the gates to Pompey, admitting the Romans to the city and palace. While Pompey made plans for an assault on the Temple, Hyrcanus and his supporters "willingly assisted him in all ways" (*Ant.* XIV.60) "with their advice and services" (*War* I.144), just as a client king would be expected to do.

After lengthy preparation and a three-month siege (*War* I.145–49; *Ant.* XIV.64–68), the Temple fortifications were scaled. Josephus reports that twelve thousand Jews perished in the capture:

> Most of the slain perished by the hands of their countrymen of the opposite faction. . . . The priests, seeing the enemy advancing sword in hand, calmly continued their sacred ministration, and were butchered in the act of burning incense; putting the worship of the Deity above their own preservation. (*War* I.150)

Some cast themselves off the precipices; others set fire to buildings around the walls and were consumed in the flames (*Ant.* XIV.169–71; *War* I.151).

Pompey manifested what the onlookers and later Jewish generations viewed as absolute audacity: he and his staff "penetrated to the sanctuary [the Holy of Holies], entry to which was permitted to none but the high priest, and beheld what it contained. . . . However, he touched neither these nor any other of the sacred treasures" (*War* I.152–53; *Ant.* XIV.71–72). This, however, would not have been construed as audacity by the Romans, and given the sectarian differences still existent at this time, it may not have been construed as such by all Jews even within the Temple state. The latter, however, we cannot know. But we must remember that for some, the sanctuary had become polluted as soon as Judas Maccabeus became high priest, and it continued to be polluted by the successive Hasmonaean high priests. For some, the fact that they held the office *de facto* and *de iure civile* did not justify their doing so precisely because this was out of accord with "biblical" law, which would have excluded them from that office. In any case, when Pompey went into the Holy of Holies, he did not act as if he had conquered Yahweh by storming Jerusalem. He did not remove the Temple property to take back to Rome as if he had taken Yahweh into captivity, as the Babylonians had done in 586 B.C.E., when they brought the Temple accoutrements to Babylon along with the Judahite aristocracy. In fact, Pompey merely looked at what was in the Holy of Holies and the Temple. The burning of its walls was another matter, which we will discuss below. Although Josephus attributes Pompey's actions within the Holy of Holies and the Temple to Pompey's piety (*Ant.* XIV.72), we do not know why it happened. More likely it reflected his political astuteness.

Following Hyrcanus's victory, which was effected by Pompey, the latter took several steps to pacify Judea. In so doing, Pompey made the Roman suzerainty over the client kingdom more obvious than it had previously been, thereby showing that it was effectively under Roman control. The fact that his (and subseqently Gabinius's) measures were meant to stabilize matters in this region of the now defunct Seleucid empire (*War* I.153–58; *Ant.* XIV.73–79) was not ideologically important to those whose sources Josephus used. Although Pompey might have been operating on the assumption that the area would soon become a directly governed Roman province, this is not only not clear but also doubtful and unlikely. Even at this time in Rome's history, the undertaking of direct governance was not likely to be particularly pleasing to any Romans but the *equites* (Roman knights, the aristocratic class involved in business, trade, money-lending, and tax farming) or those who would benefit financially from its direct governance. Moreover, such a consequence was out of accord with Rome's general "instinct" to allow control of any area to remain in the hands of a client king unless there was danger that Rome would have to go to war or to expend monies to keep the area quiet.

Pompey's measures, described below, seem to support the idea that he wished to keep Judea as a peaceable and well-regulated client state, but one of more limited proportions than it had been previously.

1. The Temple servants were ordered to cleanse the Temple and reinstitute the customary services. The Romans, in accordance with their own custom, not only did not take the "god" captive, even though Pompey had entered the Holy of Holies for whatever reason, but also they allowed the religious practices to continue as before.

2. The high-priestly office was restored to Hyrcanus II. Although in his secular authority, he was denied the title of king but given the title ethnarch, that is, "ruler" of the *ethnos* and possibly by implication of the state, this was merely a "slap on the wrist." The holder of the high-priestly office effectively held the rights and privileges of rule over the Temple state.

3. The leaders of the war were executed by beheading. This is particularly interesting because it means they were given an "honorable" death. That is, they were not treated as rebellious slaves or a "subspecies" of humans, which would have required crucifixion, but rather as those who had violated the Roman *maiestas*. (This is a pregnant word, possibly eliciting a "knee jerk" reaction among Romans. It means "majesty," at the very least, but it also implies honor, prestige, dignity, greatness, and all that was special about Rome. The *crimen maiestatis* included "high treason, sedition, criminal attack against a magistrate," and so on. One did not have to be a Roman citizen or in Roman territory to commit it.) Pompey was therefore allowing the thin veil of nonincorporation to remain, and the war to be construed as civil and local rather than as something that had to do with Rome.

4. The walls of the Temple and city were razed and Jerusalem was made tributary to the Romans. But this too was a slap on the wrist. It was a diminution of status to be sure. A walled temple, particularly one located on a citadel, is a fortress, and a walled city held special status in antiquity. So, even though he razed the walls, by Roman definition, Pompey had not violated the Temple Precinct itself, and thereby he had not perpetrated an act of impiety. Such an act would have been construed by the Romans themselves as making illegal anything he did in having quashed the rebellion, insofar as it would have been viewed as "unjust and impious," a very serious legal matter. By making the Temple state "tributary," he was taking away a privilege sometimes but not always granted to a client state, be it a city-state or a Temple state.

5. Cities that the Jews had conquered along the Mediterranean coast and in the northern Transjordan were detached from Jewish control.

6. The nation was confined within limited borders.

7. Some cities even within the interior of the Hasmonaean state—such as Samaria and Gabal—were given the status of "free cities" (a technical term which does not imply "freedom" as we would construe it) and annexed to the Roman province of Syria.

8. The Jewish nation was placed under tribute to the Romans, who in a short time exacted more than ten thousand talents.

9. Aristobulus II and his family, along with thousands of his supporters, were taken away in chains to be marched through Rome in Pompey's triumphal procession (see Plutarch, *Pompey* 39.3; 45.5; *GLA* I.564–65). This, however, was in accord with Roman custom in such a circumstance and is not to be construed as unique. Many conquered kings or tribal chiefs or leaders, together with their followers, were led in chains in a Roman "Triumph." During the Republic a Triumph was not automatically given to a victorious general. Rather, it was an honor voted on by the Roman Senate, and it was the only occasion on which a general or his army could bear arms within the Roman *pomerium* (sacred protective "wall"). The conquered, who were led in chains, might then be put to death, or they might be made into slaves. Conquered kings and chiefs, and occasionally even their followers (as in the case of Polybius himself) were sometimes treated as "honored" detainees and kept in Rome under very reasonable circumstances.

10. Judea, along with the area between Egypt and the Euphrates, was placed under the authority of Scaurus, who was left in the region with two legions of Roman troops.

Pompey's actions seem to have had the goal of rendering the Jews ineffective in certain political and economic spheres, and less strong in others. They were cut off economically from maritime trade, and reduced in status and territory. They were not restricted from participating in trade, and they were not denied the right to act in accord with the sovereignty Rome accorded a client kingdom. The fact that they had been left with unaggressive leadership may not even have been at Pompey's design, although he was the initiator and the arbiter of the matter. Pompey, who was well versed in Roman law, knew that the recognition of a high priest or other type of potentate was a prerogative of the Roman Senate. Clearly even *imperium maius* would have given him the right to arbitrate regarding those who had been conquered, with or without the presence of a *decemviri,* that is, a group of ten advisors traditionally appointed by the Senate to accompany and to give on-the-spot advice. He could have expected the Senate to ratify his decisions. Whatever Pompey's intent, he acted well and properly. It was to Rome's advantage to have a strong but pro-Roman ruler in any client state. Possibly Pompey did not realize how weak Hyrcanus II actually was.

Roman and Jewish relationships under Aristobulus had suffered under what would seem to have been very antagonistic and hostile conditions. The Hasmonaean Aristobulus II and his followers took an uncompromising attitude toward the Romans. They unrealistically believed that the Temple state really was independent of Rome, and they may have believed their own ideology, that they were an independent state, merely being bound to their patron Rome by virtue of their *amicitia,* which by that time had been turned into a *societas et amicitia,* a less desirable type of diplomatic bond. True independence was an option that the Romans never permitted their clients. (One must remember that "freedom" was a technical term in the Hellenistic and the Greco-Roman world. It represented a specific status that allowed for subordination to the hegemony or even the suzerainty of a greater power.)

Because the Romans exerted their hegemony and eventually suzerainty over the Temple state in a pyramidal type of structure—whereby that state was for most of its history from 196 B.C.E. onward subordinate to both them and to the Seleucid monarch, who was also subordinated to them—they considered Palestine as an extension of Syria and thought of Palestinian politics as part of a larger arrangement in the area. The Romans certainly could not have granted real independence to a Jewish state lying between Syria to the north and the agriculturally rich Egypt to the south. And, in fact, real independence was unheard of in antiquity for any but a "superpower" such as Rome itself.

After the defeat of Aristobulus II, Pompey had effectively dismembered the Hasmonaean state and reversed trends that had been developing and even become dominant in the area for decades. This can be seen especially in three areas:

1. For years, the Hasmonaeans had followed a program of territorial expansion. Pompey not only put an end to this policy of expansion but also confined Jewish authority to a very limited and greatly reduced territory — consisting of Judea, Galilee, part of the region of Samaria, eastern Idumea, and a strip of Transjordan (Perea)—with Jerusalem as the only city of any size.

2. The Hasmonaeans had followed a policy of annihilating or expelling populations under their control who did not convert. In liberating cities under Jewish control and establishing new towns, the Romans not only forced Jews and non-Jews to live in close proximity but also repatriated dispossessed Jewish and non-Jewish people. Many Temple state Jews who had settled in the expanded Hasmonaean territory were now dispossessed. In returning to Temple state Jewish territory they must have greatly swelled the population, creating a large landless class, a seedbed of discontent and anti-Roman revolutionary sentiments. This explains some of the subsequent rural and peasant support for Aristobulus's family (see *War* I.153).

3. Access to Mediterranean trade and the control of Palestinian coastal regions and towns had been long sought and hard fought for by the Hasmonaeans and now had to be surrendered. This constituted a severe blow to the economic life of the Jewish people.

There is no reason to believe that the Roman Senate would have disapproved of Pompey's actions in this matter. So it does not really matter if Pompey was acting on his own initiative or if he was following some type of senatorial precept. We must not overlook the possibility that what he did had the support of Roman businessmen *(equites)* who had ventures in Palestine and elsewhere in the East, a topic that Josephus seems to ignore.

Early Roman Rule in Palestine

After several decades of what may have been incorrectly interpreted as independence (in the modern sense) because neither Jannaeus nor Alexandra seemed to have renewed the *amicitia* with Rome, thereby repudiating their state's status as a Roman client, Aristobulus II and Hyrcanus II acknowledged that the Jews of Judea were clearly and without doubt under Roman domination. And this was affirmed by Pompey's actions in that land. What we must not forget is that Pompey did not take back a state that had rebelled against Rome. Rather, he as a Roman magistrate who had been given extraordinary police powers *(imperium maius)* with the charge of settling the problems in the East took Jerusalem as an invited police action. This police action, moreover, was effected in a Roman client kingdom, located within his assigned sphere of duties and commands. That is, it was part of what the Romans had defined as a *provincia* centuries prior to their acquisition of territorially defined provinces.

The years 65–40 B.C.E. were a transition period that produced a mix in which three components were the principal ingredients:

1. First, Roman overlordship exercised itself more openly than it had before in determining the structure of the client state. Judea remained a client state, but it was placed under the oversight of the new Roman territorial province of Syria. (In other words, Judea became a part of the assignment, of whatever magistrate was given the governance of Syria as his *provincia*, both territorially defined and as a sphere of duty.) As such, Judea was subject to the Roman legates holding *imperium* in Syria, and an attitude of hospitality toward them was at least expected. Judea was obligated to pay tribute and was expected to offer some services for the occupational forces. The Romans had basically one goal in mind: to preserve a peaceable order in the area and thereby facilitate the collection of tax revenues and military operations. As a rule, Roman provincial government cooper-

ated with the local aristocrats and the wealthy, that is, with the local power structures, which were usually pro-Roman. The Romans had always sought out and supported the pro-Roman factions in any sphere of operations, and from a sociological perspective, it is interesting that almost inevitably these factions were upper class. So the Roman cooperation with the local aristocrats and the wealthy was not the result of a class prejudice, but rather of a desire to favor those who favored and supported Rome.

On the Roman side, two factors contributed to the heightening of tensions. One of these was the strain that lack of understanding created between the occupying force, when such occupation was necessary, and the Jewish populace, whose religious and social sensitivities and scruples exceeded normal expectations. A second area of problems resulted from the frequent ineptitude and possibly greed displayed by Roman administrations ruling over the population.

2. A second ingredient that contributed to strife in the area was what is treated as the unquenchable yearning and widespread Jewish support for the ousted Hasmonaeans to regain the throne. This most likely emanated from the anti-Roman factions, in this case the lower classes, who would not have approved of a ruler whom they must have viewed as arbitrarily placed in power by a Roman over territory that they construed to be only a segment of Judea. When Pompey left Palestine, he carried away the deposed king Aristobulus II, his father-in-law, his two daughters, and two sons, Alexander and Antigonus, but for some reason not his wife (*War* I.158; *Ant.* XIV.79). Both father and sons eventually escaped Roman custody to return and fail in efforts to retake their homeland. Only when the last of the three was executed by Mark Antony in 37 B.C.E. did the family cease to be a thorn in Roman flesh.

We must not forget, however, that Pompey did not completely remove the Hasmonaean family from ruling the now diminished kingdom. Pompey had reinstated Hyrcanus II as high priest (*War* I.153; *Ant.* XIV.72) and ruler, but not as king. This, however, was merely an act of psychological warfare. By withholding the kingship from Hyrcanus, Pompey made him thoroughly aware that it was Rome's right to determine who ruled its client kingdom. It was the alteration in Jerusalem's status to one that was neither free nor nontributary, rather than Pompey's withholding of the kingship, that is the basis of Josephus's statement: "We became subject to the Romans" (*Ant.* XIV.77–78). The high priest in the Temple state was a "priestly" ruler, and therefore acted as king whether or not he had the title, and Pompey would have been aware of this. So, in effect Hyrcanus was king until Gabinius stripped him of his ancestral "right," held by virtue of being high priest, to exercise legal authority in civil matters.

3. A final ingredient in the Palestinian mix was the ambition of Antipater

and his family. Antipater was from Idumea (though not necessarily non-Jewish) and had served earlier as governor over Idumea under King Alexander Jannaeus and Queen Alexandra. Josephus tells us that he had, "by kind offices and hospitality, attached to himself persons of influence in every quarter" (*War* I.181), "having a large fortune and being by nature a man of action and a trouble-maker" (*Ant.* XIV.8). Antipater first became a powerful voice in Judean politics when he orchestrated Hyrcanus's struggles against Aristobulus. With the appointment of his son Herod, "from a house of common people and from a private family" (*Ant.* XIV.491), as king of the Jews, the family's success probably even exceeded the ambitions of the old patriarch.

Hasmonaean Efforts
to Regain the Throne

Alexander, the older son of Aristobulus, escaped from Pompey before the latter's entourage set sail for Rome. Unwilling to give up the ideal of a Jewish monarchical state free from direct Roman control, Alexander mustered a sizable following of ten thousand infantry and fifteen hundred cavalry. In spite of having occupied and fortified several fortresses as well as having begun the reconstruction of Jerusalem's walls, Alexander was no match for the Roman forces under Gabinius, the newly appointed legate over Syria. After a siege in which Mark Antony distinguished himself, Alexander was forced to give up his stronghold at Alexandrium (*War* I.160–68; *Ant.* XIV.82–89).

Alexander's attempt to regain the land from the Romans demonstrated to Gabinius the necessity of more drastic action to restructure Jewish political life and to curb the potential for uprisings. He took four steps that involved rather radical alterations for the Jews, and a fifth that was just as radical from the perspective of the Roman economy. (1) In the reorganization, Hyrcanus II seems to have been stripped of his civil authority, which Pompey had allowed to him, and restricted to purely cultic functions: he had custody of the Temple (*War* I.169; *Ant.* XIV.90). (2) Ruined and unoccupied cities were restored and resettled throughout the region, continuing the policy of Pompey of effectively hemming in the Jewish areas with ties to the Temple state with strong and politically independent cities. Josephus refers to colonists who gladly flocked to these towns to repopulate them. Although no explicit reference is made about the identity of these new inhabitants, some of them were undoubtedly Roman businessmen and opportunists, while others were repatriated non-Jewish natives (*War* I.166; *Ant.* XIV.88; see also XIV.83). Some may have been Yahwistic people who did not adhere to the precepts of Judaism practiced within the Temple state. (3) The area was subdivided into five separate administrative districts, each

with its own capital, and placed under the civil jurisdiction of five aristocratic councils or synods (*War* I.170; *Ant.* XIV.91). Rome was here attempting to weaken national unity so as to preempt effectively further trouble by
dissipating authority and tying the hands of effective leadership. (4) The
mountaintop fortresses of Hyrcania, Machaerus, and Alexandrium were
demolished "to prevent their serving as a base of operations for another
war" (*War* I.168; *Ant.* XIV.89). (5) At the same time Gabinius tried to help
the Judeans maintain their economic well-being. We cannot presuppose
that this was done for altruistic reasons since Gabinius's actions vis-à-vis
the *publicani* ("tax farmers") in Syria, and his other actions in his *provincia*,
reflect his greed, as Cicero (*pro Sestio* XLIII.93) mentions. So it is extremely
significant that he treated the *publicani* in Judea repressively, rather than
supportively (Cicero, *De provinciis Consularibus* V.1). This may have been of
greater importance to the life of most of the populace in Jewish Palestine
during that period than any of the first four measures.

In any case, another war soon broke out. Aristobulus II escaped from
Rome and returned to Palestine, where many of his countrymen flocked to
his support "both on account of his former glory and especially because
they always welcomed revolutionary movements" (*Ant.* XIV.93). The former king's plans to regain the country were hastily executed and his hopes
just as quickly shattered. With Gabinius in pursuit, he fled from the decimated remains of Alexandrium only eventually to have to surrender amid
the ruins of Machaerus. Along with his younger son Antigonus, who had
shared his flight from Rome, he was returned in chains to the capital city.
On the basis of an earlier promise made to Aristobulus's wife, however,
Gabinius successfully petitioned the Roman Senate to allow the sons
Alexander and Antigonus to return to Judea (*War* I.171–74; *Ant.* XIV.92–97).

While Gabinius was on an Egyptian campaign, Alexander raised
another army "and proceeded to massacre all Romans in the country" (*War*
I.176). Upon Gabinius's return, Alexander was defeated in a pitched battle
near Mount Tabor, and his followers were either annihilated or dispersed
(*War* I.175–78; *Ant.* XIV.98–102). Even a nonmember of the Hasmonaean
family was willing to lead a revolutionary movement on behalf of Aristobulus. Peitholaus, a former combatant in Rome's support and second in
command in Jerusalem, raised the banner of revolt, "endeavoring to rally
the partisans of Aristobulus," but was quickly disposed of by Cassius
(legate from 53 to 51 B.C.E.), and thousands of his followers were sold into
slavery (*War* I.162, 172, 180; *Ant.* XIV.84, 93, 120).

Aristobulus and Alexander eventually fell victims to the rivalry between Julius Caesar and Pompey. Caesar released Aristobulus from prison
and armed him with two legions, intending to send him into warfare
against his rival's supporters in Syria, but Pompey's patrons poisoned

Aristobulus shortly after his arrival on the coast. His corpse lay "preserved in honey" for a long while, until Antony finally sent it back to Judea and had it placed "in the royal sepulchers" (*War* I.183–84; *Ant.* XIV.123–24). Alexander was placed on trial in Antioch by Scipio, Pompey's father-in-law, and subsequently beheaded (*War* I.185–86; *Ant.* XIV.125–26).

Roman Legates in Syria

Judea's fate during this period of struggle for Roman power was intertwined with that of Syria and was subjected to the aims of Roman policy and the whims of Roman governors. In the twenty-five years from Rome's takeover of Syria in 65 B.C.E. until Herod was designated king in 40 B.C.E. fourteen different Roman administrators governed Syria. Greed and insensitivity were characteristic of many of them, and their activities contributed to Judea's difficulties and its lack of wholehearted support for this foreign imperial power.

Scaurus, the first governor (65–62 B.C.E.), initially had supported Aristobulus on the basis of a bribe (according to *War* I.128). Gabinius (57–55 B.C.E.), infamous for his corruption and extortion, was publicly attacked in speeches by Cicero and eventually convicted in Rome on grounds of extortion. He was dismissed from his position in Syria after invading Egypt in 55 B.C.E. (*War* I.175; *Ant.* XIV.98) against the explicit opposition of the Senate.

Gabinius's successor, Crassus (54–53 B.C.E.), no longer depended upon mere bribery and extortion but engaged in open robbery in the style of Veres. To help finance a campaign against the Parthians, he ignored Roman precepts regarding the conduct of a *bellum iustum piumque* (= a just and pious war). Roman faith demanded that each war be *bellum iustum piumque.* This means that even non-Roman gods and their temples were to be respected since the Parthians were not under Roman suzerainty. When Crassus stripped the Jerusalem Temple of its gold in spite of a Jewish attempt to ransom and save some of the treasure (*Ant.* XIV.105–9; *War* I.179), he violated Rome's customs. With Crassus's death in the Parthian campaign, his successor, Cassius, further embittered the Jews when he sold many of them into slavery. During his second period of rule in Syria (44–42 B.C.E.), following Caesar's assassination, Cassius laid heavy tribute on the entire area, extracting seven hundred talents of silver from Judea. Four Jewish cities that could not muster their quota were reduced to servitude (*Ant.* XIV.271–76; *War* I.218–22). Nevertheless, he had won over some Jews (Dio Cassius, *Roman History* XLVII.28.3). Widespread Jewish dislike for the Romans was fed not only by the humiliation of the loss of statehood but also by the humiliation of oppressive Roman policies and practices (see also Dio Cassius, *Roman History* XLIX.22.4).

The Consolidation of Antipater's Control

One party—Antipater, his family, and supporters—made the most of Roman control. This shrewd Idumean realized what Aristobulus's family never admitted: the arrival of Roman imperialism in Syria and Palestine meant that the possibility of an independent Judea had been irreparably shattered. Antipater's goal was to function as the *de facto* head of the Judean people and to do so as far as possible without any precipitate ostentation. He pursued his goal by offering cooperative support to the Romans that went beyond the limits of ordinary expectations. In return, his loyalty was rewarded with ever-increasing compensations. He seems to have been given, quite early in the Roman *dominatio* (= domination), an administrative position—probably with the responsibility of tax collection—as the first of ever-greater increments of power (see *Ant.* XIV.103, 127, 139).

When Caesar returned to Syria in 47 B.C.E. after settling matters in Egypt with Antipater's help, Antigonus, the sole surviving son of Aristobulus, appealed to him for redress of grievances, claiming that the deaths of his father and brother in Caesar's cause should have some recompense. When Antigonus's appeal progressed to an attack on Antipater, the latter outmaneuvered him. Antipater appealed to his own unfailing loyalty and displayed the scars he had gained in fighting for the Roman cause. He charged that Antigonus had inherited his father's passion for revolution and was only seeking the opportunity to sow sedition. With no record of devotion to the Roman cause, Antigonus's play for the office of high priest failed to impress Caesar, and he was forced to return to his exile in Chalcis. His uncle Hyrcanus II was reconfirmed in the post and apparently given the office of ethnarch (see *Ant.* XIV.191), a move that restored to the high-priestly office some of the political functions removed by Gabinius.

Caesar proceeded to take actions reversing Judea's earlier humiliations. A Hasmonaean estate in the Plain of Esdraelon was restored to Jewish control as well as the toparchies of Lydda, Ephraim, and Ramathaim and the coastal city of Joppa (*Ant.* XIV.202–10). Judea was exempt from the levying of Roman auxiliary troops and from requisitions for winter quarters and other services (*Ant.* XIV.195, 204). Judea was thus treated as a client kingdom, not as a Roman province.

Antipater was rewarded with "the privilege of Roman citizenship with exemption from taxes, and by other honours and marks of friendship which made him an enviable man. It was to please him that Caesar confirmed the appointment of Hyrcanus to the office of high-priest" (*War* I.193–94; *Ant.* XIV.137). Apparently at this same time, Caesar decreed that Hyrcanus II "and his children shall be ethnarchs of the Jews and shall hold the office of high priest of the Jews for all time in accordance with their national customs, and that he and his sons shall be our allies and also be numbered among our particular friends; and whatever high-priestly rights or other privileges exist in accordance with their laws, these he and his children shall possess by my command. And if, during this period, any question shall arise concerning the Jews' manner of life, it is my pleasure that the decision shall rest with them" (*Ant.* XIV.194–95). This would suggest that significant authority was restored to the Jerusalem Sanhedrin also. Antipater as "procurator" was granted permission, either in 47 B.C.E. or after Caesar returned to Rome, to restore the fortifications of Jerusalem previously destroyed by Pompey and the reduction of taxes to finance the project (*War* I.195–200; *Ant.* XIV.140–44). He had clearly become Rome's resident representative, the guardian of Roman financial interests in the country.

Although he shared administrative powers with Hyrcanus II, whom the Jews called king (*War* I.202, 209; *Ant.* XIV.157, 162), Antipater consolidated his power so as to take the organization of the country into his own hands but without disturbing the titular authority of Hyrcanus, whom Josephus described as "indolent and without the energy necessary to a king" (*War* I.203; *Ant.* XIV.158). The walls of Jerusalem, which Roman soldiers would be forced to scale again a century later, were rebuilt. Local disturbances were quelled. Attempts to cajole the population were made on the premise that support for Hyrcanus and thereby Antipater and Rome would result in peace, prosperity, and tranquillity, whereas if they revolted, "they would find in himself [Antipater] a master instead of a protector, in Hyrcanus a tyrant instead of a king, in the Romans and Caesar enemies instead of rulers and friends" (*War* I.201–3; *Ant.* XIV.156–57).

The Rise of Herod

The most consequential move of Antipater, in the exercise of his "power to rule in whatever form he preferred" (*Ant.* XIV.143), was the appointment of two of his sons as governors. Phasael was made governor of Jerusalem and its environs, and Herod was sent to Galilee with the same position (*War* I.203; *Ant.* XIV.158–59). Herod's impulsive and inflexible determination, fed by an energetic spirit, was quickly given occasion for expression. Upon taking up his post, he was confronted with the activity of a certain Hezekiah whom Josephus describes as "a brigand-chief, at the head of a large horde" (*War* I.204). He was ravaging the Syrian border, that is, probably engaging in anti-Roman activity and banditry. Hezekiah may have been primarily a pro-Hasmonaean nobleman supported by pro-Hasmonaean elements and serfs and landless groups in Galilee. Herod captured him and, presumptuously without trial, had him and many of his

CHART V. The Herodian Era (40–4 B.C.E.)

Roman Affairs	Major Events	Roman Administrators in Syria
	Herod proclaimed king of the Jews in Rome (40)	
	Hasmonaean Antigonus ruled as king and high priest in Jerusalem (40–37)	39–38 P. Ventidius Bassus
	Portions of Galilee, Joppa, and Idumea taken by Herod (39)	
38 Ventidius, inflicted major defeat on Parthians at Gindarus; Parthian crown-prince Pacorus killed	Herod's first siege of Jerusalem failed (39/38)	
	Jericho and parts of Galilee taken (38)	
	Herod journeyed to see and secure help from Antony (38)	38/37 Gaius Sosius
	Herod married the Hasmonaean Mariamne at Samaria while Jerusalem was under siege	
	Jerusalem captured by Herod and the Romans under Sosius (37)	
	Hananel appointed high priest (37)	
	Antony's initial grant to Cleopatra of Herodian territory (36?)	
36 Antony in the east; with Cleopatra in Syria and then in Egypt	Hyrcanus returned from Parthian imprisonment (36)	
	Aristobulus III made high priest and then ordered drowned by Herod (35)	35 L. Munatius Plancus
	Herod appeared before Antony to explain the death of Aristobulus (34)	
	Joseph executed without a hearing (34)	

Roman Affairs	Major Events	Roman Administrators in Syria
	Cleopatra visited Jerusalem (34)	34–32 L. Culpurnius Bibulus
32 Antony-Octavian War	Herod's war with the Nabateans (32–31)	
31 Battle of Actium		
30 Death of Antony and Cleopatra; Egypt became a Roman province	Hyrcanus II executed (30) Herod allied himself with Octavian following Actium Octavian presented Herod with his first extension of territory	30 Q. Didius
	Mariamne executed (29) Alexandra executed Costobar executed	29 M. Valerius Messalla Corvinus 29–27? (27–25?) M. Tullius Cicero 24–23? Varro (probably M. Terentius Varro)
27 Octavian accepted title of "Augustus"		
25	Samaria rebuilt and named Sebaste	
23 Augustus accepted lifelong tribuneship; end of the Republic	Alexander and Aristobulus, sons of Hasmonaean Mariamne, sent to Rome to be educated Herod given Trachonitis, Batanea, and Auranitis by Augustus Work begun on Caesarea	23–13 M. Vipsanius Agrippa
20 Augustus stabilized the eastern frontier with Parthia	Augustus presented Herod with the territory of Zenodorus Herod reduced taxes by one third Rebuilding of the Temple begun Herod visited Rome, brought home Alexander and Aristobulus	
15		
	Further reduction in taxes Dissension with Alexander and Aristobulus began;	

	Antipater brought to court and sent to Rome	
	Herod accompanied Alexander and Aristobulus to Rome to accuse them before Augustus; all three sons returned with Herod	
10	Dedication of Caesarea Herod's family troubles worsened	ca. M. Titius
		9–ca. 6 Sentius Saturninus
	Augustus granted Herod permission to deal with his sons	
	After a trial at Berytus, Alexander and Aristobulus were strangled at Sebaste	
	Pharisees executed	6–4 P. Quinctilius Varus
	Herod's first will	
	After a stay in Rome, Antipater returned to Judea and was placed on trial	
5	Herod ill; made second will naming Antipas as his successor	
4	Uprising led by Judas and Matthias suppressed	
	Antipater executed	
	Herod made third will	
	Herod died five days after Antipater's execution	

followers executed. The feat delighted the Syrians and pleased the Roman governor Sextus Caesar (47–46 B.C.E.), gained the youthful Herod an instant reputation, but aroused strong consternation among the aristocracy in Jerusalem when "they saw how powerful and reckless Herod was and how much he desired to be a dictator" (*Ant.* XIV.158–65; *War* I.204–7).

The Jerusalem aristocrats convinced Hyrcanus to place Herod on trial before the Sanhedrin, claiming that the high priest's inactivity was "to rear kings to his own undoing" and that Herod had carried out the death

penalty in violation of Jewish law, which required an action of the Sanhedrin (*War* I.208–9; *Ant.* XIV.165–67). Hyrcanus's own anxiety (*War* I.208)
and the appeal of the mothers of the slaughtered (*Ant.* XIV.168) were said
to have helped push Hyrcanus to the point of a decision, inconclusive and
indecisive as it was.

Herod promptly appeared before the court, armed, attended by a contingent of bodyguards, robed in purple, and with his hair well-groomed,
not at all like normal defendants, even when innocent, who came when
charged in criminal cases in a supplicating mood, dressed in black, and
with unkempt hair. Because of contradictions in Josephus's account, it is
not certain whether Herod was tried and acquitted or whether Hyrcanus
simply postponed the trial or whether Herod fled to escape condemnation,
but, at any rate, Sextus Caesar wrote urging Hyrcanus to acquit Herod
(*Ant.* XIV.169–79; *War* I.210–11).

Herod took refuge in Damascus with Sextus, a relative of Julius Caesar,
who appointed him military governor over Coele-Syria (the cities of the
Decapolis) and the city of Samaria. Probably with Sextus's permission,
Herod marched against Jerusalem, both to exact vengeance on those who
dared to accuse him and to depose Hyrcanus. The intervention of Antipater and Phasael finally quieted his impetuosity. Herod withdrew to
Galilee, "believing that it was enough for his future plans merely to have
made a show of his strength to the people" (*Ant.* XIV.180–84; *War*
I.212–16).

The internal struggles that were tearing at the fabric of the Roman Republic had their repercussions in Jewish life, especially following the assassination of Julius Caesar. To secure Herod's support, Cassius and
Brutus provided him with additional troops, including infantry, cavalry,
and ships; appointed him governor of Coele-Syria; and, more important,
"promised to appoint him king of Judea after the war which they had just
then begun with Antony and the young Caesar [Octavian]" (*Ant.* XIV.280;
War I.225). Josephus reported that "these powers and brilliant expectations
of the son proved in the end the occasion of his father's destruction" (*War*
I.226). An aristocratic supporter of Hyrcanus II, Malichus, who had previously had troubles with Cassius (*War* I.220–22; *Ant.* XIV.273–76), con-
spired to have Antipater poisoned, either "thinking that his death would
make for the security of Hyrcanus's rule" (*Ant.* XIV.277) or dreaming "of
deposing Hyrcanus without difficulty, and of mounting the throne himself" (*War* I.232). Contemporaneous with, but probably unrelated to, Antipater's death, sedition broke out in Samaria and had to be put down by
Herod (*War* I.229). Herod was able to avenge his father's death, with the
compliance of Cassius, but not before Hyrcanus and Malichus succeeded

in momentarily barring Herod and his non-Jewish troops from Jerusalem during a festival (*Ant.* XIV.285–93; *War* I.229–35).

After Cassius departed Syria in 42 B.C.E. general anarchy broke out in Palestine, creating conditions that did not abate until five years later. A certain Helix, one of Hyrcanus's commanders, along with Jerusalemite citizens, marched against Phasael, seeking to avenge the killing of Malichus, but Phasael subdued the insurgents (*War* I. 236–37; *Ant.* XIV.294–95). Malichus's brother led a revolt and seized several Judean fortresses, including Masada, but was suppressed by Herod (*Ant.* XIV.296; *War* I.237). Antigonus, the surviving son of the Hasmonaean Aristobulus II and an exile in the princedom of Chalcis in the Lebanon valley, thought that the time was propitious to regain the Judean kingdom. With the support of his host Ptolemy, Marion (the prince of Tyre), and Fabius (the Roman general in Damascus), Antigonus and his supporters moved into Galilee and met with initial success. Herod repulsed the invasion but was unable to recapture all the territory occupied by the Tyrians (*War* I.238–40; *Ant.* XIV.297–99, 314–18).

The attempt of Antigonus to retake the leadership of the Jewish people brought Hyrcanus II, the high priest, and Herod into closer cooperation. The strained relationship that had frequently existed between the two was transcended in the threatening appearance of a common enemy. An indication of this new association was Herod's engagement to Mariamne, the granddaughter of both Hyrcanus II and Aristobulus II (*Ant.* XIV.300; *War* I.241).

When Mark Antony and Octavian triumphed at the Battle of Philippi (42 B.C.E.), Herod found himself with a history of support for the losing side. Antony took over control of Asia, and when he arrived in Bithynia, he was greeted by numerous national embassies, including Herod and a delegation of leading Jews bringing accusations against Herod and Phasael. Antony refused to hear the charges against the Idumeans (*Ant.* XIV.301–3; *War* I.242). At Daphne, near Antioch, Antony was met by a second embassy of a hundred Jewish officials whose charges against Herod and his supporters were heard. Antony, relying upon Hyrcanus's opinion, favored Herod and "created the brothers tetrarchs, entrusting to them the administration of the whole of Judea," and placed fifteen of the Jewish delegates under arrest when their indignation exceeded protocol (*War* I.243–45; *Ant.* XIV.324–26). When Antony reached Tyre, he was confronted with a third embassy—a thousand clamoring Jewish representatives anxious to state their case against the Herodians. Although possessed of sufficient passion for Cleopatra (VII), who had met him in Cilicia (*Ant.* XIV.324; *War* I.243), Antony possessed no patience for the persistently protesting Jewish representatives. Local troops were ordered to silence the crowd. Appeals from Herod and Hyrcanus failed to calm the embassy's fury, and the troops took action. Many were killed, more wounded, and in his exasperation Antony had his Jewish prisoners from the second delegation put to death. The surviving members of the delegation fled (*Ant.* XIV.327–29; *War* I.245–47).

In 40 B.C.E., while Antony was spending his time "in idleness and revelry" with Cleopatra in Egypt, the province of Syria was overrun by the Parthians. Syria, Phoenicia, and Palestine as well as territory to the east came under their control. In general, this invasion allowed all the subjected peoples in the area to give expression to their fierce anti-Roman sentiments. (Antony had only shortly before exacted enormous tribute in his passage through the area.) In Judea, it provided opportunity to vent the pent-up hatred of the Idumean-duo. Antigonus seized the occasion and the cooperation of the Parthians—who were promised a thousand talents and five hundred women—to regain the throne of his fathers. The invading Parthians, whom many Jews had revered for decades as deliverers, were greeted almost everywhere with open arms. As the invaders marched toward Jerusalem, "Jews flocked to Antigonus in large numbers and volunteered" (*War* I.250). After initial skirmishes around Jerusalem, Herod and Phasael were besieged in the city, their enemy forces being swelled by "the arrival of the multitude from the country . . . for the celebration of Pentecost . . . tens of thousands of armed and unarmed men" (*Ant.* XIV.337–38). Phasael and Hyrcanus were persuaded by a Parthian commander to leave the city, ostensibly to discuss peace plans. Both were placed in chains (*Ant.* XIV.330–48; *War* I.248–60).

Herod decided that his only hope was flight. With his family, he fled at night toward Idumea. Along his route, "he found . . . the Jews even more troublesome than the Parthians, for they perpetually harassed him" (*War* I.265). After several minor and one major skirmish, Herod reached the fortress of Masada. There he left his family with eight hundred troops and sufficient supplies and set out for Petra (*Ant.* XIV.349–62; *War* I.261–67).

With Herod's departure from Jerusalem, Antigonus and the Parthians were free to act at will. They ravaged and pillaged not only Jerusalem but also the general countryside. The discovery that Herod had escaped with some of the women and had earlier sent much treasure and wealth to Idumea antagonized the looters, who vented their frustrations on the general populace. Hyrcanus and Phasael were turned over to Antigonus. Hyrcanus was disqualified from holding the office of high priest when Antigonus bit or cut off his ears (see Lev. 21:17–23). Phasael either committed suicide or was poisoned by Antigonus. Hyrcanus was carried away as a prisoner to Parthia, and Antigonus was set up as king (*Ant*. XIV.363–69, 379; *War* I.268–73). Coins struck during his short reign bear the inscriptions "King Antigonus" and "Mattathias [his Hebrew name] the high priest, the congregation of the Jews."

Herod made good his escape. Rebuffed by the Nabatean king Malchus I (ca. 56–28 B.C.E. [*Ant*. XIV.370–73; *War* I.274–76]), Herod headed for Egypt. There he was greeted in Alexandria with "a magnificent reception from Cleopatra [VII], who hoped to entrust him with the command of an expedition which she was preparing" (*War* I.279), probably to reclaim Palestine as part of her ancestral Ptolemaic inheritance, but Herod had eyes for Rome and set sail in spite of autumn storms, which had already begun (*Ant*. XIV.374–76; *War* I.277–79). In Rome, Antony and Octavian championed his cause before the Senate, which unanimously approved Herod as "King of Judea" (*Ant*. XIV.377–89; *War* I.280–85).

Herod Becomes King

Numerous reasons contributed to the Roman willingness to appoint Herod, and Josephus noted that many of these were discussed by members of the Senate. (1) The family that had ruled over Judea for years was now in complete shambles: Antigonus had been placed on the throne by the Parthians, the mutilated Hyrcanus was a Parthian prisoner, and the only viable Hasmonaean candidate for any major post was Mariamne's brother, still a minor. (2) The entire family of Antipater had a history of hospitality and invariable loyalty toward the Romans, and with Phasael dead, Herod had no strong kinsmen to create family rivalry. (3) Governing the Jews and combating the Parthians to Roman advantage were tasks that required a strong ruler and a steadfast supporter, and only Herod filled this bill. (4) Since Herod was unqualified for religious office, he could not hold the positions of both king and high priest. This existence of two power poles—crown and priesthood—within the community was no doubt viewed by the Romans as a factor in their favor. (5) Herod was viewed as a good, actual and potential, source of funds, bribes, and gifts.

Following formal festivities, including a sacrifice on the Capitol and a banquet given by Antony, and the official depositing of the senatorial decree, Herod left Rome after a stay of only seven days.

For Herod, the appointment to kingship with authority to act and the full exercise of royal power were separated by many months of struggle and warfare. His kingdom was overrun by foreigners and another sat upon the throne. While Herod was sailing for home, Antigonus was extending his control into Idumea and besieging the fortress of Masada, where Herod's family successfully held out, but only after a timely rain replenished the cisterns. In 39 B.C.E. the Roman legate Ventidius (39–38 B.C.E.) successfully drove the Parthians out of Syria. This gave him opportunity to move against Antigonus, but the Roman only took action strong enough to elicit "as much money as he wanted." After "glutting his avarice," he withdrew, leaving behind a small force under his subordinate Silo, who was as amicable toward the receipt of bribes as his superior (*Ant.* XIV.390–93; *War* I.286–89).

Herod put ashore at Ptolemais and began the task of raising an army. The Roman commanders in the area had been enjoined to give him assistance against Antigonus, but Silo did so with the remorse and enthusiasm of a parasite losing its host. Apparently unable to make much headway in Galilee, Herod moved down the coast, taking Joppa, and then into the more friendly territory of Idumea. He rescued his relatives from Masada and moved north to lay Jerusalem under siege. In spite of Herod's proclamation that "he had come for the good of the citizens and the welfare of the city, bearing no grudge even against those who were openly his foes, but, on the contrary, being ready to forget the offenses his most determined adversaries had committed against him," Antigonus and his followers did not slacken their opposition, but waited for the anticipated return of the Parthians to rescue them. When Silo proved to be more a burden than a help, Herod raised the siege of Jerusalem and returned to Galilee (*Ant.* XIV.394–412; *War* I.290–302).

The subjugation of Galilee proved to be a lengthy and arduous chore. Sepphoris fell without a contest, but vast hordes of brigands and Herodian opponents occupied caves, particularly in the vicinity of Arbela. The last of these were finally routed only by lowering soldiers in boxes over a cliff to gain access to the opponents in the caves. While Herod was away in the friendly city of Samaria, where he had placed his family, his commander in Galilee was killed by "the usual promoters of disturbance," and general insurgency, probably with pro-Hasmonaean sympathies, flourished until his return. Later, while Herod was meeting with Antony and aiding in repelling the Parthians, at Samosata along the Euphrates River, his brother Joseph was killed and his body mutilated by Antigonus in a battle near Jericho. The defeat again brought out the Galilean opponents to Herod. Herod's partisans and Galilean nobles were dragged from their homes and drowned in the Sea of Galilee. Insurrection also broke out in the south (*Ant.* XIV.413–50; *War* I.303–27).

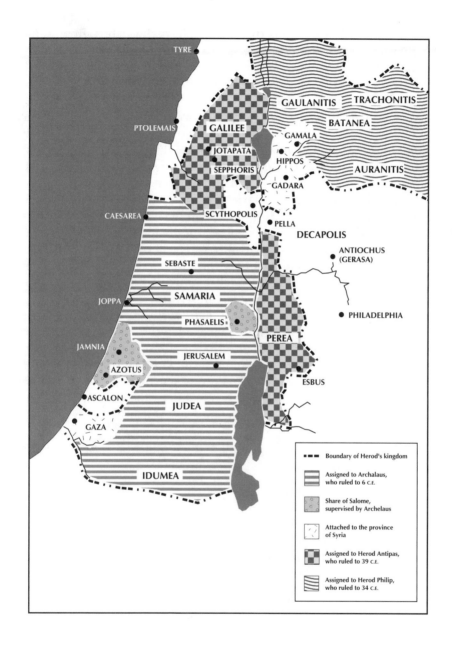

TYRE

GAULANITIS TRACHONITIS

PTOLEMAIS

GALILEE BATANEA

GAMALA

JOTAPATA HIPPOS

SEPPHORIS AURANITIS

GADARA

CAESAREA SCYTHOPOLIS

PELLA

DECAPOLIS

ANTIOCHUS
(GERASA)

SEBASTE

SAMARIA

JOPPA PHILADELPHIA

PHASAELIS

JAMNIA PEREA

JERUSALEM

AZOTUS

ASCALON ESBUS

JUDEA

GAZA

IDUMEA

- - - Boundary of Herod's kingdom

Assigned to Archalaus,
who ruled to 6 C.E.

Share of Salome,
supervised by Archelaus

Attached to the province
of Syria

Assigned to Herod Antipas,
who ruled to 39 C.E.

Assigned to Herod Philip,
who ruled to 34 C.E.

MAP 3.
EXTENT OF HEROD'S KINGDOM
AND ITS DIVISION AT HIS DEATH

Herod hastened home to Palestine to avenge his brother's killing and once and for all establish his rule. Unlike his earlier return from Rome, his return now was with the strength of Rome at his disposal: "Antony entrusted Syria to Sosius [38/37 B.C.E.] with instructions to aid Herod . . . and so Sosius sent two legions ahead to Judaea to assist Herod, and himself followed with the greater part of his army" (*Ant.* XIV.447). Galilee was subdued, an army of Antigonus was defeated, and Pappus, Antigonus's military commander, was slain. Jerusalem was laid under siege. Herod "appointed his army their several tasks, cut down the trees in the suburbs, and gave orders to raise three lines of earth-works and to erect towers upon them," while he himself went off to Samaria to consummate his marriage with Mariamne after a five-year betrothal. "So contemptuous was he already of the enemy, he made his wedding an interlude of the siege" (*War* I.344). Following the wedding, he returned to Jerusalem, where he was joined by Sosius. The two forces numbered several thousand troops: "an army of eleven divisions of foot-soldiers and six thousand mounted men, as well as auxiliaries from Syria" (*Ant.* XIV.469). The defendants held out gallantly, being encouraged by "invocations made about the temple, and many were the things said to encourage the people, to the effect that God would deliver them from danger" (*Ant.* XIV.470), some of these being uttered by persons who "indulged in transports of frenzy and fabricated numerous oracular utterances to fit the crisis" (*War* I.347). Forty days after the bombardment began, the outer wall was breached; after fifteen more days, the second wall was taken. Finally, the Temple area and upper city also fell (*Ant.* XIV.451–78; *War* I.328–51).

When the inner city was captured, in the summer of 37 B.C.E., the survivors were treated with great brutality. Josephus reports:

> Soon every quarter was filled with the blood of the slain, for the Romans were furious at the length of the siege, while the Jews on Herod's side were anxious not to leave a single adversary alive. And so they were slaughtered in heaps, whether crowded together in alleys and houses or seeking refuge in the temple; no pity was shown either to infants or the aged, nor were weak women spared, but even though the king sent word around, urging them to forbear, not one of them held his hand, but like madmen they fell upon persons of every age. (*Ant.* XIV.480)

Having become master over his enemies, Herod now had trouble exercising mastery over his foreign allies, who rushed to enter the Temple and sought to plunder without limits. Appeals and threats, tempered with Herod's distribution of monetary rewards, quelled the fury of the soldiers. Antigonus surrendered, throwing himself at the feet of Sosius and begging for mercy. The Roman commander ridiculed him, designating him Antigone—the feminine form of his name. The deposed monarch was led away in chains. Sosius delivered him to Antony, who had him executed, an act that did not displease Herod (*Ant.* XIV.479–91; *War* I.352–58). Dio Cassius reported that before Antigonus was beheaded, he was first scourged while bound to a cross and thus subjected to a punishment "which no other king had suffered at the hands of the Romans" (*Roman History* XLIX.22.6; *GLA* II.360–61). Antony "became the first Roman who decided to behead a king, since he believed that in no other way could he change the attitude of the Jews so that they would accept Herod" (*Ant.* XV.9). Herod, a product of Rome's eastern policy combined with the ambitions of would-be Roman leaders, was now king in Jerusalem.

Herod's Reign

The years of Herod's monarchy may be divided into three fairly distinct periods: the early part of his rule (until about 30 B.C.E.), during which it was difficult for him to solidify his authority because of internal matters and the role of Antony and Cleopatra in the area; the middle portion (until about 10 B.C.E.), which was an age of prosperity and success but with some major domestic troubles; and the latter years of his rule (until his death in 4 B.C.E.), which were characterized by dissipating domestic turmoil and some international tensions. Throughout these three periods, two things remained constant: the dominating presence of the Romans and the character and personality of Herod (see Text 8).

The Early Period (37–30 B.C.E.)

The early years of Herod's reign were characterized by his efforts to establish his rule throughout the state, by attempts of the Hasmonaeans to regain authority, and by Cleopatra's designs on his territory.

After the capture of Jerusalem, opposition to Herod ran deep. Support for the previous Hasmonaean dynasty (*Ant.* XV.10) against that of "a commoner and Idumean, that is, a half-Jew" (*Ant.* XIV.403), meant that Herod had to establish his throne over the graves of many of his opponents. In spite of the fact that forty-five leading members of Antigonus's supporters, and probably members of the Sanhedrin, were

TEXT 8:
JOSEPHUS'S DESCRIPTION OF HEROD

Herod's genius was matched by his physical constitution. Always foremost in the chase, in which he distinguished himself above all by his skill in horsemanship, he on one occasion brought down forty wild beasts in a single day. As a fighter he was irresistible; and at practice spectators were often struck with astonishment at the precision with which he threw the javelin, the unerring aim with which he bent the bow (*War* I.429–30).

Now it has occurred to others to wonder at the inconsistency of Herod's natural tendencies. For when, on the one hand, we consider his munificence and the benefactions which he bestowed upon all men, it is impossible for anyone, even for those who have very little respect for him, to refuse to agree that he had a most beneficent nature. But when, on the other hand, one looks at the punishments and the wrongs which he inflicted upon his subjects and his closest relatives, and when one notes how harsh and inexorable his character was, one is forced to regard him as bestial and lacking all feeling of moderation. For this reason they think that there were divergent and warring tendencies within him. But I myself have a different view and believe that both these tendencies had the same cause. For Herod loved honours and being powerfully dominated by this passion, he was led to display generosity whenever there was reason to hope for future remembrance or present reputation, but since he was involved in expenses greater than his means, he was compelled to be harsh toward his subjects, for the great number of things on which he spent money as gifts to some caused him to be the source of harm to those from whom he took the money. And though he was aware of being hated because of the wrongs that he had done his subjects, he decided that it would not be easy to mend his evil ways—that would have been unprofitable in respect of revenue—, and, instead, countered their opposition by seizing upon their ill-will as an opportunity for satisfying his wants. In fact, among his own people if anyone was not deferential to him in speech by confessing himself his slave or was thought to be raising questions about his rule, Herod was unable to control himself and prosecuted his kin and his friends alike, and punished them as severely as enemies. These excesses he committed because of his wish to be uniquely honored. . . . For the very same attentions which he showed to his superiors he expected to have shown to himself by his subjects, and what he believed to be the most excellent gift that he could give another he showed a desire to obtain similarly for himself. But, as it happens, the Jewish nation is by law opposed to all such things and is accustomed to admire righteousness rather than glory. It was therefore not in his good graces, because it found it impossible to flatter the king's ambition with statues or temples or such tokens. And this seems to me to have been the reason for Herod's bad treatment of his own people and his counsellors, and of his beneficence toward foreigners and those who were unattached to him. (*Ant.* XVI.150–59)

executed and their property confiscated (*Ant.* XV.6), opposition to Herod ran so deep that Antony was forced to leave a Roman legion "encamped about the city [Jerusalem] to protect the king's position" (*Ant.* XV.72). The fortress at Hyrcania, a few miles southeast of Jerusalem, held by a sister of the Hasmonaean Antigonus, only fell into Herod's hands five years after the capture of Jerusalem (*War* I.364). This suggests that Herod was incapable of immediately overcoming and disposing of all his opponents. Those who had sided with Herod were honored; among them were "Pollion the Pharisee and his disciple Samaias," who had reprimanded the Sanhedrin in Herod's initial appearance before that body (in 47 B.C.E.; *Ant.* XIV.172–76), then predicted his ultimate success, and finally recommended that Jerusalem be surrendered to Herod during the siege (*Ant.* XV. 3).

Although Antony had put to death the Hasmonaean Antigonus, the Hasmonaean family had not relinquished its desire to rule. The ardent holders of this imperishable hope were now members of Herod's immediate family—his wife Mariamne and her mother, Alexandra. When Herod brought a priest from Babylonia, Hananel, and installed him as high priest, the king not only broke with the normal practice of retaining the high-priestly office within the same family but also infuriated Alexandra by passing over Aristobulus (III), her young son—and grandson of both Hyrcanus II and Aristobulus II—disregarding Caesar's promise that the office would be hereditary in the Hasmonaean family (*Ant.* XIV.194–95). Alexandra immediately initiated contact with Cleopatra to gain her assistance in getting Antony to force Herod to appoint her son to the post (*Ant.*

XV.22–24). When Antony showed an interest in Aristobulus and Mariamne, Herod temporarily capitulated and removed Hananel, the recent appointee, and appointed Aristobulus, who at the time was only seventeen years old (*Ant.* XV.22–41). The young priest's first appearance at the Feast of Tabernacles produced what Herod feared the most: a widespread popular response.

> Aristobulus was a youth of seventeen when he went up to the altar to perform the sacrifices in accordance with the law, wearing the ornamental dress of the high priests and carrying out the rites of the cult, and he was extraordinarily handsome and taller than most youths of his age, and in his appearance, he displayed to the full the nobility of his descent. And so there arose among the people an impulsive feeling of affection toward him. . . . Being overcome, they gradually revealed their feelings, showing joyful and painful emotion at the same time, and they called out to him good wishes mingled with prayers, so that the affection of the crowd became evident, and their acknowledgment of their emotions seemed too impulsive in view of their having a king. (*Ant.* XV.51–52)

Herod's jealous insecurity led him shortly thereafter to have Aristobulus III drowned at a swimming party at Jericho (*Ant.* XV.50–56; *War* I.437). Herod no doubt had fears that Cleopatra might convince Antony of the attractiveness of her ruling over Judea, with this handsome and popular young Hasmonaean as her vassal.

Undeceived by Herod's public tears, excessive mourning, and lavish burial rites, Alexandra intuited the truth and set about to find revenge. Pleading her case through Cleopatra, Alexandra succeeded in getting Antony to question Herod at Laodicea when the former passed through Syria on his way eastward. Herod's defense—garnished with rhetorical skill and undergirded with a bribe—led to his acquittal (*Ant.* XV.57–67, 74–79).

With the death of Aristobulus, Mariamne became the pivotal point in Herod's personal life. Alexandra hoped to exploit Mariamne's great beauty and Antony's proclivity for erotic pleasures in order to recover the throne for her family. Earlier, she had sent portraits of her two children to Antony, but Herod had prevented the youthful Aristobulus from visiting Antony, ostensibly fearing that he would become the object of the Roman's erotic passions (*Ant.* XV.26–30). Herod's love of Mariamne was not only skewed by extreme jealousy and abnormal cruelty but also by a justifiable sense of Alexandra's ambitions. Herod upon his return from Laodicea had his brother-in-law, Joseph, put to death. According to Josephus, Joseph had been left in charge of the affairs of the realm and secretly commissioned to kill Mariamne should anything fatally befall Herod. "He was very much in love with his wife and feared the outrage (it should be to his memory) if ever after his death she were pursued by another man [especially Antony] because of her beauty" (*Ant.* XV.65). A false report of Herod's death sent Joseph, Alexandra, and some friends scurrying to the Roman troops in the hope of making the most of the new situation. This was later reported to Herod by his ever loyal and perpetually pernicious mother and his sister. The latter, Salome, accused her husband Joseph of "having frequently had intercourse with Mariamne" (*Ant.* XV.81). When Herod discovered that Joseph had revealed his secret orders to Mariamne, this was sufficient to confirm the king's fears. Joseph was executed without the privilege of an audience before the king. Alexandra was temporarily placed in chains and under guard (*Ant.* XV.65–73, 80–87).

Throughout the early years of his reign Herod was under the constant harassment of Cleopatra of Egypt. Her ancient reputation was built on her political sagacity, her affairs with Julius Caesar and Mark Antony, and her ruthless extermination of relatives. Following her marriage to Antony in the winter of 37/36 B.C.E., Cleopatra intensified her hounding of Antony for the extension of her domain, hoping to restore the Ptolemaic glory of the third century B.C.E. She convinced him to execute Lysanias of Chalcis and give her his territory (*Ant.* XV.92). On more than one occasion, Antony presented gifts to Cleopatra that reduced Herod's territorial holdings. (Both the extent to which Antony reduced Herod's kingdom and the dates of these gifts are matters of dispute; see *Ant.* XV.79, 95–96; *War* I. 361–62, and the descriptions of Plutarch [*Vita Antonii* 36.3–4] and Dio Cassius [*Roman History* XLIX.32.4–5]; *GLA* 1.568–69; 2.362.) After receiving Chalcis, Coele-Syria (the Decapolis), Cilicia, Cyprus, and most of the Palestinian coastal area, apparently including Joppa, which had been restored to the Jews in 47 B.C.E., Cleopatra set out to take over all of Judea and Arabia. Antony balked at her blatant request but granted her control over the valuable balsam and palm plantations in the region of Jericho as well as territory along the eastern shore of the Dead Sea with its bitumen industry, which belonged to Malchus, the Nabatean king. Herod felt that submission was the better means for preventing further encroachments. He was forced to stand surety for the annual fee of two hundred talents imposed on Malchus and the Nabateans for their continued use of her newly acquired property and in the end agreed to pay her two hundred talents annually to lease the lands that had been detached from his own realm (*Ant.* XV.88–107; *War* I.360–63). Shortly before the Battle of Actium (2 September 31 B.C.E.), Malchus fell into arrears with his annual payments and war seemed the only means to collect. Cleopatra convinced Antony "to entrust

CHART VI. Partial Genealogy of the Herodian Family

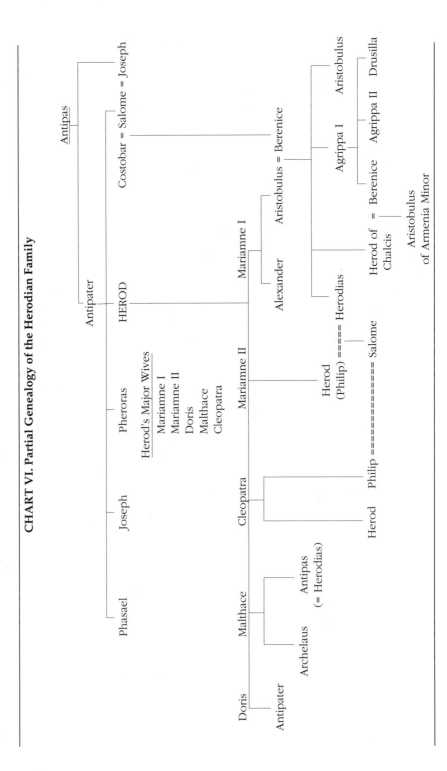

the war against the Arabs to Herod, hoping, if he were successful, to become mistress of Arabia, if unsuccessful, of Judaea, and by means of one of the two potentates to overthrow the other" (*War* I.364–65). Herod suffered a humiliating defeat at Canatha at the hands of the Nabatean Arabs, aided on Cleopatra's orders by one of her generals, but rallied his troops after Judea was devastated by a major earthquake in 31 B.C.E. (*War* I.364–85; *Ant.* XV.108–60). Herod's preoccupation with the Nabateans, however, had its beneficial side; it effectively removed him from direct participation in the conflict between Antony and Octavian.

Herod's Successful Years
(30–10 B.C.E.)

With the death of Antony and Cleopatra and the incorporation of Egypt into the Roman (territorial) provincial system, a new day dawned for Herod and the Jewish state, just as under Octavian, a new day dawned for the Roman Empire. Herod appeared before Octavian at Rhodes to offer his submission, having taken several actions that were no doubt in his favor in the long run. Before leaving for his engagement with the Nabateans, he had finally captured the last Hasmonaean outpost at Hyrcania (*War* I.364). The aged Hyrcanus II, who had earlier been returned from Parthia, where he had the strong support of the Jewish community (*Ant.* XV.11–22), was executed for treason on grounds that must have been widely recognized as dubious (*Ant.* XV.161–82; *War* I.431–34). This removed the last Hasmonaean male who might have moved, or been used, to replace Herod. In addition, although Herod had initially had every intention of fighting for Antony (*War* I.364; *Ant.* XV.109–10), his war with the Arabs had kept him from real embarrassment. In his Nabatean wars, however, Herod had proven himself a capable military leader, which was certainly in his favor. He was able to go to Octavian having in fact already demonstrated his support. After the Battle of Actium, Herod had come to the side of Octavian by joining with the Syrian governor Didius in halting the movement of Antony's gladiators to Egypt, where they planned to join their master in his struggles (*Ant.* XV.195; *War* I.392).

Octavian took a favorable attitude toward Herod, who confessed his previous loyalty to Antony (*Ant.* XV.183–93; *War* I.386–90) but asked that his new master be concerned not with "whose friend, but how loyal a friend" he had been (*War* I.390). Herod was affirmed in his position as king (*Ant.* XV.194–97; *War* I.39–93) and "returned to Judaea with even greater honour and freedom of action, thereby causing consternation among those who had expected the contrary" (*Ant.* XV.198). Later in the year, Herod entertained Octavian at Ptolemais and supplied him with provisions for his invasion of Egypt (*Ant.* XV.198–201; *War* I.394–96).

The triumph of Octavian (subsequently named Augustus [in 27 B.C.E.]) and the subsequent relationship between him and Herod created a period of major prosperity for the Herodian state. Herod and Judea no longer had to live with an Egyptian Cleopatra meddling in internal Judean affairs and nibbling away at Judean territory and wealth. Herod subsequently received three major territorial grants from him. (1) While Octavian was still in Egypt, he returned to Herod "the territory which Cleopatra had appropriated [Jericho], with the addition of Gadara, Hippos, and Samaria and the maritime towns of Gaza, Anthedon, Joppa, and Strato's Tower" (*War* I.396; *Ant.* XV.217). This grant provided Herod with a firm base along the maritime plain and thus access to the sea as well as cities in Transjordan that had been taken from Judean control by Pompey. (2) Later, in 24 or 23 B.C.E., Herod was given the districts of Trachonitis, Batanea, and Auranitis in the northern Transjordan (*Ant.* XV.343–48; *War* I.398–400). This territory had been taken from Zenodorus, who was unable or unwilling to police the area properly. (3) In 20 B.C.E., upon the death of Zenodorus and while Augustus was in Syria, Herod was presented additional territory near the headwaters of the Jordan between Trachonitis and Galilee (*War* I.400; see *GLA* II.362–63). Thus Herod came to rule over a region almost as extensive as that of the Hasmonaean kingdom at its height. Herod had become an important element in the eastern holdings of the Romans. As their "ally and friend" (*socius et amicus populi Romani* = a legal status which by this time merely defines a client king as having a diplomatic relationship with a Roman suzerain; see [*Ant.* XVII.246]), Herod could operate with virtually absolute power in his own realm. Only foreign alliances and the waging of war required the full approval of Rome.

Even with Cleopatra out of the picture and no longer able either to serve as the model of a female head of state or to encourage Hasmonaean disdain for Herod, the king's problems with the Hasmonaeans continued. Before Herod left for Rhodes to meet Octavian, he placed Mariamne and her mother, Alexandra, in the fortress at Alexandrium under heavy guard and appointed his brother Pheroras as head of state (*Ant.* XV.185–86). All of Herod's children, including Mariamne's, were sequestered at Masada under the eagle eye of Herod's sister and his mother. Upon his return, relations between Herod and Mariamne reached the breaking point. The king eventually had her tried and executed (*Ant.* XV.202–39). Although Josephus presents the case as one of Herod's jealousy about a suspected intimacy between Mariamne and her guard—an Iturean named Soemus, who was executed as well—no doubt following what was the court's version of affairs, political issues were undoubtedly involved. The Hasmonaean women felt that they and their family had been duped out of dominion and treated as if they were commoners. One can imagine that the earlier reign of a Hasmonaean queen must have frequently crossed their minds and stimulated their imaginations. While Herod was in Samaria, despondent and even physically ill over his loss of Mariamne, Alexandra moved to gain control of the Jerusalem garrison and support for herself and her grandchildren, but her efforts were reported to Herod and he ordered the immediate execution of his mother-in-law (*Ant*. XV.240–52). A final purge was related to the continued pro-Hasmonaean sympathy. Herod had appointed a native Idumean, named Costobar, as governor of Idumea (probably in 37 B.C.E.) but was unaware that the latter was harboring either some distant members of the Hasmonaean family or its supporters whom he had smuggled out of Jerusalem after its capture by Herod. Costobar subsequently made contact with Cleopatra about her securing control over Idumea with Antony's help. When the effort was vetoed by Antony, Herod was unable to take action against Costobar because of Cleopatra's influence. Herod was finally able to do away with Costobar and his supporters, probably in 27 B.C.E., after having married his sister Salome to him, following the execution of her first husband Joseph in 34 B.C.E. Following her divorce of Costobar, Salome supplied evidence against him and others who were still waiting for an occasion to lead an uprising against Herod (*Ant*. XV.253–66).

Already before the death of Antony, Herod had begun the refortification of his kingdom. After years of Hasmonaean civil war and Hasmonaean attempts to regain their kingdom, the invasion of the Parthians, and Herod's wars to acquire his kingdom, Palestine must have been greatly war-ravaged and run-down. The old fortress that stood to the north of the Temple precincts and housed the ceremonial vestments of the high priest was rebuilt on a grander scale, perhaps even to serve as a royal residence. Herod named the new fortress Antonia, or Antony's tower (*Ant*. XV.409). The fortifications of Jerusalem were repaired and three large towers built into the walls and named after Herod's brother Phasael, his wife Mariamne, and his friend, Hippicus.

A series of primary fortresses, some with palaces, was established throughout his realm. These fortresses were either recommissioned Hasmonaean strongholds or new royal creations. Three guarded Judea in the south and west: Hyrcania, Cypros, and Herodium. Masada, the most impregnable, guarded Idumea and was probably part of a string of forts against the Nabateans. Alexandrium offered protection to Samaritis, while two fortresses, Machaerus and a second Herodium, kept watch over Perea.

Among Herod's major rebuildings outside Jerusalem were Samaria and Strato's Tower; in honor of Augustus, they were renamed Sebaste and Caesarea respectively. The city of Samaria had had good relationships with Herod from the time before his designation as king (*Ant*. XIV.284), had supported him in the early days of his monarchy (*Ant*. XIV.411–13; *War* I.314), and was the scene of his marriage to Mariamne (*Ant*. XIV.467; *War* I.344). As

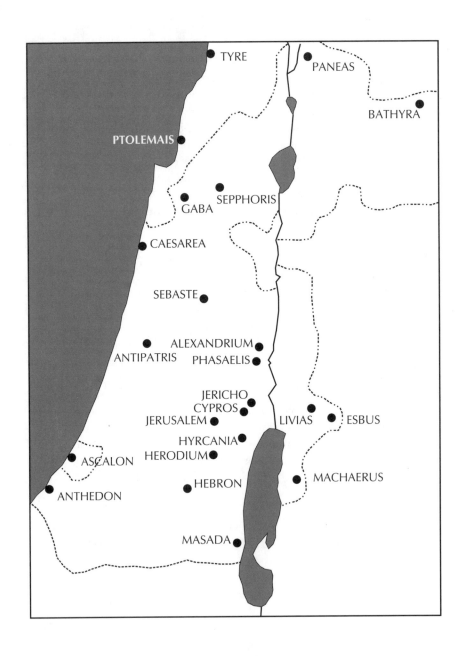

**MAP 4.
HERODIAN CONSTRUCTION SITES
IN PALESTINE**

a reward for its support, Samaria was turned into one of Herod's major strongholds. The city was completely rebuilt, its territory extended, its citizenry enlarged by six thousand, a new constitution provided, and a temple constructed for the imperial cult and dedicated to Augustus (*Ant.* XV.292–98; *War* I.403). The transformation of the decaying port of Strato's Tower into the vibrant harbor of Caesarea, which was more than a decade in the doing, provided Herod and the Jews with a first-class seaport and a bigger share in Mediterranean trade; its dedication, in 12 or 10/9 B.C.E., proved to be the occasion for a great international celebration (*Ant.* XV.331–41; XVI.136–41; *War* I.408–16). The city would later serve Judea as the administrative capital.

Under Herod, Jerusalem was transformed into what the first-century Latin author Pliny the Elder (23–79 C.E.) described as "easily the most outstanding city in the East" (*Natural History* V.70). A palace constructed in the upper city (*Ant.* XV.318–19; see *War* V.156–83) allowed Herod to move his living quarters out of the Antonia. A theater and an amphitheater were built, dedicated to the honor of Caesar, and quadrennial festivals with athletic contests and gladiatorial shows were inaugurated (*Ant.* XV.267–76). The trophies with their image shapes and inscriptions dedicated to Caesar triggered the opposition of some Jews, but even Josephus reports that their feelings were unfounded (*Ant.* XV.277–80). In Jerusalem, Herod's most spectacular achievement was the rebuilding of the Temple (*Ant.* XV.380–425). The Temple enclosure was greatly expanded and the sixth-century building replaced with one of great splendor. A saying of the time indicates the magnificence of the Herodian structure: "Whoever has not seen Herod's building [temple], has never seen anything beautiful."

In addition to his Palestinian projects, Herod made contributions to many cities outside his kingdom. Such gifts not only demonstrated his loyalty to the Roman Empire and emulated the royal practices of the time but also were efforts to enhance his prestige in the outside world. Most of the cities to whom he was a benefactor contained large Jewish settlements. Cities as far removed from Palestine as Athens and Sparta were objects of his bounty. Gifts ranging from temples, baths, markets, city streets, gymnasiums, and aqueducts to such mundane items as seeds for planting constituted his gift list to Lycia, Pamphylia, and Cilicia in Asia Minor, to the isle of Rhodes, and to Phoenician and Syrian cities nearer home (*Ant.* XV.311–16; XVI.18–19, 146–49; *War* I.422–28).

The Waning Years (10–4 B.C.E.)

The last years of Herod's rule were trouble-filled. The family intrigue and quarrels that had nagged his personal life throughout his reign crested in his old age as the interest in inheriting his mantle reached a crescendo.

Troubles with the Nabateans eventually led him to initiate warfare, an action that precipitated the disfavor of Augustus. Opposition to his rule surfaced, and various actions by his subjects required force to preserve Herodian authority. Let us now examine these three aspects in more detail.

1. The shadow of the Hasmonaeans continued to darken Herod's path. Even though Herod had had his Hasmonaean wife Mariamne, her mother Alexandra, and her brother Aristobulus put to death, Hasmonaean blood, even when mingled with his own, still haunted him. His two sons by Mariamne, Alexander and Aristobulus, were eventually executed by Herod in about 7 B.C.E. on the charge of high treason (*Ant*. XVI.361–94; *War* I.538–51). These sons, who had been given pride of place among Herod's children and sent to Rome for their education in about 22 B.C.E. (*Ant*. XV.342), were the object of jealousy on behalf of Herod's other children, especially Antipater, the son of Doris, the first of Herod's ten wives. The latter son and his mother had been banished from court at an early point but returned when troubles with Aristobulus and Alexander developed (*Ant*. XVI.66–99). The dissension against the children of Mariamne had been constantly fed by Salome, Herod's sister. Antipater's contribution to the family strife and a conspiracy he plotted against Herod finally led to his trial and execution only five days before the ailing monarch himself passed away.

The turmoil in Herod's family, the uncertainty about the succession, eradication of the most capable sons, and Herod's production of three wills in the last two years of his life are hardly the ingredients from which stable political conditions accrue. As we shall see in the next major section, Herod's family was incapable of holding matters together after his death; in a way, the old king's treatment of his offspring probably predisposed conditions toward failure.

2. Tensions between Herod and the Nabateans eventually led to open warfare. The Trachonites, whose territory Herod had acquired and whose brigandage he had suppressed, rose in revolt in 12 B.C.E. while the Judean king was in Rome. Upon his return, the revolt was suppressed, but the Nabatean commander and spurned suitor of Herod's sister, Syllaeus, allowed the Trachonites a haven from which they could continue raids on Herod's kingdom. With the approval of the Roman legate in Syria, Herod took action against the brigand's hideout but was also forced to fight a Nabatean army, killing its commander. Syllaeus, in Rome at the time, took the matter directly to Augustus. Because Herod had marched his army across the Judean boundary and thus broken the *Pax Romana,* Augustus took a harsh attitude toward him, refusing to receive the embassy Herod sent to Rome (*Ant*. XVI.271–94). For the first time, Herod fell out of favor with Augustus. At least two years passed before he was willing to enter-

CHART VII. The Later Roman Era—I (4 B.C.E.–44 C.E.)

Roman Affairs	Jewish Affairs	Roman Prefects in Judea	Jewish High Priests
23 B.C.E.–14 C.E. Augustus *princeps*	4 B.C.E. Death of Herod; disturbances in Judea; Archelaus made ethnarch of Idumea, Judea, and Samaritis Antipas made tetrarch of Galilee and Perea Philip made tetrarch of Batanea, Trachonitis, Auranitis, Gaulanitis, and Panias		4 B.C.E. Joazar ben Boethus 3 B.C.E. Jesus ben Sie 5–6 C.E. Joazar reappointed
6 C.E. Sulpicius Quirinius legate in Syria	6 C.E. Archelaus deposed and banished to Gaul; Judea made Imperial Province 6/7 Quirinius's census of Syria; Judas the Galilean and Saddok the Pharisee led uprising	6–8 C.E. Coponius	6 Ananus ben Seth
		9–11 Marcus Ambibulus	
14 (19 August) Death of Augustus		12–14 Annius Rufus	
14–37 Tiberius emperor		15–26 Valerius Gratus	15–36 Ishmael ben Phabi Eleazar ben Ananus Simon ben Camithus Caiaphas (son-in-law of Ananus)

Roman Affairs	Jewish Affairs		Roman Prefects in Judea	Jewish High Priests
26 Tiberius "retired" to Capri: influence of Sejanus became important factor in Roman politics	26–36	Antipas divorced daughter of Aretas of Nabatea to marry Herodias Pilate sent Roman troops into Jerusalem, carrying effigies of emperor, withdrew after protest Pilate built aqueduct in Jerusalem, using Temple funds; quelled protest with violence Shields with names of Pilate and Tiberius placed on Herod's palace Pilate's troops attacked Samaritans at Mount Gerizim; Pilate ordered to return to Rome	26–36 Pontius Pilate	
31 Sejanus executed	33/4 36	Death of Philip (September) Agrippa I imprisoned by Tiberius		
35–39 Vitellius legate in Syria	36/37	War between Antipas and Aretas the Nabatean; Antipas appealed to Vitellius for aid	36–37 Marcellus (Marullus?)	37 Jonathan ben Ananus

Date	Emperors and Events	Prefects	High Priests
37	(16 March) Death of Tiberius		37 Theophilus ben Ananus
37–41	Gaius Caligula emperor	37–41 Marullus	
37	Agrippa I made king over Philip's tetrarchy		
38	Agrippa left Rome for Palestine		
39/40	(Winter) Gaius ordered erection of statue in Jerusalem Temple		
40	(Spring) Antipas appealed to Gaius but was deposed		
40	(Fall) Agrippa I given Antipas's territory in Galilee and Perea		
40	(September) Agrippa convinced Gaius to give up statue project		
41	(14 January) Gaius assassinated		41 Simon Cantheras
41–54	Claudius emperor		41 Matthias ben Ananus
41	Agrippa I made king over Judea, Idumea, Samaritis		
44	(Summer) Death of Agrippa I in Caesarea		

tain the Jewish delegation headed by Herod's advisor and tutor, Nicolas of Damascus (7 B.C.E.; *Ant*. XVI.335–55).

3. Serious tensions developed between Herod and some religious leaders. Perhaps to demonstrate his loyalty to Rome and to win back Augustus's favor, Herod required his subjects to pledge jointly their loyalty to himself and to the emperor, as he had done earlier in his career (*Ant*. XV.368–71). On the earlier occasion, Pharisees and Essenes who objected were exempted from the oath, but now Herod had them fined for failure to swear loyalty (*Ant*. XVII.41–45). For meddling in court affairs and possibly fomenting a conspiracy against the king, some Pharisees were executed.

When Herod's health began to deteriorate rapidly, two Jewish educators, probably rabbis and possibly Pharisees, excited a crowd of youth into pulling down the golden eagle that the king had erected over one of the gates to the Temple. The instigators of the act, along with many of the perpetrators, were burned alive as punishment, important community leaders were reprimanded for allowing such behavior, and the high priest was dismissed from office (*Ant*. XVII.49–67). Herod's reaction to the Pharisees' unwillingness to pledge their loyalty and to the removal of the eagle from the Temple was out of line with his earlier public policy of suppression but not ferocious punishment of dissenters. Undoubtedly, physical and family problems had produced mental instability. The old man had outlived his rationality.

In spite of serious health problems and an attempt at suicide, Herod lived long enough to see his son Antipater exposed as a conspirator, tried, and executed. But now that Alexander, Aristobulus, and Antipater were dead, Herod was left with no son who had been groomed for the office to succeed him. In the four days between Antipater's and his own death, Herod wrote a third will that left his kingdom to three of his sons but did so in a manner that predisposed the arrangement to failure, as we shall see. Herod's final disposition of his kingdom can be viewed as the old monarch's ultimate indecisiveness and sadism toward his children.

Herod died in Jericho, probably early in 4 B.C.E., just before Passover (*War* II.10; *Ant*. XVII.213), after a rule of thirty-seven years (*War* I.665; *Ant*. XVII.191). An elaborate funeral cortege bore his body to Herodium, on the edge of the Judean Wilderness. There it was interred, as Herod had stipulated.

An Appraisal of Herod's Reign

In both Judaism and Christianity, Herod has served as a paradigm of the evil ruler. That he has had a bad press is an understatement. The negative colors with which his portrait has been painted make any positive portrayal of the man appear to be special pleading. Several factors about his rule, however, ought to be noted in summary.

1. His harsh, sadistic treatment of his family and of any actual or potential competitors has rightly been seen as hardly reflective of a normal personality. His acts appear to have been fueled by a sense of insecurity and inferiority. As the product of Hasmonaean ineptitude, Idumean opportunism, and Roman contrivance, Herod had no firm base within his kingdom that could count him as its own, and vice versa. Herod's suspicious nature was fed by continuing disdain shown him by the Hasmonaean family and by pro-Hasmonaean sentiment in his kingdom. His suspicion was exacerbated by a similar feeling among his relatives and family members. Herod's murderous acts of brutality toward his family and his elimination of opponents, however, pale in magnitude when compared to those of his predecessors Aristobulus I and Alexander Jannaeus.

2. Economically and culturally, the Judean state under Herod probably enjoyed its high-water mark, even exceeding the time of Solomon and the reign of the Omrides. Although Herod's rule was no doubt an expensive administration, employment must have been high, and on at least two occasions Herod reduced taxes (*Ant.* XV.365; XVI.64). His construction projects indicate a high level of prosperity and full Judean participation in the trade and life of the Mediterranean world. According to Josephus, Herod once reminded his subjects that such a feat as rebuilding the Temple had been unrealizable during the 125-year reign of the Hasmonaeans (*Ant.* XVII.62).

3. Herod's relationship to Jewish religious institutions and groups was somewhat ambivalent, but he can hardly be condemned for lack of respect for Judaism. Several incidents and activities would suggest his positive regard for Jewish religion. (a) His reconstruction of the Jerusalem Temple was executed with respect for the fears and religious scruples of the population. Demolition of the old edifice was carried out only after full preparations, including the training of priests in construction work (*Ant.* XV.388–90, 421). (b) Archaeological and architectural remains from the traditional burial place of the patriarchs at Hebron and from the site associated with Abraham at Ramet el-Khalil are certainly to be connected with projects of Herod's day. Herod's constructions at these sites would indicate respect for the national heritage. (c) When the Nabatean military commander Syllaeus wished to marry Herod's sister Salome, Herod refused to approve the marriage because the former was unwilling to convert to Judaism (*Ant.* XVI.200–205). (d) His gifts to cities with large Jewish communities may be seen as compensation for the loss of revenues incurred by the annual Jewish payment of the Temple tax to Jerusalem, if we could ascertain that all Jews really did pay it as alleged. (e) The Greek pun about

Herod, attributed to Augustus (Macrobius, *Saturnalia* 2.4.11), that declared it was better to be Herod's pig (*hus*) than his son (*huios*) could indicate that the king even practiced Jewish dietary customs. (f) Although Herod clearly participated in the general Hellenistic culture of the empire and would have liked to see Judea more in the cultural mainstream of the day, there is no evidence that he ever attempted to force Hellenistic practices and thought upon unwilling Jews within his kingdom. He employed Greek tutors for his sons (*Ant.* XVI.242), studied Greek philosophy, rhetoric, and history, and constructed temples in the newly founded cities of Sebaste and Caesarea but carefully avoided what would seem to be non-Jewish worship in Jewish territory (*Ant.*XV. 328–30).

On the negative side, Herod certainly used the office of high priest, although he could not occupy it. He appointed Hananel, whom Josephus calls "a rather undistinguished priest from Babylon," as high priest in 37 B.C.E.; subsequently he deposed Hananel to appoint Aristobulus (III), his brother-in-law, only to reinstate the former after the latter's death (*Ant.* XV.22, 34, 39–41, 56). Other high priests were deposed: Jesus son of Phiabi, so Herod could elevate his future father-in-law, Simon son of the Alexandrian Boethus, to an office and thus to social prominence (*Ant.* XV.322); and Matthias, whom he blamed for failure to prevent "the eagle episode" (*Ant.* XVII.164–67). The use of the office to suit the king must have resulted in a loss of respect for the occupants and the office.

Little is heard of the Sanhedrin in Herod's day. He seems to have gotten rid of most of its members at the time of his capture of Jerusalem in 37 B.C.E. and to have controlled its membership thereafter (*Ant.* XIV.175; XV.5).

From Kingdom to Province

In his last days, Herod altered his will twice in rapid succession. First, he removed Antipater as sole successor and named Antipas, his youngest son and offspring of his wife Malthace from Samaria, to succeed him (*Ant.* XVII.146–48; *War* I.644–46). In the interval following Antipater's execution, Herod again changed his will, naming Archelaus, the elder son of Malthace, to succeed him as king, with Antipas to become tetrarch over Galilee and Perea, and Philip, the son of Cleopatra of Jerusalem, to occupy the same post over Gaulanitis, Trachonitis, Batanea, and Panias (*Ant.* XVII.188–90; *War* I.664). Although Caesar had given Herod the right to name his successor or successors, Herod's arrangements had to be confirmed in Rome. Since cases had to be argued before Augustus, there was no immediate succession to power in Palestine; instead, a period of turmoil and general uprisings ensued.

Disturbances at the Death of Herod

After being widely acclaimed during the seven days of mourning for his father, Archelaus as he prepared to journey to Rome was soon involved in a public audience in which favors, reduction of taxes, release of prisoners, and abolition of duties were requested of him (*Ant.* XVII.200–205; *War* II.1–4). The various demands eventually related to and emanated from the "eagle episode." Crowds, as Josephus calls those desiring revolutionary action (*Ant.* XVII.206; *War* II.5), sought to have Herod's brutality in the event avenged. They also sought to have Joazar, whom Herod had appointed as high priest, deposed. Matters moved from protest to riot, with Archelaus having to be polite in order to be politic, and to exercise power before having been invested with authority. At Passover, tensions led to clashes between segments of the populace—represented by Josephus as if they were the entirety of that populace—and the police, which resulted in the death of large numbers in the Temple (*Ant.* XVII.206–18; *War* II.8–14). After dispersing the crowds, Archelaus and many of the Jewish leaders departed for Rome.

Conditions, already on the brink of anarchy, were only aggravated by the subsequent actions of Sabinus, the Roman official charged with oversight of the finances for the province of Syria. When, at the time of Pentecost, Sabinus moved into Jerusalem and sought to seize Herod's treasury and to occupy the citadels, the Jewish "populace" surrounded the Roman soldiers in the city and a battle ensued. The porticoes of the Temple were burned and the Temple treasury looted by the Romans, with Sabinus's participation. The populace, joined by some of Herod's troops, finally besieged Sabinus in Herod's palace (*Ant.* XVII.221–23, 250–68; *War* II.16–19, 39–54).

With Romans under siege in Jerusalem, revolution broke out throughout the kingdom under a motley array of leaders. (1) A contingent of Herod's troops in Idumea rebelled and took up arms against royalist forces led by one of Herod's cousins (*Ant.* XVII.269–70; *War* II.55). (2) At Sepphoris in Galilee, Judas, the son of the rebel leader Hezekiah whom Herod had killed about 47 B.C.E., seized the royal arsenal and he and his followers sought to control the area (*Ant.* XVII.271–72; *War* II.56). (3) Simon, a handsome slave of Herod's, was proclaimed king by a band of followers. He and his army burned several royal palaces, including the one at Jericho, and ravaged Perea before he fell in battle, beheaded by a Roman commander (*Ant.* XVII.273–77; *War* II.57–59). Tacitus (56–120 C.E.), an embittered Roman historian noted for his "yellow journalism" and "pointed style," later took note of Simon's revolt: "After Herod's death, a certain Simon assumed the name of king without waiting for

Caesar's decision" (*Histories* V.7.2; *GLA* II.29). Tacitus did not mention the other disturbances, but his comment on Simon would seem to indicate that uncertainty about the succession contributed to the rise of claimants to the throne. According to Josephus, a shepherd, Athronges, supported by his four brothers and a large force, claimed the title of king and began killing Romans and royalists in Judea (*Ant.* XVII.278–84; *War* II.60–64).

These and other acts of brigandage and revolution turned much of the country into a "scene of guerrilla warfare" (*War* II.65). Except for the area of the northern Transjordan and the district of Samaria, all of the kingdom was involved in the turmoil of the pretenders to the throne. Only in Perea, against Simon, were the Roman soldiers of the legion under Sabinus able to suppress an uprising. Peace was restored to the area only when Varus, the Roman legate of Syria, moved into Palestine with two additional Roman legions and a variety of regional auxiliaries and suppressed the uprisings with great vigor. After some fierce fighting in Galilee, where rebellion was the most widespread, Varus's approach raised the siege of the Roman force that was with Sabinus in Jerusalem, and he put down dissident elements and crucified about two thousand rebels. Ten thousand armed men in Idumea, now supported and led by some of Herod's kin, disbanded without a battle, and only the leaders were arrested (*Ant.* XVII.286–98; *War* II.66–79). The various factions were not finally suppressed until after Archelaus had returned to Judea, since he aided in the capture of Athronges's brothers (*Ant.* XVII.284; *War* II.64).

In the conditions prevailing after Herod's death, we can see many of the patterns and possess evidence to hypothesize about some of the causes of actions and reactions that would characterize Palestinian affairs for decades. (1) The diversity of movements and splinter parties in Judaism, often violently opposed to one another, surfaces. (2) The contributions to unrest made by Roman ineptitude and/or greed are already clear in the case of Sabinus. (3) The ineffectiveness of native leadership when caught between the wishes of the local population and the demands of a foreign occupying force can be seen in the case of Archelaus. (4) The struggle of the Jews to gain independence and self-government—which we must remember did not mean total freedom, but without either a clear program or a common consensus of how that freedom and self-rule should function, is graphically illustrated. As later, opposition to foreign oppression found expression in the form of civil strife. (5) Messianic aspirations and apocalyptic visions undoubtedly triggered disturbances and gave rise to self-appointed and follower-proclaimed leaders.

The Rule of the Herodians

Herod's will was challenged in Rome, and Augustus Caesar listened to various parties on two occasions before rendering a verdict. (1) Antipas, supported by many members of Herod's family, claimed that since his father's earlier will had bequeathed the kingdom to him and since Archelaus was not competent to rule, he should have the throne (*Ant.* XVII.224–39; *War* II.20–32). (2) A "delegation of Jews, which Varus had permitted the nation to send," as Josephus refers to them (*Ant.* XVII.300), pleaded for autonomy (*Ant.* XVII.299–314; *War* II.80–92), that is, "that they be delivered from kingship and such forms of rule, be joined to (the province of) Syria, and be made subject to the governors sent there" (*Ant.* XVII.314). Josephus mentions neither the supporters nor the constitution of this group of fifty delegates other than to say that they represented the nation, the same terminology he had used earlier in describing the anti-Hasmonaean delegation that made similar requests of Pompey the Great in Damascus (*Ant.* XIV.41). The group, allegedly supported by several thousand Jews in Rome, could have represented an (or the) anti-royalist faction that wished to live in a theocratic state under the governance of the high priest. (3) Archelaus through Nicolas of Damascus responded to both factions (*Ant.* XVII.240–47, 315–16; *War* II.33–36, 92). (Philip, who had initially been left behind in Judea by Archelaus [*Ant.* XVII.219; *War* II.14], put in an appearance, to support Archelaus and his own possible inheritance [*Ant.* XVII.303; *War* II.83].)

Shortly after the second council hearing, Augustus handed down his decision. It followed, but not completely, the lines of Herod's will (*Ant.* XVII.317–24; *War* II.93–100; terms of the will are given in *Ant.* XVII.188–90; *War* I.668). The disposition of Herod's kingdom made by Augustus was as follows. (1) Archelaus was made ethnarch, not king (a title dangled before him by prospects of a possible future bestowal), over Idumea, Judea, and portions of Samaria, with the cities of Caesarea, Sebaste, Joppa, and Jerusalem subject to him. This gave him an income of six hundred talents a year (according to *Ant.* XVII.320; or four hundred according to *War* II.97). Archelaus was not given any superior status over his brothers. Rather, the men's territories were independent. (2) The towns of Gaza, Gadara, and Hippos were detached from the principality and attached directly to the province of Syria. (3) Salome, Herod's sister, was given the towns of Jamnia, Azotus, and Phasaelis and other bequests, with an income of sixty talents annually. (4) Antipas was made tetrarch over Galilee and Perea, with an annual income of two hundred talents. (5) Philip received territory whose extent is not quite certain but included Batanea, Trachonitis, Auranitis, Gaulanitis, and Paneas, with an income of one hundred talents yearly. (6) Other family members received various gifts. (7) As a reward for not participating in the recent revolts, the inhabitants of the region of Samaria received a 25 percent reduction in their taxes.

In his divisions of Herod's territory, Augustus probably weakened the Herodians as much as possible without outrightly disregarding Herod's will. No one was made king; no son was given dominance over the whole of what had been Herod's kingdom. Major cities were detached from the old principality.

On the other hand, it was in the best interests of Rome to maintain the appearance that the kingdom was still in existence. In accord with the traditional Roman methods of governing those under Rome's hegemony, whereby client rulers governed, thus sparing Rome expense and difficulty, Augustus decided that it was best for the sons of Herod, rather than Rome directly, to deal with the anarchic conditions. Although some see this as a "set up" so as to enable Rome to inherit the domain under more favorable circumstances, this is a perspective that is colored by modern imperialistic methods. The history of the Roman Republic and of the early Principate makes it clear that Rome only stepped in and governed any portion of its domain directly when there was no choice in the matter. Rome was reluctant to expend the money and manpower. Unfortunately, during the early Principate, Rome was required to do so fairly often despite the costs incurred in the process precisely because of the troubled conditions in various parts of Rome's domain.

Archelaus (4 B.C.E.–6 C.E.)

Tradition has preserved little about the ten-year reign of Archelaus (*Ant.* XVII.339–55; *War* II.111–16). Of the three brothers, Archelaus inherited the most difficult task: the government of Judea, which included the supervision of Jerusalem, the religious capital for Yahwists both within and without the borders of Judea proper. The fact that Archelaus had been pushed to the point of military confrontation and massacre even before his departure for Rome meant that his earlier popularity had soured considerably. He had earlier loosed both his infantry and his cavalry forces upon the crowds, an act that earned him all the liabilities of office before he had been awarded the prestige of a position (*Ant.* XVII.215–18; *War* II.12–13).

None of the grandeur of Herod's reign can be associated with Archelaus. He is credited only with rebuilding the Jericho palace, with constructing one village, that of Archelais, north of Jericho and named after himself, and with establishing a palm grove irrigated by depriving the village of Neara of half its water supply. Presumably he repaired the damage done to the Temple porticoes. Archelaus kept his promise to remove the high priest appointed after the eagle affair. As successor he chose Joazar's brother Eleazar, but he was quickly replaced by Jesus son of Sie, although Joazar was soon reinstated. Such rapid turnover in the office could indicate difficulties over the appointments. Archelaus's divorce of his wife and his marriage to Glaphyra, the widow of his executed brother Alexander, irritated the sensibilities of the Pharisees and other Yahwists who accepted pentateuchal law as authoritative civil law, since the requirements of levirate marriage were not involved (see Lev. 18:16; 20:21; Deut. 25:5–6).

Leaders in Judea and Samaria eventually united to bring a case against Archelaus for cruelty and tyranny. Augustus, perhaps figuring that it would be less costly in both money and manpower to impose direct Roman rule, deposed Archelaus and banished him to Vienne in Gaul. His principality was placed under the administrative supervision of the province of Syria.

Philip (4 B.C.E.–33/34 C.E.)

Of Herod's successors, only Philip reigned until his death and only he seems to have never given any cause for scandal or charge of incompetence (*Ant.* XVIII.27–28, 106–8, 237; *War* II.167–68, 181). Philip's territory was primarily populated by Gentiles or those thought to be Gentiles. The main Jewish settlements in his tetrarchy were in western Gaulanitis, adjoining Galilee. At least one strong Jewish community existed in Batanea since the elder Herod had settled a military colony of Babylonian Jews in the region to help control the brigands preying on the countryside.

Philip carried out two major city reconstructions. The city of Paneas was rebuilt, named Caesarea Philippi after the emperor, and turned into his capital. He fortified and raised to city status the village of Bethsaida on the northern shore of the Sea of Galilee, renaming it Julias after Augustus's daughter. Both of these projects were carried out early in his career.

The Romans granted only Philip, of the three sons, the strictly guarded privilege of minting coins. His were imprinted with the imperial portraits of the emperors Augustus and Tiberius, the likeness of a temple, and perhaps an issue with his own image. Such coinage in a predominantly non-Jewish area seems not to have met with Jewish opposition in spite of its use of human effigies.

Josephus (or his sources) eulogizes Philip for his just and efficient administration of his realm. He died after a reign of thirty-seven years. Although married, Philip died childless. (Salome, the daughter of Herodias, remembered in history for requesting the head of John the Baptist, was his [only?] wife; *Ant.* VIII.136.) Following Philip's death, his territory was placed under the administration of the Roman legate in Syria, but its revenues were kept separate. The emperor Caligula later awarded the region to his friend Agrippa I.

Herod Antipas (4 B.C.E.–39 C.E.)

Antipas ruled longer than any other son of Herod, and accordingly we possess much more information about him than about either of the other two (*Ant.* XVIII.27, 36–38, 101–5, 109–26, 240–56; *War* II.167–68, 181–83). During his reign, we hear of no major tensions between him and his subjects, and his rule was terminated as a consequence of his and his wife's personal aspirations rather than as a consequence of incompetency or inhumaneness.

Antipas was noted for his building projects. He rebuilt Sepphoris in Galilee, fortified Betharamphtha in Perea, which had been damaged by Simon's forces in 4 B.C.E. (*Ant.* XVII.277, 289; *War* II.59, 68), and founded a new capital on the western shore of the Sea of Galilee, named Tiberias after the emperor. Of the three sons, Antipas had the most illustrious international reputation and "a high place among the friends of Tiberius" (*Ant.* XVIII.36). Antipas married a daughter of the Nabatean king Aretas IV (ca. 9 B.C.E.–40 C.E.), an arrangement that brought peace between the two for several years. The Jewish tetrarch was selected to entertain the Parthian king and the Roman legate at their meeting on the Euphrates in 36 C.E., a meeting called to negotiate peace terms between Parthia and Rome.

Antipas is also remembered for the execution of John the Baptist. Josephus's account of the episode (*Ant.* XVII.116–19) indicates that Antipas feared that John's movement might lead to some form of political unrest: "Herod decided therefore that it would be much better to strike first and be rid of him before his work led to an uprising, than to wait for an upheaval, get involved in a difficult situation and see his mistake." John was imprisoned in Machaerus and then put to death.

Josephus makes no connection between the execution of John the Baptist and the latter's condemnation of Antipas's "unorthodox" marriage, as do the Gospels (Matt. 14:3–12; Mark 6:14–29; Luke 3:1–20). Antipas, while visiting his half brother Herod, son of Mariamne II (who had been named as second in the succession to Antipater in Herod's original will), fell in love with Herod's wife Herodias, the daughter of the elder Herod's executed son Aristobulus. Herodias agreed to break with her husband if Antipas would divorce his Nabatean wife. With both conditions fulfilled, the marriage was consummated in spite of its transgression of pentateuchal law forbidding marriage to a brother's wife. After his daughter fled to Petra, the Nabatean ex–father-in-law of Antipas set out to punish the Jewish king. Aretas's forces defeated an army of Antipas in a battle in which neither king participated. Antipas's appeal to the emperor led to Tiberius's order that Aretas be taken dead or alive, since he had disturbed the *Pax Romana* by initiating hostile action.

Antipas's affair with Herodias eventually led to his downfall. After Caligula awarded Agrippa I, Herodias's brother, the title of king, Herodias pushed Antipas, who was "content with his tranquillity" (*Ant.* XVIII.245), to appeal for a like title. Agrippa I, a close friend of the new emperor, convinced Caligula that Antipas was engaged in conspiratorial activity, since the latter had accumulated equipment for seventy thousand heavily-armed infantry (*Ant.* XVIII.251). Antipas was deposed and exiled to Lyons in Gaul (or Spain, according to *War* II.183). Agrippa I was rewarded with his tetrarchy.

Judea as a Roman Province (6–41 C.E.)

As a consequence of Augustus's dismissal of Archelaus from office, the Judean community secured what representatives of the nation had requested ten years earlier: that it "be delivered from kingship and such forms of rule, be joined to (the province of) Syria, and be made subject to the governors sent there" (*Ant.* XVII.314).

Judea with Samaria was incorporated into the Roman Empire as an imperial province and thus under the emperor's direct control. Since it was a small province and could be protected militarily by the four Roman legions in Syria, the officials appointed to govern Judea were from the lower administrative echelon of the equestrian order. The earliest appointed officials were apparently designated as "prefects." The more widely known title of "procurator" seems to have been employed primarily during Judea's second phase as a territorial province, after the short reign of Agrippa I (41–44 C.E.), but without any distinction being made in the function of the office.

Judea had paid Rome tribute officially since 63 B.C.E., but now that Judea was a province, various taxes payable to Rome were imposed and yet others, previously paid to her own monarchs, were increased. In addition to paying the land tax, customs, and various indirect taxes, the citizens of a province were liable to a personal or head tax, the *tributum capitis*, paid annually. In order to assess the tax liability of a province, the Romans carried out a census to determine population and financial resources. Thus in 6 or 7 C.E., Augustus commissioned the newly appointed legate of Syria, Quirinius, to carry out the census, with Coponius being appointed as prefect over Judea (*Ant.* XVII.355–XVIII.1–3; *War* II.117; see Luke 2:1–3). Opposition to the census was widespread. Joazar, the high priest, who had apparently been restored to his post by Archelaus (see *Ant.* XVII.339), argued that the census should not be opposed. A significant group violently repudiating the census was led by the Pharisee Saddok and a certain Judas from Gamala, east of the Sea of Galilee, whom Josephus calls Judas the Galilean (*Ant.* XVII.4–10, 23–25; *War* III.118). Josephus tells us little about the actions and fate of Judas and leaves unrelated this Judas and the earlier Judas, son of Hezekiah, who was a pretender to the throne in 4 B.C.E. Acts 5:37 suggests that the opposition to the census took armed form and that Judas was killed in conflict with the Romans and that his followers were scattered. Josephus does report something about the beliefs and pronouncements of Judas's movement, which he dubs "the fourth philosophy" of Judaism in addition to that of the Pharisees, the Sadducees, and the Essenes: (1) To submit to the census and the assessment was to submit to downright slavery; (2) God alone should be leader and master of the people; (3) violence and vengeance in the name of the cause of independence were acceptable; (4) martyrdom and suffering for the cause of independence would be necessary; (5) independence from Rome and service to God were intricately related.

Josephus relates the beginning of this group to the final downfall and destruction of Jerusalem and the Temple in 70 C.E. Later, however, when he discusses these events, he makes no specific mention of Judas. The activity of Judas, like that of Theudas (Acts 5:36) and numerous other knowns and unknowns of the era, was expressive of the discontent with the status quo widespread in Jewish circles. Such discontent was fed by a number of factors ranging from nationalist urges for independence, to hopes for theocratic government, to utopian disillusionment with historical existence, to personal greed and ambition.

Little is known about Judean life under the early prefects. Some general patterns, however, are clear and must have been instituted already under Coponius. (1) Caesarea on the coast became the military headquarters and administrative capital for the Romans. Here the prefect spent most of his time, putting in an appearance in Jerusalem only when conditions required his presence—for example, at the time of major festivals. (2) No major concentration of Roman troops was centered in the region. The forces employed in the area consisted of no more than a few thousand auxiliary troops recruited locally from the non-Jewish population. Of these, only one cohort was stationed in Jerusalem, where it was garrisoned in the Antonia. (3) The appointment of the high priest and the supervision of the high-priestly robes became prerogatives of the Romans. Before Quirinius returned to Syria, he installed Ananus as high priest (*Ant.* XVIII.26). (4)

Daily sacrifices of two lambs and a bull were offered for the emperor's well-being in the Jerusalem Temple (*War* II.197, 409). (5) The collection of most direct taxes was carried out by the Roman officials. As a consequence of Augustus's recent tax reforms, indirect taxes such as customs taxes were farmed out to tax collectors (*publicani*) who were natives—in this case Jewish. The intensity of feeling about taxes can be seen in the fact that as late as the ministry of Jesus, the question was not, "Are the taxes too high?" but, "Should one pay taxes to Caesar?" (Luke 20:22).

The Early Roman Administration

Little is known of the rule of the seven, or perhaps six, prefects who governed the region prior to the temporary reestablishment of native kingship under Agrippa I in 41 C.E. Coponius seems to have ruled for two or three years. Josephus reports only one event associated with his reign, namely, the profanation of the Jerusalem Temple by Samaritans who scattered human bones in the porticoes and courtyard (*Ant.* XVII.29–30). Such a prank, while not involving the Romans, illustrates the form that religious rivalry and sectarian animosity could sometimes take.

Under Marcus Ambibulus (9–11 C.E.), Herod's sister Salome died, willing her holdings at Jamnia, Phasael, Azotus, and Archelais to Julia (Livia), the wife of Augustus (*Ant.* XVIII.31). What this did was to create large and very profitable estates owned directly by absentee Roman landlords. To see such wealth and acreage, in Yahweh's land, controlled and administered by foreign Romans must have greatly rankled landless Jewish masses.

Caesar Augustus died (19 August 14 C.E.) during the governorship of the otherwise unknown Annius Rufus (12–14 C.E.) and was succeeded by Tiberius (14–37 C.E.), his stepson (*Ant.* XVIII.32; *War* II.168). The new emperor appointed Valerius Gratus (15–26 C.E.) as the new prefect for Judea (*Ant.* XVIII.33–36), and, as was customary under Tiberius, who was noted for his procrastination, Gratus's term of service was lengthy (see *Ant.* XVIII.172–76).

Tacitus notes, in discussing Judean affairs, that "under Tiberius all was quiet" (*Histories* V.9.2: *GLA* II.29). Only two bits of information about Judea are known from the time of Gratus. Josephus reports that in rapid succession four high priests were appointed (*Ant.* XVIII.34–35). The first (Ishmael son of Phabi) held office only for a short time. The second (Eleazar son of Ananus) and third (Simon son of Camithus) held office for only one year each, although the fourth (Joseph Caiaphas, son-in-law of Ananus) served for years, probably until 36 C.E. Tacitus reports that when Tiberius's adopted son Germanicus was in the East in 17 C.E., "Syria and Judaea, exhausted by their burdens, were pressing for a diminution of the tribute" (*Annals* II.42.5). If this tribute protest and the rapid succession of high priests are related, this could suggest unrest in Judea early in his tenure, which Gratus felt was not sufficiently handled by the high priests in office.

Pontius Pilate (26–36 C.E.)

Information on the fifth prefect, Pilate, is reasonably full. Both Josephus (*Ant.* VIII.55–64, 85–89; *War* II.169–77) and the Alexandrian Jewish writer Philo (ca. 20 B.C.E.–50 C.E., in his *On the Embassy to Gaius*) as well as the New Testament Gospels report incidents about Pilate. Tensions between the Roman occupants and their Jewish subjects, probably already building under Gratus, reached the explosive point under Pilate. Tiberius "retired" to the island of Capri in 26 C.E. After this, his prefect over the praetorian guard, Aelius Sejanus, wielded enormous power for a time. Sejanus was strongly anti-Jewish, and his influence has been used to explain Pilate's actions and disrespect for the Jews, but with little or no evidence to prove such a theory.

Philo, quoting Agrippa I, describes Pilate as "naturally inflexible, a blend of self-will and relentlessness," and speaks of his conduct as full of "briberies, insults, robberies, outrages and wanton injuries, executions without trial constantly repeated, ceaseless and supremely grievous cruelty" (Philo, *Embassy*, 301–2). Philo's assessment is obviously biased, but the evidence we possess suggests Pilate's high degree of insensitivity to Jewish religious and social customs as well as of impetuosity in behavior. Several incidents described or alluded to during his tenure illustrate the growing tensions between Romans and Jews, although the episodes remained for the time being of only local and internal concern:

1. In order not to trample on Jewish sensitivities, Pilate's predecessors had stationed troops in Jerusalem whose standards were not decorated with medallion busts of the emperor. Apparently in his first year in office, Pilate sent troops by night carrying the effigies of the emperor into Jerusalem (*Ant.* XVIII.55–59; *War* II.169–74). Pilate was confronted shortly in Caesarea with a protesting crowd requesting the removal of the standards. After several days of entreaty and demonstration and a public confrontation in the stadium, Pilate chose to withdraw the standards rather than resort to violence.

2. Pilate sought to improve the Jerusalem water supply by constructing a new aqueduct, but to finance the project he confiscated Temple funds (*Ant.* XVIII.60–62; *War* II.75–77). Again the crowds protested, but this time Pilate was not cowed. Soldiers armed with clubs and dressed as civilians were sent into the crowds and on signal beat the protesters, injuring many

and killing some. Such indiscriminate police tactics brought the demonstrations to a halt.

3. The New Testament alludes not only to suppressive acts of Pilate but also to open acts of insurrection against his rule. Luke 13:1 refers to "the Galileans whose blood Pilate had mingled with their sacrifices" but provides no specific details. In conjunction with the crucifixion of Jesus, reference is made that "among the rebels in prison, who had committed murder in the insurrection, there was a man called Barabbas" (Mark 15:7). Again no specifics are given, but an armed uprising is indicated. Jesus' death at the hands of the Romans must also be seen as the suppression of what Pilate felt was a potentially threatening situation.

4. Philo reports an episode involving gold-plated shields that Pilate placed on the palace of Herod in Jerusalem (*Embassy*, 299–305). The shields with no images and no inscription other than the name of Pilate and Tiberius raised a storm of protest. The Jewish crowds, represented by members of the Herodian family and the Sanhedrin, appealed for redress but were rebuffed. Eventually the Jewish leaders wrote to Tiberius, who ordered the shields removed. (It was probably during Pilate's rule that widespread sentiment developed for the restoration of Herodian rule and led to the formation of the Herodian party; Mark 3:6; 12:13.)

5. A final encounter of Pilate with his subjects led to his dismissal from office (*Ant.* XVIII.85–89). When a large group of armed Samaritans followed their leader to Mount Gerizim with the expectation that the sacred tabernacle vessels hidden there by Moses would be unearthed, Pilate, probably fearing that some military purpose was hiding behind their religious zeal, took action. His troops blocked the procession of pilgrims; a battle ensued; casualties resulted; and Pilate executed the ringleaders and the most influential figures among the Samaritans. The Samaritans appealed to Vitellius, the Roman legate in Syria, who ordered Pilate to Rome for trial.

Vitellius, the Syrian legate, replaced Pilate temporarily with an otherwise unknown Marcellus (*Ant.* XVIII.89), who may be the same person as Marullus appointed by Gaius Caligula (*Ant.* XVIII.237), the successor to Tiberius who had died before Pilate arrived in Rome. In addition, Vitellius took other actions to ameliorate the conditions created by Pilate's rule and to placate Jewish feelings (*Ant.* XVIII.90–95). He went up to Jerusalem at Passover, where he was received in magnificent fashion. He proceeded to remit all taxes on the sale of agricultural produce and granted the priests custody of the high-priestly vestments, thus removing them from Roman control and putting them under Jewish control. Caiaphas was removed as high priest and replaced with Jonathan son of Ananus. Shortly after (*Ant.* XVIII.120–24), Vitellius, headed for a military campaign against Aretas IV, agreed that his troops should bypass rather than carry their standards through Jewish territory. While offering sacrifice at the festival, he was warmly received by the Jewish multitude. The legate replaced Jonathan as high priest with his brother Theophilus. While he was in Jerusalem, word arrived of the death of Tiberius, and Vitellius administered to the people the oath of loyalty to Gaius the new emperor, the son of the popular Germanicus. The Jews were thus, as Philo says, "the first of the inhabitants of Syria to show our joy . . . and it was from our city [Jerusalem] that the glad tidings spread. Our temple was the first to accept sacrifices on behalf of Gaius's reign" (Philo, *Embassy*, 231–32). The joy of the Jews, however, would shortly turn to wails of sorrow.

The Gaius Affair

The inauguration of the reign of Gaius Caligula ("little boots") was hailed enthusiastically throughout the empire. For some, Gaius's new wine, however, soon turned sour: "He administered the empire quite high-mindedly during the first and second years of his reign [see Philo, *Embassy*, 13]. By exercising moderation, he made great advances in popularity both with the Romans themselves and with their subjects. But as time went on, he ceased to think of himself as a man and, as he imagined himself a god because of the greatness of his empire, he was moved to disregard the divine power in all his official acts" (*Ant*. XVIII. 256).

Alexandrian Jewry was the first to feel the consequences of the anti-Judaism that sailed in the wake of Gaius's promotion of himself as god. Jews unwilling to join in adoration of the emperor as divine became the object of abuse. In Egypt, pent-up anti-Judaism and the desire of the governor, Flaccus, to ingratiate himself with Gaius saw the Jews greatly abused. According to Philo, there were three stages in the hostilities: (1) Emperor images were installed in the synagogues; (2) Alexandrian Jews were deprived of their citizenship rights; and (3) Jewish property was plundered as if the Jews were citizens of a conquered city (Philo, *Flaccus*, 40–47, 52–57; see *Ant*. XVIII.257–60). Eventually, while appeal was being made to Gaius, troubles of a similar nature broke out in Palestine.

Non-Jews in the town of Jamnia, an imperial estate that had been a legacy from Salome, Herod's sister, set up an altar to the emperor which was demolished by the Jewish population (in the winter of 39/40 C.E.). This action and reaction set the stage for what we have called "the Gaius affair." A narrative of the events is given by both Josephus (*Ant*. XVIII.261–309; *War* II.184–87, 192–203) and Philo (*Embassy*, 188, 198–348), although with some significant differences in detail.

The imperial procurator of Jamnia reported the destruction of the altar to

Gaius, who responded with an order to the Syrian legate, Petronius, that, as punishment, the Jerusalem Temple was to be converted into a shrine for the imperial cult, with a statue of the emperor placed in it. Petronius was ordered to have the statue fashioned in Syria, escorted with half the Roman forces in the province (two legions), and placed in the Temple. Petronius, like Vitellius before him, was sensitive to Jewish religion and realized the uproar this would cause. (Philo reports that he had studied Jewish thought in preparation for his stint as Syrian legate; *Embassy*, 245.) Petronius took various measures to deal with what he rightly sensed would be widespread opposition and demonstrations. (1) The statue was commissioned in Sidon, well outside Jewish terrain. (2) Jewish leaders were summoned for an audience and entreated to encourage their fellow citizens to submit with resignation, if not with grace. (3) When he came to Ptolemais and was confronted with an enormous crowd of Jewish protesters, he stalled for time, informing the artisans that they need be in no hurry to complete the work. (4) In the light of the demonstrations, he hastened to Tiberias, the Galilean capital, to appraise matters there. In Tiberias, he encountered the same enthusiastic opposition and was appealed to by Aristobulus, the brother of King Agrippa, and other Jewish leaders. (5) The legate took the advice of the Jewish leaders and wrote directly to Gaius, offering reasons for not carrying through on the project: first, the crops in the area were being neglected and might be destroyed, thus producing an inconvenient situation when Gaius traveled down the coast on his forthcoming visit to Alexandria, and second, a revolt, with accompanying loss of revenue, would probably be inevitable if the statue were erected.

Gaius responded, somewhat politely, perhaps out of respect for an official supported in the field by four legions, but insisted that the statue be installed. Petronius continued, however, to procrastinate. In the meantime, Agrippa I had arrived in Rome and learned of Gaius's order. After suffering a "seizure" when he heard of the proposed desecration of the Temple, Agrippa appealed in writing to his old friend Gaius, pleading that the toleration shown the Jews by previous Roman officials be the present course of action. Gaius issued orders to Petronius, dropping the projects but requiring the Jews to repay toleration with toleration, that is, not to interfere with the erection of imperial altars outside Jerusalem. Thus ended a major period of tension between Rome and Jerusalem which, without proper handling by Petronius, could have eventuated in rebellion and war.

Philo reports that Gaius later backed down on his word and ordered that a statue be made in Rome that he could take on his eastern trip and set up personally in the Temple (*Embassy*, 337–38), but whether this is merely embellished legend remains uncertain. At any rate, the emperor was assassinated on 24 January 41 C.E.

The Reign of Agrippa I

One consequence of the death of Gaius was the temporary restoration of Herodian rule over the whole of Palestine. Agrippa I, who had recently played an important role in Roman and Jewish relations, was elevated to the old throne of Herod by Gaius's successor. Josephus has provided a long, detailed, and rather gossipy account of Agrippa's career, although focusing on the years before his reign (*Ant.* XVIII.143–239; XIX.274–359; *War* II.178–82, 206–22).

As the son of the executed Aristobulus (son of Mariamne I and the grandson of the elder Herod), Agrippa possessed both Hasmonaean and Herodian blood in his veins. Prior to his rise to kingship over territory exceeding in size that of his grandfather's, Agrippa had already experienced a checkered career with periods of poverty and plenty. Born in 10 B.C.E. (*Ant.* XIX.350), he was sent to Rome for his education. There, he and his mother Berenice, who accompanied him, became a part of the imperial social world. Berenice was a friend of Antonia, the mother of the future emperor Claudius, and Agrippa became a close companion of Tiberius's only son Drusus as well as, later, of Gaius who succeeded Tiberius. Extravagant spending throughout his early years left him only one step ahead of his creditors, whom he generally paid with funds borrowed in ever larger quantities from other creditors. After Drusus's death in 23 C.E., Agrippa lost support at the court and drifted back to Palestine. There he was employed temporarily and as an act of mercy by his uncle and brother-in-law Antipas. After disputes with Antipas and Flaccus, the Roman legate in Syria, he made his way back to Italy, financing his journey and staying solvent by means of additional loans. Through Tiberius he became friends with Gaius but was thrown into prison when he expressed the hope that Tiberius would soon be succeeded by Gaius. When the latter took the throne in 37 C.E., he rewarded his friend with release from prison and with the territory previously ruled by Philip as well as the title of king. Probably Abilene, the tetrarchy of Lysanias, was bestowed on him at the same time. Agrippa did not return to Palestine until 38 C.E. His journey there via Alexandria helped precipitate anti-Jewish riots in Egypt (Philo, *Flaccus*, 25–26). Agrippa's triumphal return to Palestine with the coveted title of king rankled his sister Herodias, who considered her brother one of the oddest sheep in the Herodian flock. Her jealousy, as we have already noted, led to her husband Antipas's downfall. After Gaius deposed Antipas, he presented his territory to Agrippa.

Fortunately for the Jews, Agrippa was in Rome when the Gaius affair regarding placing the emperor's statue in the Jerusalem Temple reached its crisis point. His persuasion convinced Gaius to retract his order. Agrippa was still in the city when Gaius was assassinated and played a significant role in convincing Claudius and the Senate that Claudius should become ruler of the empire. The new emperor confirmed Agrippa in his royal holding, and, having inherited the imperial province of Judea, he bestowed this upon Agrippa. Agrippa's position was confirmed by treaty (*Ant.* XIX.362) and in an edict inscribed on bronze tablets and deposited in the Capitol. The Jewish king now reigned over territory larger than that ruled by Herod (see *Ant.* XIX.274–75; *War* II.214–17). His brother Herod was simultaneously given the kingdom of Chalcis.

Agrippa returned to Palestine as "Great King, Friend of Caesar and Friend of Rome." He also returned as the friend of the Jews, for his intercession with Claudius led the emperor to issue an edict restoring the civil rights of Jews in Alexandria (*Ant.* XIX.279–85) and a subsequent edict ordering "the same privileges to be maintained for the Jews throughout the empire under the Romans as those in Alexandria enjoy" (*Ant.* XIX.288). Claudius's edicts and his appointment of Agrippa were no doubt intended to soothe Jewish wounds and restore stability to the region following "the Gaius episode."

Only a few items and events are reported for Agrippa's short reign, and these may be summarized as follows:

1. Virtually all ancient Jewish sources speak in glowing terms of Agrippa's piety and devotion to his people and the law (see *Ant.* XIX.330–31). Upon returning to Jerusalem, he offered sacrifice and presented to the Temple the gold chain that Gaius had presented him as a remembrance of the one he wore in prison. He also defrayed the expenses involved in fulfilling the vows of a number of Nazirites (*Ant.* XIX.292–94). He also is reported to have been careful about laws of cleanliness (*Ant.* XIX.332–34). When a statue to the emperor was placed in a synagogue by a youthful gang in the Phoenician town of Dora, Agrippa petitioned Petronius personally. The legate ordered the image removed and insisted on compliance with Claudius's edicts (*Ant.* XIX.300–311). The Mishnah has preserved a tradition, perhaps legendary, that suggests that Agrippa, unlike his grandfather Herod, was widely received by his fellow countrymen. At the Feast of Booths in 41 C.E., he is said to have been reading the book of Deuteronomy (as was customary in sabbatical years; see Deut. 31:9–13) and began to weep when he reached Deut. 17:15. To his tears, the crowds yelled out, "Grieve not Agrippa. You are our brother! You are our brother!" (Sotah 7:8). To show his gratitude to the Jerusalemites for their enthusiastic friendship, he remitted the property tax on all the houses in the city (*Ant.* XIX.299).

2. Two actions of Agrippa raised the opposition of Roman administration, although the motivations of the Jewish king remain uncertain. He

began the construction of a wall to the north of Jerusalem that would enclose the new suburb of Bezetha and offer work to the area's unemployed. Josephus reports that the wall would have provided a fortification that would make the city almost impregnable. Before the work had advanced significantly, the Roman legate in Syria, Marsus, sent a report to Claudius, who ordered the cessation of work on such a major project undertaken without the requisite Roman approval and supervision. The emperor is said to have feared that a revolution was afoot. Apparently Agrippa gave up his project without protest (*Ant.* XIX.326–27; *War* II.218; V.152). The second incident was a meeting with five minor kings from the region just north of his kingdom. The visiting kings came to Tiberias, but their meeting was terminated by Marsus, who suspected that the affair was prejudicial to Roman interests (*Ant.* XIX.338–42).

3. Christian tradition recalls Agrippa as a persecutor of the developing church. According to Acts 12:1–19, he had James the son of Zebedee beheaded and Peter arrested, although the latter escaped from prison. Tensions with the cities of Caesarea and Sebaste also developed. We are uninformed about their nature, but the citizens of these two cities celebrated rather than mourned the death of Agrippa (*Ant.* XIX.356–59). Acts 12:20 also notes that there was fierce hostility between Agrippa and the cities of Tyre and Sidon. A border dispute with the city of Philadelphia was left hanging by Agrippa's demise (*Ant.* XX.2–4). In some of these cases, it is possible, but not certain, that Agrippa's desire to appear highly pro-Jewish and thus impress his subjects may have led him to take action against Christians and the Gentile communities in these cities.

4. A cluster of factors suggest that at least some of Agrippa's actions were unconcerned with Jewish scruples. His coins were hardly aniconic. Most were struck with human images, including those of Gaius, Claudius, himself, and his son, not to mention those showing a pagan temple, pagan sacrifice, and a city goddess. Statues of his daughters were set up at Caesarea and Sebaste (*Ant.* XIX.357). Among his gifts to cities outside his domain, Berytus (Beirut) received a theater, an amphitheater, baths, and porticoes (*Ant.* XIX.335–37). The amphitheater was dedicated with a grand gladiatorial battle in which fourteen hundred combatants, malefactors to be sure, slaughtered one another for the pleasure of the general public. In his last public appearance, at a festival in honor of Caesar in a theater in Caesarea, Agrippa, dressed in a garment of woven silver, was greeted as a god (so Josephus, *Ant.* XIX.343–49, and Acts 12:20–23), a greeting he is not said to have repudiated.

5. During his brief reign of only three years over Judea and Jerusalem (*Ant.* XIX.343; *War* II.219), Agrippa continued the Roman policy of creating instability in the high-priestly office. Four high priests served under him, and

a fifth declined appointment (*Ant.* XIX.297–98, 313–16, 342). (During his reign of thirty-three years, the elder Herod had appointed only five different persons in the office.) It is impossible to know why there was such a turnover in the office under Agrippa, but it could hardly have been an expression of piety. One suspects political expediency.

Agrippa died, apparently deeply in debt, as was his manner, in Caesarea at the age of fifty-four (*Ant.* XIX.350–52). His last five days were spent in great abdominal agony, possibly from peritonitis precipitated by appendicitis aggravated by roundworms, which Josephus, like Acts 12:23, regarded as divine judgment.

Agrippa left behind three children, the oldest of whom was a seventeen-year-old son (*Ant.* XIX.354). Claudius, following high-level advice, decided not to appoint Agrippa's son to succeed him, offering his youth as the reason (*Ant.* XIX.360–463). Agrippa's border disputes, his troubles with neighboring cities, and his debts may have suggested that better arrangements could be made. At any rate, Agrippa's kingdom passed again into direct Roman rule.

CHAPTER 4

The Jewish-Roman Wars

With the death of Agrippa I, Judea again was subjected to direct Roman rule as in the years between Archelaus's deposition in 6 C.E., and Claudius's appointment of Agrippa as monarch in 41 C.E. The old apprehensions and tensions of earlier days returned, or merely intensified, as well. This was exacerbated by the Roman presence in Judea, which of necessity curtailed certain aspects of what some sectarian groups, particularly the more restrictive elements within the state, thought of as the Jewish way of life. This caused a gradual but steadily increasing breakdown of law and order, which first led to conditions approaching outright anarchy and then to open warfare.

Liberty as we construe it was not a conceptually valid construct in either the Greek or the Roman world. A state could have liberty and still be subject to another state. The Romans were therefore reflecting a common worldview when they did not acknowledge any province or client state as independent of the empire. Precisely because they construed provinces and client states as having liberty but liberty under Rome, the Romans could only construe the uprising in Judea as a revolt. They did not and could not view this as a "war" since that would imply an interaction between two sovereign powers. And, as we have seen, the nature of Roman rule from 196 B.C.E. onward shows that Rome considered foreign rulers under its suzerainty answerable to Rome. So, from the Roman perspective, Judea was no more sovereign after the installation of Agrippa than it had been before that event. It simply had the appearance of sovereignty, without its reality.

The Romans deemed what was happening in Judea a revolt. They acted no differently in pursuit of victory, however, than they would have were it a war against a sovereign king or monarch. But because this was a revolt and not a war, they could pursue it without having the approval of the gods, which would be necessary for a declaration of war. It could be pursued and concluded differently. Most important, the aftermath of the revolt was of necessity different. The successful outcome under Flavian leadership did not result in a treaty of any sort in 70 C.E., when the Temple in Jerusalem was destroyed. Likewise, there was no treaty (with its requisite treaty oath) in 73 C.E. when the entirety of Judea was pacified, but without a "peace." Rather, Judea suffered the arbitrary type of pacification and punishment that Rome used against rebellious subjects who had offended Rome's *maiestas*. Instead of a war indemnity per se, the tax that those circumcised Jews (despite ideology to the contrary, not all Jews were circumcised) who acknowledged the Jerusalem Temple as the focus of worship (not all Jews saw the Jerusalem Temple as such) used to pay to that Temple was now to be paid to the Roman "purse," the *Fiscus Iudaecus*.

The Road to Rebellion
(44–66 C.E.)

Following the death of Agrippa I, Claudius returned his kingdom to imperial provincial status, and he continued to appoint as administrators procurators of equestrian rank. This revived province of Judea was now, of course, a much larger entity than had been the case following the death of Archelaus. The territory now included the old domains of both Philip and Antipas.

We are not sure how this new province was governed. Tacitus wrote that "Claudius made Judaea a province and entrusted it to Roman knights or to freedmen" (*Histories* V.9.3; *GLA* II.29), which itself is a problematic statement. We do not know if it reflects the reality of what happened or Tacitus's well-honed use of inference and innuendo. This was a method, which scholars call his "pointed style," whereby he could slander whom he would by an "either-or" statement. Tacitus did this frequently so as to make his reader believe what we would call a worst-case scenario. Moreover, each time Tacitus did so, his presentation was sufficiently probable so that the reader could or would believe it. Had it not been so, Tacitus's attacks on those he hated would not have been so effective. Consequently we may say that it is possible that Claudius used either equestrians or freedmen or both to govern. The use of freedmen in administration was something that began to develop during the early Empire. It was not to be found in the old Roman Republic, which ended when Octavian (not yet called Augustus) won at Actium in 31 B.C.E., at which time the Empire may be said to have begun.

The Early Procurators

Cuspius Fadus (44–46 C.E.)
Claudius relieved Marsus, the legate of Syria with whom Agrippa had clashed, and replaced him with Cassius Longinus. Fadus was simultaneously sent to Judea as procurator, with two immediate assignments (*Ant.*

XIX.360–66). He was to punish the cities of Sebaste and Caesarea "for their insults to the deceased, and for their intemperate attack on his [Agrippa's] still living daughters." In addition, the troops, a squadron of cavalry and five cohorts of infantry (about three thousand troops), which had been recruited from Caesarea and Sebaste, were to be transferred out of the region. They were to be replaced by non-Palestinian troops from the Roman legions stationed in Syria. The troops, however, appealed to Claudius and were allowed to remain in the area. Josephus was of the opinion that the retention of these forces was one of the causes for the later warfare. Soldiers recruited outside the area probably would have done a better job in policing the area than locals with their vested interests, local loyalties, and regional commitments and animosities.

Fadus and his successor, Josephus tells us, "by abstaining from all interference with the customs of the country kept the nation at peace" (*War* II.221). Although it is true that no major disturbances erupted during the period, nonetheless there was certainly a foretaste of things of come. The procurator had first to deal with a border dispute and hostilities between some of the Pereans and the independent city of Philadelphia (*Ant.* XX.2–5). The trouble seems to have been caused by freewheeling marauding bands of Jews that raided in Philadelphian territory. Such robber bands were apparently preying on victims not only in the Philadelphia region but also in Idumean and Nabatean territory across the border. Fadus executed two brigand chiefs, exiled two others, and sought to wipe out such gangs throughout Judea.

One of Fadus's conflicts was of his own doing. He decided that the vestments of the high priest should be returned to Roman custody (*Ant.* XX.6–14). This was a major "power play." The high priest had the power to rule the Jews politically, and therefore his vestments were symbolic of that power. This was an attempt to "instruct" the Jews in the reality of Roman rule, in particular direct rule under provincial status. Only the Romans had the right to rule; they could however allot that right to whom they chose, including the high priest.

Fearing that violence might result from the popular indignation stirred up by Fadus's plans, Longinus with a large force put in an appearance in Jerusalem and brought the developing controversy to a standstill. Claudius, after a Jewish appeal and a personal intercession by Agrippa II, sided with the Jews rather than with Fadus. This was of particular symbolic and admonitory importance since it reminded the Jews that the ultimate decision about who could hold the high priesthood rested with the suzerain, Rome, as represented by the emperor himself. It was the emperor's decision whether Rome would give (or not give) its approval to whosoever was recommended under local auspices to that office.

CHART VIII. The Later Roman Era—II (45–70 C.E.)

Roman Affairs	Jewish Affairs	Roman Procurators in Judea	Jewish High Priests
41–54 Claudius emperor	Herod of Chalcis granted supervision of the Temple and the right to appoint high priests	44–46 Cuspius Fadus	44 Elionaeus ben Simon Cantheras
44–50 Cassius Longinus legate in Syria	Theudas killed	46–48 Tiberius Julius Alexander	46 Joseph ben Camithus
	Two sons of Judas the Galilean executed		
	Death of Herod of Chalcis; Agrippa II made his successor	48–52 Ventidius Cumanus	48 Ananias ben Nebedaeus
49 Expulsion of the Jews from Rome	Passover riot in Jerusalem		
50–60 Ummidius Quadratus legate in Syria	Torah scroll burned		
	Samaritan-Jewish clashes	52–58/9 Antonius Felix	
	Agrippa II received the territory previously ruled by Philip		
	Felix married Drusilla, sister of Agrippa II		ca. 55 Jonathan
54 (13 October) Death of Claudius			

Roman Affairs	Jewish Affairs	Roman Procurators in Judea	Jewish High Priests
54–68 Nero emperor	Agrippa II given four additional regions: two on the western coast of the Sea of Galilee and two in southern Perea		
	Rebel leader Eleazar captured and sent to Rome		
	Rise of the *Sicarii*		
	Episode of the Egyptian prophet		
	Priestly conflicts in Jerusalem		
	Riots in Caesarea		
	Paul arrested in Jerusalem		ca. 59 Ishmael ben Phabi
60–63 Domitius Corbulo legate in Syria Caesarea	Nero's verdict denying the Jews full civil rights in	60–62 Porcius Festus	
	Conflict between Agrippa II and Jerusalem leaders		ca. 61 Joseph Kabi ben Simon Cantheras
	Stoning of James, brother of Jesus		62 Ananus ben Ananus
63–66 Cestius Gallus legate in Syria	Conflict over high-priestly office	62–64 Lucceius Albinus	62 Jesus ben Damnaeus
			63/4 Jesus ben Gamaliel

			High Priests
		64	Matthias ben Theophilus
		67	Phanni ben Samuel
64–66	Gessius Florus		
67–69	Vespasian		

Work on the Temple completed

64 Christians persecuted in Rome

66 Cestius visited Jerusalem (March–April)
Turmoil in Caesarea
Florus raided Temple treasury; battles in Jerusalem followed
Masada captured
Imperial sacrifices terminated
Jewish-Gentile massacres
Cestius and twelfth legion defeated (October)

67 Jewish government set up
Jewish coins struck
Vespasian moved into Galilee (May–June)
John of Gischala entered Jerusalem
Northern Palestine subdued (November)
Vespasian moved to isolate Jerusalem

68 (9 June) Death of Nero

Roman Affairs	Jewish Affairs	Roman Procurators in Judea	Jewish High Priests
68–69 (9 June–15 Jan.) Galba emperor			
69 (15 Jan.–17 April) Otho emperor	Simon ben Gioras admitted to Jerusalem (March/April) Factional battles in Jerusalem		
69 (17 April–21 Dec.) Vitellius emperor	Vespasian subjugated the areas where Simon ben Gioras had operated (May/June)	69–70 Marcus Antonius Julianus	
69 (July) Vespasian proclaimed emperor by his troops			
69–79 Vespasian emperor			
70	Jerusalem laid under siege (March/April) Temple burned (August) Upper city captured (September)		

Although there is no known case of Rome rejecting a nominee during the early empire, we may be quite certain that the *princeps's* veto would have been meaningful should it have been given at any time. Even under the Republic, Rome had supported nominees who were attuned to the scenario Rome wished to have developed. (We must not forget that Rome supported the early Hasmonaean high priests even though they were not of a high-priestly family. In doing so, they thereby implicitly and, although we do not have direct literary data to this effect, possibly explicitly vetoed the more "legitimate" nominee. In any case, their action in supporting the Hasmonaean high priesthood helped the Hasmonaeans to retain the rulership of the Temple state.) Thus Claudius's role in the matter of the vestments must be seen as consequential. In fact, the dispute over the vestments may have convinced Claudius, who had the right to make the determination, to grant Herod of Chalcis the right to be in charge of the Temple, the holy vessels, and the selection of high priests (*Ant.* XX.l5–16).

One final episode is reported from Fadus's tenure in office: the appearance and execution of the prophet Theudas (*Ant.* XX.97–99; Acts 5:36 could be speaking of the same figure but chronologically out of order). Theudas was less a bandit/terrorist type than an idealistic messianic figure. He and his followers (about four hundred, according to Acts 5:36) gathered at the Jordan River, which he claimed would part just as Josh. 3:15–17 indicates it had done at the time of the conquest of Canaan. Fadus, unlike the Canaanite kings of old, sent a squadron of cavalry to stop the procession. For whatever reason, violence broke out. Theudas was captured, decapitated, and his head carried to Jerusalem. This is particularly interesting, however, because it means that Theudas suffered an honorable death. He was not crucified as a traitor, which is what we would have expected and what should have happened according to Roman tradition. Perhaps the Romans, having learned from what transpired when Jesus had been crucified, not much earlier, were unwilling to have another messianic martyr on their hands.

TIBERIUS ALEXANDER (46–48 C.E.)

The successor to Fadus, from a prominent and wealthy Alexandrian family, was a nephew of the famous Jewish philosopher Philo (*Ant.* XX.100–104). Alexander had repudiated his Jewish faith. Unlike most of the Roman administrators, he would have possessed an intimate knowledge of Jewish life and practices, at least as lived and practiced in Alexandria. Thus he would have known the potential consequences of infringing the Mosaic law and scruples resultant on its interpretation sufficiently well so as to avoid doing so. The members of his family were also friends of Agrippa I. During his tenure, Palestine suffered from a severe famine. Some relief was obtained from Queen Helena and the royal house of Adiabene. These recent converts to Judaism supplied funds to buy grain from Egypt and dried figs from Cyprus (see *Ant.* XX.17–96, especially 49–53; Acts 11:28–30).

Josephus provides no negative comments about Alexander. Given his later outstanding administrative record, he may have ruled exceptionally well. That terrorist and national liberation movements were still afoot is indicated by the fact that Alexander crucified two of the sons of Judas the Galilean. We must remember that crucifixion was the specific Roman punishment for rebellion of subjects or slaves against Rome. This was construed as harmful to Rome's *maiestas,* and therefore as an act of treason against Rome. Additionally it had been practiced from early on as the punishment for the same crime in various mainland Greek city-states. Crucifixion was not the common type of execution used for other types of capital crimes. Since Judas had led a major anti-Roman uprising at the time of Quirinius's census in 6 C.E., his sons too must have been engaged, or must have been conceived of as having been engaged, in anti-Roman activity. Josephus merely says that they "were brought up for trial and, at the order of Alexander, were crucified" (*Ant.* XX.102) because it was not necessary for him to describe completely the nature of their crime for his Roman or his Jewish audience.

This same Alexander was procurator at the time of the death of Herod of Chalcis. Herod himself had acquired the right to appoint high priests, which was an acknowledgment of his position in Judea, but again under Rome. He had exercised this very important prerogative twice (*Ant.* XX.16, 103). Claudius bestowed Herod's kingdom upon his nephew, the young Agrippa, and with the new appointment went the right to fill and supervise the high-priestly office. One measure of Roman control, however, was that the right to rule the client kingdom did not automatically mean that the king himself would be appointed high priest. This is of major significance. (1) It means that those sectarian groups that would have questioned Herod's or Agrippa's Jewishness would not be offended by the appointment of someone *they considered* a non-Jew. (2) It also means that there was a division of "power," whereby rulership was not concomitant with the exercise of the high priesthood, which was also a form of rulership. Although Herod and Agrippa had the right to appoint a high priest, what that high priest did once in office was or at least could be another matter. "Divide and conquer" was certainly applicable to the Roman exercise of power in the political as well as the military arena.

VENTIDIUS CUMANUS (48–52 C.E.)

The difficulties under Fadus and Alexander appear minor when viewed in the light of the troubles under Cumanus. The outbreaks of violence during his tenure illustrate the manner in which seething tensions ignite, as if by spontaneous combustion, when the catalytic provocation occurs. The first upheaval occurred at Passover (*Ant.* XX.105–12; *War* II.224–27). When Jewish pilgrims filled the Temple courtyard and Roman troops as usual stood guard on top of the Temple porticoes, one of the soldiers publicly exposed "his backside to the Jews, and made a noise in keeping with his posture" (*War* II.224). The crowd of worshipers called upon Cumanus to punish such lewdness. Some people accused Cumanus of having instigated the episode, while others began hurling stones at the troops before the procurator had time to act. Disdainful provocation produced crowd reaction, which in turn precipitated the procurator's call for reinforcements. Josephus says that in the skirmish and stampede that followed, twenty thousand (*Ant.* XX.112) or thirty thousand Jews (*War* II.227) were killed. Although the figures appear exaggerated, the impact of such deaths at a festival would have been significant. On such an occasion people were assembled from throughout the province. The deaths would have embittered those from outlying regions who suffered loss. So those families that did not yet resent, or had not previously resented, Roman rule, would be brought into the fray.

In the next episode, provocation came from the Jewish side (*Ant.* XX.113–14; *War* II.228–29). A slave of the emperor was robbed on a public thoroughfare. With the culprit unapprehended, Cumanus sought rectification by plundering the villages near the incident's locale and by holding the local leaders responsible. In the process of sacking the villages, a copy of the Torah was found, then torn in half and burned by a soldier (*Ant.* XX.115–17; *War* II.229–31). When crowds of protesting Jews raised a clamor in Caesarea, Cumanus, who clearly understood the potential the event had for rallying yet more to the rebel causes, had the soldier beheaded for the sacrilege. We must not construe Cumanus's action in executing the soldier as solely one of attempting to preempt further trouble with the Jews. The Romans were scrupulously aware that disfavor of the gods could bring disaster on them. Their own religiosity necessitated that sacrilege, against any god, although not necessarily against the subjects of that god, be treated appropriately.

A third episode arose out of Judean and Samaritan hostilities. It was a consequence of purely local and internal animosities but eventually involved the Roman emperor and led to the recall of Cumanus (*Ant.* XX.118–36; *War* II.232–46). A Galilean (*War* II.232; or a number of Galileans [*Ant.* XX.118]) on pilgrimage to Jerusalem was killed while passing through Samaritan territory. When Cumanus did not act promptly against the Samaritans, armed Judeans joined with the Galileans to take justice in their own hands. Two brigand leaders of Jewish gangs operating in the mountains were called in for assistance. The armed crowds attacked

Samaritan villages near Shechem, "massacred the inhabitants without distinction of age and burnt the villages" (*War* II.235). The procurator led his Sebastenian troops and government-armed Samaritans against the marauding Jews, slaying some and capturing many. Jerusalem leaders intervened to persuade the others to stop the fighting. The Samaritans appealed to the Syrian legate Quadratus.

Tacitus paints an even more drastic picture of this situation than does Josephus: The province would have been "ablaze with war but for the intervention of Quadratus, the governor of Syria" (*Annals* XII.54.3; *GLA* II.77). Quadratus held two hearings on the matter. One was at Samaria (or Caesarea, according to Josephus, *War* II.241), after which he blamed the Samaritans but crucified both Samaritan and Jewish participants. The second was at Lydda, after which more Jews were executed on suspicion of rebellion (*Ant.* XX.125–30; *War* II.240–42). Eventually Quadratus sent members of the various factions to Rome: the high priest and other Jewish leaders in chains; Cumanus, the procurator; high Samaritan officials; and a military tribune named Celer but not further identified. Intervention with the empress Agrippina and the emperor Claudius by Agrippa II, who happened to be in Rome at the time, led to a decision against the Samaritans, whose representatives were executed. Cumanus was convicted of the charges brought against him and sent into exile. The unidentified Celer, who may have been a Roman attaché under Cumanus, was returned to Jerusalem, dragged around the city in a public spectacle, and then put to death (*Ant.* XX.131–36; *War* II.243–46).

From Bad to Worse

In the middle of his discussion of the immediate successor of Cumanus, Josephus declares that "matters were constantly going from bad to worse" (*Ant.* XX.160). This assessment was accurately descriptive not of just a limited period or the tenure of a particular procurator but of matters in general, until war eventually broke out.

ANTONIUS FELIX (52–58/59 C.E.)

To replace Cumanus, Claudius appointed Felix, a brother of the freedman Pallas, who, as a favorite of Claudius, had risen to great prominence, power, and wealth in Rome. According to Tacitus, Felix had already served in a post in Samaria during the Jewish and Samaritan imbroglio under Cumanus (*Annals* XII.54.1–4; *GLA* II.77), although Josephus makes no reference to any such arrangement. Felix may have been Quadratus's temporary replacement for Cumanus when the latter was ordered to Rome (see *Ant.* XVIII.89; XX.137, however, says that Claudius "sent" Felix out as procurator). Felix had been requested to fill the post by Jonathan the ex–high priest who had been in Rome at the hearing before Claudius (*Ant.* XX.162). Tacitus castigated Felix as one of the major contributors to the later Jewish-Roman war. "Felix practiced every kind of cruelty and lust, wielding the power of king with all the instincts of a slave" (*Histories* V.9.3; *GLA* II.29). We must not forget, however, Tacitus's hatred of everyone connected with the Julio-Claudian or subsequent Flavian rule. Additionally, Tacitus seems to have had a prejudice against freedmen, particularly those who were being used by the emperors in governance. As frequently happened when Tacitus was attacking by inference and innuendo, he supplied no details to support his accusation.

Felix was remembered in Roman circles for his three marriages, always to members of royal families (so Suetonius, who called him the "husband of three queens" [*Divus Claudius* 28; *GLA* II.117]). One of his wives was a granddaughter of Antony and Cleopatra and thus he was a grandson-in-law, as Claudius was the grandson, of Antony (Tacitus, *Histories* V.9.3; *GLA* II.29). The other known wife of Felix was Drusilla, the daughter of Agrippa I and sister of Agrippa II (*Ant.* XX.139–44; Acts 24:24). This Jewish princess had married the king of Emesa while still an early teenager. When Felix became procurator she was about fourteen years old. Felix was so fascinated by her great beauty that he persuaded her to divorce her husband ("transgress the ancestral laws" [Josephus, *Ant.* XX.143]) and marry him (in 54 C.E.). This surely did not ingratiate the Roman official to the general Jewish population but did provide him with a close associate conversant with Jewish life and practices.

During the early days of Felix's service, the influence of Agrippa II in Palestine was greatly increased. Claudius bestowed on him the old territory ruled by Philip as well as other grants but deprived him of Chalcis (*Ant.* XX.138; *War* II.247). When Nero became emperor in 54 C.E., he reconfirmed Felix in his post. He also transferred to Agrippa four districts as a reward for his contribution of troops for engagements with the Parthians. These were Tiberias and Tarichaea on the western coast of the Sea of Galilee and Abila and Julias (Livias) on the southern border of Perea. Nero also awarded the kingdom of Armenia Minor to another Herodian, Aristobulus, son of Herod of Chalcis and cousin of Agrippa II (*Ant.* XX.158–59; *War* II.252). Agrippa enlarged and improved the city of Caesarea Philippi, renaming it Neronias in honor of his patron, and later struck coins bearing Nero's image (*Ant.* XX.211). There is no evidence of any contact between Agrippa II and Felix, but Agrippa's new status and location provided him with an increased number of Jewish subjects and easier access to Judea and Jerusalem.

Troubled conditions seem to have grown more anarchic under Felix.

Josephus's report is clearly an obvious exaggeration. So we may not take it for granted that "not a day passed, however, but that Felix captured and put to death many . . . impostors and brigands" (*Ant.* XX.160), crucifying the leaders and their supporters. (Again, remember that crucifixion was the means by which the Romans executed those subjects and slaves whose actions were treasonable.) Felix was able to capture Eleazar, the leader of a group that had ravaged the country for more than twenty years. He and his supporters were sent to Rome for trial (*Ant.* XX.121, 161; *War* II.253).

New means of opposition to the Romans and their Jewish supporters developed under Felix, apparently as a consequence of his suppression of the groups operating in the countryside. The terrorists began to conceal short daggers beneath their robes and while mingling with the crowds in the city or Temple would stab their victims, quickly hide their weapons again, and pretend to share in the alarm over the murder (*Ant.* XX.162–65; *War* II.254–57). One of the early victims, if not the first, was the high priest Jonathan. In the *Antiquities,* Josephus reports that Jonathan's assassination was the result of a bribe from Felix, who was exasperated by Jonathan's nagging for better governmental administration (*Ant.* XX.163). This hardly rings true, since Jonathan was clearly pro-Roman and had helped secure the post of procurator for Felix. In *War* II.256, no connection is made between Felix and Jonathan's murder, which is presented as the spontaneous act of the nationalistic terrorists who would have been a natural enemy of Jonathan. These assassins, or "dagger-men" (*sicarii,* from *sica,* a curved-blade dagger), were able to eliminate many victims and spread terror throughout the land.

The multiple possibilities for disorder existent at the time are illustrated by three other circumstances from Felix's tenure. Would-be redeemers and messianic/prophetic figures continuously put in appearances. The most significant of these was an Egyptian Jew who rallied a following and promised that while standing on the Mount of Olives he would destroy the walls of Jerusalem with a command (*Ant.* XX.167–72; *War* II.258–65; Acts 21:37–38). The sources speak of his following as being in the thousands. Felix sent his forces against the crowds, hundreds were killed or captured, but the Egyptian escaped. That the apostle Paul was later suspected of being this Egyptian implies that the Romans continued to be on the alert for him (Acts 21:38). Josephus notes that three factors were part of these messianic/impostor movements: hostility toward Rome, an assertion of Jewish independence, and the pillage, looting, and burning of the homes and villages of the wealthy. Thus class conflicts as well as nationalistic and religious sentiments can be seen in these movements.

Another form of class struggle, which also involved the general populace, broke out between the different levels of the priesthood (*Ant.*

XX.179–81). Josephus associates this particular trouble with Agrippa II's appointment of Ishmael the son of Phabi as high priest. The high-priestly families, that is, the families of those who had served in this office, and the remainder of the clergy clashed, collected gangs, and engaged in general harassment of one another. The high-priestly group, because of their economic means, were able to send slaves and others into the fields and threshing floors to collect tithes and thus deprive the local people of the option of giving the tithes to the lower clergy (see Num. 18:21–25). The Babylonian Talmud, a late and secondary source, has preserved what may be a memory of Ishmael and his tough tactics. A rabbi is quoted as saying, "Woe is me because of the house of Ishmael the son of Phabi, woe is me because of their fists" (*Pesahim* 57a). Whatever the case, this conflict had economic roots at its base. The consequence of this priestly competition and strife, according to Josephus, was that Jerusalem became a city without order and without government (*Ant*. XX.181).

Events occurring in Caesarea illustrate the strife that must have frequently developed between Jewish and non-Jewish citizens in Palestinian cities with mixed population (*Ant*. XX.173–78; *War* II.266–70). In Caesarea, Jews initially comprised a minority of the population and had the status of resident aliens rather than citizens, although they became the wealthier members of the community. A quarrel over the subject of equal civil rights arose, led to public disputes, and finally to rock-throwing mob scenes in the streets. Since the soldiers in Roman service were mostly recruits from what either was ideologically construed by Josephus as the non-Jewish population or actually was the non-Jewish, non-Yahwistic population of Caesarea and Sebaste, they tended to side with the Gentiles. After a period of general controversy over citizens' rights for the Jews, Felix turned the troops loose on a street demonstration that resulted in Jewish deaths and was followed by the looting of Jewish homes. The open expressions of hostility were temporarily suppressed. Unable or unwilling to settle the matter himself, however, Felix selected representatives from both sides and sent them to Rome for a hearing before Nero. The tensions were still smoldering when Felix's tenure in office ended.

The story of Paul's arrest and hearings in Jerusalem and Caesarea illustrate the breakdown of law and order under Felix (Acts 21:15–24:27). Paul was rescued from the crowds by Roman soldiers and kept in custody to prevent a lynching. A group of self-appointed vigilantes banded together in oath to kill Paul. Almost five hundred troops escorted him partway to Caesarea. Paul remained imprisoned in Caesarea for two years, with no verdict in the case. Felix apparently feared that he could not keep order, especially in Caesarea, if a decision were rendered. (Acts 24:26 says, in gossipy fashion, that Felix expected a bribe from Paul.)

PORCIUS FESTUS (60–62 C.E.)

When Festus arrived in Palestine (the date uncertain), he found the land overrun by gangs, Paul languishing in prison, and a controversy brewing between Agrippa II and the establishment in Jerusalem (*Ant.* XX.82–96; *War* II.271; Acts 25–26). Tradition has preserved a favorable opinion of Festus. He "proceeded to attack the principal plague of the country: he captured large numbers of the brigands and put not a few to death" (*War* II.271). His death after a short tenure meant that little progress could be made about stemming the rush toward total disorder.

Under Nero, all provincials were finding it harder and harder to obtain justice (Tacitus, *Annals* XIII.33.52; XIV.18.28). Under Festus, Nero handed down his verdict on the Caesarea situation, denying the requests of the Jews and holding Felix innocent of any wrongdoing. Josephus says that Nero authorized a rescript "annulling the grant of equal civil rights to the Jews" (*Ant.* XX.183). What such an order imported remains uncertain: the denial of all civil rights for Jews in the city? the denial of rights granted by Claudius? the denial of a bestowal of rights to Jews en masse? At any rate, the status quo was preserved or worse conditions imposed. The tensions were left to simmer and brew.

Agrippa II and his widowed sister Berenice, whom traditional gossip said lived together as man and wife, visited Festus shortly after his arrival (Acts 25:13). They heard Paul's defense and were consulted on Festus's decision to send him to Rome. The role of incidental matters in shaping a situation and in drawing in Roman involvement at the highest level is illustrated by the controversy between Agrippa II and Jerusalem leaders (*Ant.* XX.189–96). While in Jerusalem, Agrippa resided in the old Hasmonaean palace whose location on a lofty ridge provided a marvelous view of the city. Not content with the view, Agrippa added an elevated chamber to the palace to serve as a dining area, which allowed the Jewish potentate, while reclining at his meals, to watch all the activity in the Temple, including the sacrificial services. Agrippa's nosy surveillance raised the ire of Jerusalem's leaders, and they built a high wall obstructing Agrippa's view into the Temple precincts. The wall, however, also obstructed the view of Roman soldiers standing guard on the Temple porticoes, so Festus became the third party in a triangular argument. Matters were eventually appealed to the emperor, and twelve Jewish leaders were sent to Rome. Nero, influenced by his wife Poppaea, decided in favor of the Jews, thus leaving the wall intact. The Jewish high priest Ishmael ben Phabi and Helcias the keeper of the Temple treasury were retained in Rome as hostages, as was Roman custom. Thus Ishmael, who had stood up against Jewish king and Roman procurator, was forced to surrender the office.

Festus died in office, producing an interval when there was no procurator in Palestine. During this period, Agrippa II removed Joseph Kabi son of Simon, who had replaced Ishmael as high priest, and bestowed the office on Ananus son of Ananus, the fifth son in the family to hold the office. Ananus, whom Josephus describes (*Ant.* XX.197–203) as a heartless opportunist (but see *War* IV.319–25 for a totally different view), took the occasion to bring Christians to trial. James the brother of Jesus was stoned (Acts 7). Opposition to him by some leaders of Jerusalem led Agrippa to depose Ananus after only three months in office, to replace him with Jesus son of Damnaeus.

LUCCEIUS ALBINUS (62–64 C.E.)

Under Albinus, matters "went steadily from bad to worse" (*Ant.* XX.214). Josephus provides two somewhat different descriptions of Albinus's tenure; the *War* account is more critical of the procurator (*War* II.272–76) than that in the *Antiquities* (*Ant.* XX.204–10, 215). In both, the portraits are dismal.

In *Antiquities* Albinus is at least credited with having "bent every effort and made every provision to ensure peace in the land by exterminating most of the *sicarii*" (XX.204). But in the next sentence, the procurator is pictured, along with the high priest, taking bribes from the wealthy Ananus, a previous holder of the high-priestly office and an extortioner of tithes from the local population. Albinus seems to have suffered as much from despair over the situation as from self-seeking greed.

Under Albinus, the *sicarii* employed a new terrorist technique. Kidnapped victims were held hostage until prisoners were released. The *sicarii* kidnapped Eleazar, secretary of the Temple captain and son of Ananias, and held him captive until ten of their company were released. Ananias's entourage proved a productive source of hostages for such groups, since he possessed the wealth to bribe Albinus for an exchange of prisoners.

When Jesus son of Damnaeus was deposed and Jesus son of Gamaliel was appointed to succeed him, the former did not wish to vacate the office (*Ant.* XX.213). Followers of the two and hired supporters feuded and engaged in rock-tossing encounters in Jerusalem when the incumbent had to relinquish the post.

Two relatives of Agrippa, Costobar and Saul, organized gangs of their own and plundered widely (*Ant.* XX.214). Apparently they viewed themselves as an anti-insurrection, pro-Roman movement, although Josephus offers no clue to their political loyalties. Both later appear siding with the Romans (*War* II.418, 556–58).

With troubles burning on every hand, Agrippa II was rebuilding and enlarging Caesarea Philippi in order to dedicate it as "Neronias" in honor of the emperor (*Ant.* XX.211). A further factor that angered many of his subjects was the king's use of funds to provide Berytus with amenities and gladiatorial spectacles, funds collected from his subjects as taxes (*Ant.* XX.212).

Under Albinus, work on the Temple was completed and eighteen thousand laborers were threatened with unemployment (*Ant.* XX.219–22). Agrippa II, who had custody of the Temple's upkeep, refused to approve a public works project involving raising the height of the eastern Temple wall. He did give his blessing to a project for paving the streets of Jerusalem. Further work, however, was shortly resumed on the Temple when part of the foundation gave way (*Ant.* XV.391; *War* V.36).

When Albinus received word of his replacement, he sought to clear up pending cases in Jerusalem (*Ant.* XX.215). Prisoners who deserved death were executed, and others who were held for lesser or trivial charges were released. His successor could at least start with a clean slate. Albinus himself was sent to Mauretania, where he continued to conduct himself as he had in Judea (Tacitus, *Histories* II.58).

GESSIUS FLORUS (64–66 C.E.)

Jewish and Roman opinion agreed that the administration of Florus pushed conditions in Palestine toward war, but both speak more in generalities than specifics. Tacitus, for example, says, "Still the Jews' patience lasted until Gessius Florus became procurator: in his time war began" (*Histories* V.10.1). Josephus writes, "It was Florus who constrained us to take up war with the Romans, for we preferred to perish together rather than by degrees" (*Ant.* XX.257). Josephus's general descriptions of Florus's rule (*Ant.* XX.52–58; *War* II.277–79) speak of Albinus as a "paragon of virtue" compared to Florus (*War* II.277). Florus, whose wife's friendship with the empress Poppaea secured him the post, was charged with having "stripped whole cities, ruined entire populations, and almost [going to] the length of proclaiming throughout the country that all were at liberty to practise brigandage, on condition that he received his share of the spoils" (*War* II.278). Josephus declares, in what sounds like a later rationalization, that Florus actually set out to incite a Jewish revolt—"his only hope of covering up his own enormities. For, if the peace were kept, he expected to have the Jews accusing him before Caesar; whereas, could he bring about their revolt, he hoped that this larger crime would divert inquiry into less serious offences" (*War* II.282–83).

Events Precipitating the War

The movement toward open warfare progressed almost inevitably. Incident after incident, which if isolated and dealt with effectively could have been contained, snowballed and eventually turned the entire land into a battlefield. The outbreak of open warfare was preceded by a number of events involving various towns, groups, social classes, and degrees of violence. Various factions within Judaism as well as non-Jews were participants in the episodes.

Cestius Gallus's Visit to Jerusalem

Jewish animosity toward Florus found occasion for demonstration when the Roman legate in Syria, Cestius (63–66 C.E.) accompanied by Florus, paid a visit to Jerusalem at the Passover season in 66 C.E. (*War* II.280–83). The pilgrim multitudes crowded around the official, denouncing Florus and demanding relief from their oppression. Florus scoffed at the people's protest, and Cestius, like a good politician, promised that Florus would moderate his behavior in the future. With such a pledge, he returned to Antioch. Cestius's reaction or lack of action in response to the jeering Jewish crowds may have had significant impact on forthcoming events. Probably both the Jewish populace and Florus became convinced that Cestius would take no initiative to straighten out matters and that in consequence it was every group for itself. The present and potential anarchy in the country encouraged the influx already underway (*Ant.* XX.256; *War* II.279).

Civic Turmoil at Caesarea

The hostilities and conflicts that had characterized relations between Jews and non-Jews in Caesarea soon burst into open violence (*War* II.284–91). The Jewish community had sought to acquire or extend their civic rights in the city but had been rebuffed in their efforts (*Ant.* XX.173–78, 182–84). Nero's verdict against the Jews apparently was seen as condoning anti-Jewish behavior in the city. A Jewish synagogue in town adjoined a Greek-owned plot of land that the Jews had sought unsuccessfully to purchase. To harass the Jewish worshipers, workshops were built on the plot, leaving the Jews only a narrow passageway to the synagogue. Jewish youth sought to halt the construction, and violence broke out. In an effort to secure governmental intervention in their favor, the Jewish leaders gave Florus a bribe of eight talents. One of these leaders was John the tax collector. That the tax collector in a Gentile-governed city was Jewish might help to explain some of the hostilities in the community. On the following day, a Sabbath, the Jews assembling for worship were met by a Caesarean Gentile simulating the sacrifice of a bird on a pot in front of the synagogue. Such an action could, by implication, suggest that the Jews were "lepers" (see Lev. 14:4–5), a common charge leveled against them and used to explain their "expulsion" from Egypt (see, for example, Josephus, *Contra Apion* I.304–13). A fight between the two camps erupted. Jewish leaders left the city carrying along the synagogue copy of the Torah. They appeared personally before Florus, who was in Sebaste at the time, to plead their cause but were arrested and put in irons for having carried away the copy of the Torah even though they "delicately reminded him of the matter of the eight talents" (*War* II.292). Tensions became so heated in Caesarea that Florus did not dare to put in an appearance there (*War* II.296).

The Temple Treasury Episode

The Jews had fallen greatly in arrears on their payment of tribute to Caesar (*War* II.403–4). Apparently for this reason Florus sent to Jerusalem and extracted seventeen talents from the Temple treasury. This resulted in a Roman-Jewish confrontation. In the midst of the populace's demonstration, some of the group passed a basket begging coppers for the procurator (*War* II.293–96). Hearing of the uproar, Florus then put in a personal appearance in Jerusalem, held a tribunal requesting that he be given the men who had insulted him, and ended up turning his soldiers loose to plunder the city market and adjacent area (*War* II.305–6). Numerous persons were caught, scourged, and crucified. Josephus claims that Florus proceeded "to do what no one had ever done before, namely, to scourge before his tribunal and nail to the cross men of equestrian rank, men who, if Jews by birth, were at least invested with that Roman dignity" (*War* I.307–8). This, of course, is problematic, and Josephus's bias may be showing. Florus was crucifying rebels, who were citizens of a subject state. There is no other evidence that he was so arrogant or so foolish as to crucify Roman citizens, so we must leave the resolution of this problem in abeyance.

In any case, Agrippa's sister Berenice appealed to the Romans to desist (*War* II.309–14), and the leading men and chief priests of Jerusalem appealed to the populace for cessation of hostilities (*War* II.315–24). When two new cohorts arrived in the city from Caesarea, and Florus ordered the local population to give them a triumphal welcome, a new confrontation occurred (*War* II.325–29). This time, however, the soldiers were forced to retreat to the safety of their Jerusalem camp. In order to prevent the troops from gaining access to the Temple, the porticoes connecting the Temple and the Antonia fortress were destroyed. Under these conditions, Florus summoned the Jewish leaders, informed them he was leaving the city, assigned them the responsibility for law and order, and left them a cohort of their choosing (*War* II.330–32).

Three reports were sent to Cestius about the events in Jerusalem, from Florus, Berenice, and the Jerusalem magistrates. Cestius, contrary to the opinion of his counselors who urged his direct personal and military intervention, sent a representative to Jerusalem to investigate matters (*War* II.333–36). The official joined Agrippa II at Jamnia, the latter returning from a visit to Egypt. Together with the Jewish group that had met the king to escort him they made their way to Jerusalem. Cestius's representative was shown the damage done in the city, observed the (temporary) peaceful demeanor of the people, offered sacrifice in the Temple, and returned to Antioch (*War* II.336–41).

The populace, convinced that Cestius was reluctant to take action, pushed Agrippa and the priestly leaders to appeal directly to Nero and denounce Florus (*War* II.342–44). Responding, Agrippa II addressed the people with a speech in which Josephus has the monarch call for submission to Rome, arguing that to tolerate even a Florus was necessary because he represented the irresistible might of an empire to whom greater powers than the Jews had acquiesced (*War* II.345–401). In practical terms, Agrippa advised the people to restore the porticoes and to pay their overdue taxes (*War* I.402–4). For a time, the people joined in following Agrippa's suggestions, collecting forty talents of tribute in the Jerusalem area (*War* II.405). When it became clear that Agrippa's program also required obeying Florus's orders until the procurator was recalled in the normal course of events rather than for trial, many Jewish factions rose up and called for the king's banishment from Jerusalem. Before his unceremonious departure to his own territory, Agrippa sent some of the Jewish leaders to Florus with recommendations about collecting the remainder of the outstanding tribute (*War* II.406–7).

The Rebel Capture
of Palestinian Fortresses

The growing strength of gangs and rebel groups in the countryside eventually led to their capture of important fortresses. The first to be taken was Masada, which Herod had so well fortified and so lavishly developed (*War* II.408). The small Roman garrison defending the site was massacred. Seizing Masada not only supplied Jewish groups with an easily defended stronghold but also provided them with weapons, since an armory was located at the site.

For a time, Masada became the headquarters for Menahem, who, Josephus reports, was a "son of Judas surnamed the Galilean—that redoubtable doctor who in old days, under Quirinius, had upbraided the Jews for recognizing the Romans as masters when they already had God [as master]" (*War* II.433). Although Josephus says that Menahem was a son of Judas, it seems more likely that he was a grandson, since it had been sixty years since Judas opposed Quirinius's census. Masada would remain in rebel hands for years and be the last bastion of the Jews' first revolt against Rome.

Other fortresses gradually came into Jewish hands. Cypros, which guarded the region of Jericho, was captured and the Roman garrison massacred. The Roman troops at Machaerus, on the eastern side of the Dead Sea, decided to vacate the site and hand over control to the local citizens in exchange for safe passage out of the area (*War* II.484–86).

The Cessation of Imperial Sacrifices

In Jerusalem, the traditional sacrifices offered in the Temple on behalf of the Roman state and the *princeps* were brought to an end by a priestly movement under the leadership of the captain of the Temple, the youthful Eleazar son of Ananias. The twice daily sacrifice of two lambs and a bull for the emperor had been instituted by Augustus (*War* II.197; Philo, *Embassy*, 157, 317), but the practice of offering sacrifices on behalf of foreign rulers can be traced back to Persian times (Ezra 6:10). Josephus saw this episode as "the foundation of the war with the Romans" (*War* II.409); it was certainly a radical assertion of breaking with Roman dominion, which Rome could read as the initiation of revolution.

The decision to end sacrifices for the Romans was supported by only a part of the Temple priesthood. Eleazar, who had earlier been kidnapped by the *sicarii*, and the young priests pushed the matter and were probably aided by the Temple police subordinate to Eleazar (*War* II.409–10). This polarization of the priesthood between the younger members and the older establishment priests had manifested itself earlier, with the younger and lower orders of the priesthood obviously getting the worse of the conflict (*Ant.* XX.179–81). A class struggle over wealth and status as well as nationalism was thus involved in the move by Eleazar and his followers. The high-priestly families and other notables—including Pharisees, who were often but not always wealthy, more pro-Roman, and had much to lose if war broke out—offered a variety of reasons in trying to convince the dissidents to permit sacrifice (*War* II.411–17). The dissenting group refused and solidified their control over the Temple precincts and the lower city.

The leading citizens, or what might be called the peace party, who opposed the cessation of imperial sacrifices and feared the consequences of such action, hastily sent embassies to both Florus and Agrippa II (*War* II.418–19). Florus declined to respond, "determined as he was to kindle the war" (*War* II.420). Agrippa, "anxious that the Romans should not lose the Jews nor the Jews their Temple and mother city" and that he lose nothing, dispatched two thousand troops to Jerusalem (*War* II.421).

Agrippa's forces and "all the people who were in favour of peace" sought to capture the Temple area and drive out the insurgents. Fierce fighting between the two forces lasted for seven days, with neither of them getting the upper hand (*War* II.422–24). On the eighth day, some *sicarii* dressed as common folks slipped into the Temple precincts during the ceremony of "wood-carrying" to supply the altar. The insurgents, reinforced and bolstered by the *sicarii,* forced the peace party, or royalists, to evacuate the upper city. Once in control of this area, the dissidents burned the house of Ananias, the palaces of Agrippa and Berenice, and the record office where the public archives were stored. They were "eager to destroy the moneylenders' bonds and to prevent the recovery of debts, in order to win over a host of grateful debtors and to cause a rising of the poor against the rich" (*War* II.428). During the next three days, the rebels captured the Antonia fortress, executed the captured garrison, burned the fortress, and besieged the troops and citizens loyal to Rome in Herod's palace (*War* II.430–32).

A new state of affairs resulted when Menahem and his followers arrived from Masada (*War* II.433–40). Coming on the scene "like a veritable king" with his bodyguards, he took over command of the palace siege. The besieged asked for terms after part of the palace defenses were demolished. Agrippa's troops and native Jews were allowed to leave the palace. The Roman troops took refuge in the three Herodian towers at the northwest corner of the city.

With the small Roman force under siege, the rebels had a temporary lull in which they could hunt out fellow countrymen and slaughter one another. The ex–high priest Ananias and his brother Ezechias, Eleazar's father and uncle, were caught and killed by Menahem and his faction (*War* II.441). Conflict then developed between Eleazar and Menahem. Josephus says that Menahem "believed himself without a rival in the conduct of affairs and became an insufferable tyrant . . . arrayed in royal robes and attended by his suite of armed Zealots" (*War* I.442–44). Eleazar and his supporters attacked Menahem and his followers. Many were caught and slaughtered. Menahem evaded capture for a time but was found, along with his lieutenant Absalom, hiding on Ophel and, after being tortured, was killed. Some of Menahem's followers escaped to Masada, among them Eleazar, son of Jair (*War* II.445–48).

After some days under siege, the Roman commander asked for terms of capitulation. Oaths and a pledge of security were granted by the Jews, who allowed the armed soldiers to leave the towers. Once the troops had laid down their arms according to the agreement, Eleazar's party fell upon them, massacring the entire unit except for the commander, who promised to turn Jew and be circumcised (*War* II. 449–56).

Massacres and Reprisals

The breakdown of authority in the country allowed smoldering tensions to become open aggressions. Hostilities between Jews and Gentiles led to massacres in many cities. In Caesarea, the Gentile population fell upon the Jews and, according to Josephus, slaughtered twenty thousand in an hour's time (*War* II.457). This Caesarean massacre can be seen as a reprisal for the slaughter of the Roman soldiers in Masada and Jerusalem. Those troops were local auxiliaries recruited primarily from Sebaste and Caesarea (*Ant.* XIX.365–66; XX.176).

Bloody battles broke out in numerous cities with mixed populations. Reprisals and counterreprisals occurred. Jews attacked and killed Gentiles in various Transjordanian and coastal towns (*War* II.457–65). In other towns—Ascalon, Ptolemais, Hippos, and Gadara—the Jews bore the brunt of revenge (*War* II.477–80). Pillage and plunder were widespread. In at least one case, Jews fought on the side of the Gentiles against their fellow religionists. At Scythopolis, this was the case, but Gentile suspicion led to the slaughter of the city's Jewish population (*War* II.466–76). Riots and fights between Jews and non-Jews spread beyond the borders of Palestine. Two Roman legions were eventually used to quell disturbances in Alexandria (*War* II.487–98).

The Opening Phase
of the First Revolt

Cestius Gallus, the Roman legate in Syria, eventually entered the field, sometime in September 66 C.E. Whether he had been awaiting directives from Rome or was overly cautious and hesitant remains unknown. Of the Empire's twenty-five legions, Cestius was in command of four—III Gallica, VI Ferrata, X Fretensis, and XII Fulminata. He left Antioch with a large force. The twelfth Fulminata and two thousand troops from each of the other legions, as well as additional cohorts of infantry and squadrons of cavalry, gave him the equivalent of two legions. Three monarchs supplied auxiliary contingents—Antiochus of Commagene and Soaemus of Emesa from northern Syria and Agrippa II together supplied about fifteen thousand additional troops. Auxiliaries and volunteers from various cities swelled the numbers even further (*War* II.499–502). King Agrippa personally accompanied Cestius.

The Roman forces moved down the coast by sea and land, burned Chabulon (Cabul) near Ptolemais and captured Joppa (*War* II.503–9). A contingent was sent into Galilee, where Sepphoris welcomed the Romans and only extremists put up much of a fight (*War* II.510–12). When the Galilean expeditionary force rejoined the main army at Caesarea, Cestius set out for Jerusalem. It was now mid-October; pilgrims were in Jerusalem for the Feast of Tabernacles. On the march, Antipatris and Lydda were taken and burned. The Roman army began setting up camp at Gabao (Gibeon), a few miles north of the Jewish capital (*War* II.513–16).

The Jews took the offensive, abandoning the festival celebration, and attacked. The Romans were caught temporarily off guard and suffered several hundred casualties. The Jewish forces attacking from the south were joined by the rebel Simon son of Gioras and his forces from the north, who made off with many of the Roman baggage mules. For a time, Jewish combatants occupied the heights and kept the Roman army penned down (*War* II.517–22). Agrippa took the occasion to resume his peace efforts. Two of his friends, well known among the Jews, were sent to negotiate, bearing a promise of pardon from Cestius if hostilities ceased immediately. Jewish rebels, enjoying the taste of victory over a real Roman army, refused any negotiation, murdered one emissary, wounded the other, and assailed the moderates who protested such behavior (*War* II.523–26).

Cestius regrouped his army and moved closer to Jerusalem, setting up camp on Mount Scopus only a short distance from the city. After waiting three days for signs of surrender, the Romans occupied and burned the suburb of Bezetha, which the Jewish forces had deserted (*War* II.527–31). With Cestius encamped opposite Herod's palace, moderate Jews inside the city sought to communicate with the Roman commander. Ananus son of Jonathan sent a message promising to open the city gates, but he and his supporters were hauled down from the city wall (*War* II.532–34). After five days, Cestius assaulted the north wall of the Temple and was at the point of undermining the wall and firing a Temple gate when his opposition suddenly stiffened (*War* II.535–37). Precipitously and for some unexplainable reason, Cestius ordered his forces to retreat from the city. Josephus claims that his camp prefect was bribed by Florus to dissuade Cestius from pursuing the attack (*War* II.531), but his explanation makes no sense. Throughout the crisis, beginning at the spring Feast of Unleavened Bread, Cestius's caution must have given the impression of inertia; now it appeared as panic. After a night spent in the camp on Scopus, Cestius and his army retreated under hot pursuit. Two days were spent at Gabao, but again withdrawal turned into frenzied flight. Military animals were slaughtered, baggage deserted, and other *impedimenta* abandoned. In the descent to Beth-horon, hordes of Jewish fighters assailed the Romans. Under the cover of nightfall Cestius fled Beth-horon, leaving behind a detachment simulating normalcy in the camp. The next day, with the Jews in pursuit, the Romans abandoned their heavy military equipment and war machines. Cestius made it to Antipatris and with the ragged remnants of the imperial forces made good his escape (*War*

II.540–53). The Jewish insurgent forces "plundered the corpses, collected the booty which had been left on the route, and, with songs of triumph, retraced their steps to the capital" (*War* II.554).

The Major Phase of the War

With Cestius's ignominious defeat, the die was cast; an all-out "war" became inevitable. Strongly pro-Roman Jews fled Jerusalem as "swimmers desert a sinking ship" (*War* II.556). Many of these had strong connections with Agrippa and the Herodians. Prominent among them were Saul and Costobar, kinsmen of Agrippa, who were sent to Nero by Cestius to report on conditions in Judah and to accuse Florus as the culprit (*War* II.556–58).

Jewish Preparations for War

Moderate pro-Romans, or the groups that had earlier argued for moderation and peace, now had to cast their lot in with the anti-Roman rebels. The moderates and the rebels cooperated to set up a government. Two men were elected, presumably by popular assembly in the Temple courtyard, to control in Jerusalem: Joseph son of Gorion and Ananus the son of Ananus the high priest. Josephus notes that Eleazar son of Simon, a major leader in the battle against Cestius and apparently leader of the groups calling themselves the Zealots, was given no post because of his despotic character and the militant nature of his admirers (*War* II.562–65). The most radical element thus failed to gain official prominence in the city. Six other districts were set up and generals placed in charge: Idumea (under Jesus son of Sapphas and Eleazar son of Neus [probably to be read Ananias]), Jericho (under Josephus son of Simon), Perea (under Manasseh), western Judea (under John the Essene), northeast Judea (under John son of Ananias), and the Galilees (or only Lower Galilee?) and the region Gamala in Transjordan (under the historian Josephus son of Matthias) (*War* II.566–68).

Two factors should be noted about the geographical districting of Jewish territory and the leaders selected to command the war effort:

First, the Sanhedrin and the high-priestly families appear to have played a significant role in the selection of leaders. In *War* II.562, Josephus implies that leaders were appointed or selected by the general population, whereas in his *Life*, 28–29, he refers to "leading men in Jerusalem" as making the choice. At any rate, most of the leaders appointed were moderates and from important Jewish families. Persons outside the aristocratic establishment were passed over. Only Eleazar son of the high priest Ananias, assuming he is to be identified with Eleazar son of Neus, possessed a past history of known militant opposition to the Romans.

Second, the territory over which control was assumed did not include the region of Samaria; thus the newly envisioned Jewish state did not include the whole of the Roman province of Judea. In addition, Galilean and Perean territory formed part of the kingdom of Agrippa II. The regions of Tiberias and Tarichaea on the western coast of the Dead Sea and Abila and Julias (Livias) in southern Perea were part of the pro-Roman king's domain. Further, independent Greek cities under Syrian supervision in the so-called Decapolis in the northern Transjordan separated Jewish populations in the north from those in the south.

Our sources provide us with detailed knowledge of only one of the districts, namely, Galilee. Josephus reports that he set up local civil administrations in Galilee, a council of seventy members with jurisdiction including the right to execute capital punishment over the entire region and local councils of seven people in each city to adjudicate local matters (*War* II.569–71; *Life* 79). Similar moves must have been taken by the leaders in the other districts. Josephus sought to surround the district with a ring of fortified cities that were provided with supplies of grains and arms (*War* II.572–75). An army was raised and training begun (*War* II.576–84).

Galilee was far from united behind either the war effort or Josephus's leadership. Sepphoris, a significant commercial center, vacillated in its commitment for a time, but eventually opposed the war (*War* II.574; *Life* 30–31). Tiberias and Tarichaea, belonging to Agrippa, were divided between pro- and anti-war factions. Members of the aristocratic and governing class, holding positions at the pleasure of the king, were pro-Roman. Tiberias fluctuated in its allegiance. The leader of the city's insurgents, Justus son of Pistus, led raids against the independent cities of Gadara and Hippos (*Life* 32–42). John son of Levi, of Gischala, became leader of a strong rebel band after Gischala was burned by forces from independent cities in the area and then retaken by John's forces (*Life* 43–45). Gaulanitis in Transjordan initially remained loyal to Agrippa under the influence of a garrison of his troops stationed in Gamala (*Life* 46–61).

Josephus's leadership was opposed by various groups, both pro-Roman and nationalistic. The most significant opponent within the war party was John of Gischala, the commander of a force of four hundred extremists. After a brief period of cooperation, John and Josephus became bitter enemies (*War* II.575, 585–94; *Life,* 70–76, 84–103). John tried to get Josephus killed and circulated the rumor that he had plans to betray the country to the Romans. After promoting opposition to Josephus, John succeeded in having him investigated by a delegation from Jerusalem (*War* II.614–31; *Life,* 122–25, 189–335). For a time, several cities defected from Josephus's command.

Preparations for war must have been carried out in the other districts, but there is little information about their course. In western Judea a foolish and unprovoked attack was made against Ascalon, which was garrisoned with two Roman auxiliary units. Jewish forces were twice defeated in the assault, and John the Essene, commander of the district, was killed (*War* III.9–28).

A self-appointed leader, Simon son of Gioras from Gerasa in the Decapolis, at the head of a band of extremists was raiding and plundering northeastern Judea (*War* II.652–54). The Jerusalem leaders had to send an army out to restrain him. Simon and his band fled to Masada and from there carried out raids in Idumea. The activities of Simon and John of Gischala demonstrate that no national unity had developed and that interfactional conflict and personal ambitions were more the rule than the exception, a situation that would continue throughout the war.

In Jerusalem, the people "busied themselves with the repair of the walls and the accumulation of engines of war. In every quarter of the city missiles and suits of armour were being forged; masses of young men were undergoing a desultory training; and the whole was one scene of tumult" (*War* II.648–49). The wall enclosing the suburb of Bezetha, begun by Agrippa I, was hastily completed, being raised to a height of about thirty-five feet (*War* II.563; V.148–55).

The Jewish government in Jerusalem seems to have begun the operation of a mint shortly after its formation. Silver coins—shekels, half-shekels, and quarter-shekels—were struck for five years. Since the fifth year of the revolt would have begun in Nisan (about April) of 70 C.E., then the first coins must have been struck before Nisan (March/April) of 67 C.E. The use of silver coinage in addition to bronze was significant. Roman provinces were not allowed to mint in silver; by using this metal, the Jewish state was giving embodiment to a claim of independence.

The Roman Offensive

The emperor Nero was in Achaia when he received word of the Jewish defeat of Cestius. The defeated commander was soon relieved of his post— Tacitus reports that "on his death, whether in the course of nature or from vexation, Nero sent out Vespasian" (*Histories* V.10), a veteran soldier with a proven war record. Vespasian sent his elder son Titus, his second in command, to Alexandria to bring from there an additional legion, the XV Apollinaris (*War* II.1–8). In the spring of 67 C.E., Vespasian assembled his forces in Antioch, where Agrippa was awaiting him. Two full legions were stationed in Syria, V Macedonica and X Fretensis, along with the decimated XII Fulminata, which remained in Antioch. In addition to the two legions, later expanded to three after Titus's return from Alexandria, Syria supplied twenty-three auxiliary cohorts (a cohort was one-tenth of a legion, or about six hundred men). Kings Agrippa, Antiochus, and Soaemus supplied forces, as they had earlier. For this campaign, the Nabatean king Malchus II (ca. 40–70 C.E.) supplied fifteen hundred troops, and the anti-Jewish city of Caesarea contributed a sizable force. In all, Vespasian had about sixty thousand troops under his command (*War* II.64–69).

When he arrived at Ptolemais and set up camp, Vespasian was greeted with a request for troops and a promise of support sent by Sepphoris, the largest city in Galilee. A contingent of Romans was already in the city (*War* II.510; *Life* 394), and the additional forces allowed the Romans to harass Galilee (*War* III.29–33; 59–60). Josephus failed in an effort to take Sepphoris (*War* II.61–63), a failure matched in the first Roman attempt to take Jotapata (*War* III.110–14). Once Titus had reached Ptolemais and the legion from Alexandria was integrated, in late May or early June, Vespasian led his troops into Galilee. Many of the Jewish forces fled, and Josephus took refuge in Tiberias (*War* II.115–31). Gabara was captured by the Romans (*War* III.132–35), who now turned to Jotapata to which Josephus had returned. The city was placed under siege but was defended gallantly. The siege lasted for several weeks (*War* III.141–288). With the fall of the city, in late July, the males were killed, the women and children enslaved, and the city's fortifications pulled down (*War* III.316–39). Josephus survived; the Jewish commander had backed down on a suicide pact and was discovered hiding in a cave (*War* III.340–91). Immediate reaction favored sending Josephus to Nero for trial, but following the Jewish general's prediction that both Vespasian and his son Titus would serve as Roman emperors, he was retained in Judea and allowed to accompany the Roman commanders (*War* III.392–408). At least this is Josephus's version of events, a version repeated by the Latin pseudo-historian Suetonius (*Vespasian*, 5–6; *GLA* II.122) and by Dio Cassius (*Roman History* LXVI.1.1; *GLA* II.371).

After the victory at Jotapata, Vespasian established permanent military bases at Caesarea and Scythopolis, both fundamentally non-Jewish cities (*War* I.409–13). Minor action was required to squelch a small Jewish fleet of pirate ships operating out of Joppa. Roman troops secured the town and a storm wrecked the makeshift fleet (*War* II.414–31).

Vespasian next turned his attention to capturing Agrippa's Galilean territory held by rebels, namely, the cities of Tiberias and Tarichaea. After being entertained at Caesarea Philippi by Agrippa for twenty days, Vespasian gathered all three legions at Scythopolis and marched on Tiberias, which immediately surrendered (*War* II.443–61). Tarichaea, enforced by rebels fleeing Tiberias and other towns, was a different matter. For a time the city held out, but soon dissension developed between Jewish factions and Titus took opportunity of the disorder to enter the city from the direction of the Sea of Galilee, its unwalled side. Attempts were made to spare Agrippa's subjects as distinguished from the rebel outsiders who had entered the city. A speedily constructed Roman flotilla chased rebels trying to escape across the sea, an event commemorated in Vespasian's legend *victoria navalis*. Of the captives, six thousand young males were shipped to Corinth to work on the canal recently begun by Nero (*War* III.462–542).

With the Roman occupation of Tiberias and Tarichaea, all the Jewish garrisons in Galilee capitulated except for those at Gischala and Mount Tabor. In the Transjordan, Gamala held out. (The region of Samaria seems not to have become involved in the war in any significant way. Josephus reports on one encounter between Samaritans and Romans, that on Mount Gerizim. It ended disastrously for the Samaritans [*War* III.307–15].)

The siege of Gamala, because of the city's naturally elevated defenses, lasted a month. Roman troops broke into the town but were repelled and finally secured the site only after heavy fighting (*War* IV.1–53, 62–83). The garrison on Mount Tabor was subdued with little trouble (*War* IV.54–61), and Gischala surrendered after John and his forces fled for Jerusalem by night (*War* IV.384–120).

With Galilee firmly in Roman control by late November 67 C.E., Vespasian moved to set up winter camp. On his way to Caesarea, he subdued the regions of Jamnia, Azotus, and Lydda (*War* IV.130, 444). The tenth legion wintered in Scythopolis and the others in Caesarea (*War* IV.87). During the winter months garrisons were established throughout captured sites in Galilee and some towns were rebuilt (*War* IV.442).

With the Romans bivouacked awaiting the better campaigning weather of springtime, Jewish factions in Jerusalem turned their attention to lacerating one another. The Roman conquest of rebel strongholds in Galilee and elsewhere created a stream of outsiders flowing into Jerusalem. The two primary groups in the city, the moderates headed by the high priest Ananus and the zealot extremists under Eleazar son of Simon (or Gion), now had to deal with other would-be leaders. John of Gischala brought a small army into the city and further incited portions of the population (*War* IV.121–37). A round of assassinations and murders eliminated members of the moderate party, including some kinsmen of Agrippa II (*War* IV.138–50). Under Ananus's leadership a countermove against the extremists was planned. When the Zealots learned of the scheme, they occupied the Temple and proceeded to select a new high priest to replace Matthias son of Theophilus (*Ant.* XX.223). The new high priest chosen by lot was Phanni son of Samuel, a reluctant and unqualified priest possessing no special qualifications (*War* IV.151–61). Calling together a general assembly of the people, Ananus denounced the Zealots, incited the populace to battle, and led the moderates to blockade the extremists in the Temple (*War* IV.162–207).

John of Gischala convinced Ananus to allow him to serve as the go-between with the Zealots, but even when bound by oath, John maneuvered for his own advantage and served the Zealots as privileged informer. By misrepresenting Ananus, he convinced the Zealots to appeal to the Idumeans for help against the moderate party (*War* IV.208–32). The Idumeans responded with a large force but found the gates of Jerusalem barred to them. They gained access to the town only when the Zealots carried out a daring sally in a raging thunderstorm and sawed the bars to the gates (*War* IV.233–304).

Once inside the city, the Idumeans with their Zealot compatriots went on a killing spree, slaughtering the soldiers under Ananus and looting throughout the town. Ananus was murdered, as well as Jesus son of Gamaliel, and members of aristocratic and noble families were tortured and killed (*War* IV.305–33). Eventually matters went to such extremes that the Idumean forces became disgusted. A prominent citizen was put on trial before a seventy-member panel of judges (parroting the Sanhedrin?). When a unanimous verdict of innocence was returned, the defendant was struck down and killed in the Temple by two Zealots who proclaimed the act as their verdict (*War* IV.334–44). The majority of the Idumean forces decided to withdraw from the city, but before they left, two thousand persons held in prison were released. Most of these left Jerusalem to join the band headed by Simon son of Gioras (*War* IV.345–53).

Antagonism between groups, laced with murder and mayhem, continued apace in Jerusalem. John of Gischala moved to assert his leadership over the extremists, and subfactions began to develop among the Zealots (*War* IV.354–65, 389–97). Vespasian gave consideration to his subordinates, but finally declined their suggestion that they take advantage of the dissension in Jerusalem and attack forthwith (*War* IV.366–76).

Other groups operated outside Jerusalem. The *sicarii*, ensconced at Masada, carried out raiding parties attacking fellow Jews. They invaded Engedi during the Feast of Unleavened Bread and caused general havoc in much of Judea (*War* IV.398–409).

As the rainy season drew to a close, Vespasian began his campaign to isolate Jerusalem prior to laying the city under siege. In late March 68 C.E., Vespasian moved into Perea and occupied Gadara, the wealthy members of the city having agreed to capitulate. Rebel fugitives from the city and the region were pursued and many slaughtered on the banks of the Jordan, choking the river with bodies. Except for the fortress at Machaerus, the whole of Perea fell into Roman control (*War* IV.410–39). Numerous towns in western Judea and Idumea were taken by Vespasian. He then swung northward; going by way of Emmaus, he passed through the region of Samaria to Shechem and then descended to the Jordan Plain, arriving in

Jericho in June (*War* IV.440–50). Perhaps at this time the Romans occupied Qumran. Attempting to invest Jerusalem in all directions, Vespasian set up a ring of camps around the city—at Emmaus fifteen miles to the west, at Adida near Lydda twenty miles to the northwest, at Jericho fifteen miles to the east, and at other sites in Idumea and Judea. The rebels' strength outside Jerusalem lay in eastern Judea and in their hold on the fortresses of Machaerus, Masada, and Herodium (*War* IV.486–90, 550–55).

Simultaneously with the internal bloodletting in Jerusalem, Rome was torn with dissension and warfare. Early in his spring offensive Vespasian had received word of the Gallic revolt against Nero led by Julius Vindex, one of the provincial governors (*War* IV.440–42). When he returned to Caesarea to finalize plans for an assault on Jerusalem, he learned of Nero's suicide on 9 June 68 (*War* IV.491–96). Vespasian waited to see what developed in Rome before attacking Jerusalem and in the meantime sent Titus, accompanied by Agrippa, to salute the new emperor, Galba. Before reaching Rome, Titus heard of Galba's assassination in the Roman forum (on 15 January 69) and returned to Caesarea, with Agrippa proceeding to Rome (*War* IV.497–502). The attack on Jerusalem was temporarily put in abeyance.

The unexpected interlude in the war resulting from the uncertainty of political affairs in Rome allowed for further episodes in the continuing drama of internecine Jewish civil war. One of the heroes of the Cestius retreat had been Simon son of Gioras (*War* II.521). (Gioras may reflect the Aramaic term for "proselyte" and thus indicate that Simon or his father was a convert.) He later became a freelance marauder but was forced to flee from northeastern Judea to Masada when Ananus sought to curb his pillage (*War* II.652–54). For a time, he and "his following of women" were given only restricted shelter by the rebels at Masada, who regarded him with suspicion (*War* IV.503–7). Upon the death of Ananus and with the reduced activity of the Romans, he left Masada, where the rebels were not adventurous enough to suit his taste, and returned to the hills. There, "by proclaiming liberty for slaves and rewards for the free, he gathered around him the villains from every quarter" (*War* IV.508).

Simon quickly became the dominant figure in his old haunt around Acraba, some twenty miles north of Jerusalem, but his ambitions far exceeded such geographical limits. The Zealots, recognizing that Simon had his sights on Jerusalem, sent out a force to attack him but were soundly defeated (*War* IV.509–14). Simon moved to overrun Idumea before attacking Jerusalem. Initially unsuccessful, Simon gained control of much of the area with the help of an Idumean traitor. Hebron fell into his hands, and eventually he was master of much of southern Judea and Idumea (*War* IV.515–37).

The Zealots tried anew to overcome Simon. An ambush led to the capture of his wife and her attendants. Until his wife was returned, Simon harassed people who tried to enter and leave Jerusalem (*War* IV.538–44). After the Zealots released his wife, Simon continued his efforts to gain control of Jerusalem. In the city, conditions under Zealot control had gotten so deplorable that the moderate party under the leadership of the high-priestly families and with the backing of the general population admitted Simon and his forces to the city in the spring of 69 C.E. as a countermove against John of Gischala (*War* IV.556–76). Simon's forces and his newly found supporters among the moderates in the city attacked the Zealots sequestered in the Temple but were unable to dislodge them (*War* IV.577–84).

While awaiting clarification on matters in Rome, Vespasian, in the late spring of 69 C.E., took matters into his own hands and led his troops on a foray through northern Judea and reconnoitered the city walls of Jerusalem. One of his subordinates moved into northern Idumea, conquering and burning several towns, including Hebron (*War* IV.550–54). The areas invaded by the Romans at this time were those where Simon and his followers had been active only shortly before. Thus Vespasian, without directions from Rome, was reasserting Roman authority in places where it had temporarily been challenged as well as "reducing the whole of the environs of Jerusalem" (*War* IV.588).

Conditions in Rome continued to deteriorate in 69 C.E. (the "Year of the Four Emperors") and to influence actions in Judea. Dislike of Vitellius, who had replaced Otho as emperor after the latter's suicide, was widespread. When his army, supported by figures such as Licinus Mucianus, the legate of Syria, proclaimed him emperor, Vespasian moved to secure control of the empire (*War* IV.585–604). His first objective was to gain the support of Egypt, often thought of as the "breadbasket" of the empire, and the two legions stationed there. He did so with the assistance of the procurator Tiberius Alexander (*War* IV.605–6; 616–21). Josephus, whose prediction appeared to be realized, was liberated and Mucianus with an army was sent to Italy (*War* IV.622–32). By 21 December 69 C.E., Vitellius had been killed and Rome was awaiting Vespasian's arrival from Alexandria (*War* IV.645–57). From Alexandria, Vespasian dispatched Titus to Caesarea with orders to crush Jerusalem (*War* IV.658–63). The winter of 69/70 C.E. was now passing, and the war against the Jews had not been pursued since Vespasian was declared emperor the previous July.

The Siege of Jerusalem

In Jerusalem, three factions had now developed, each controlling a portion of the city. The Zealots, over whom John of Gischala had temporarily held control, had split into two groups. Eleazar son of Simon, who Josephus says first led the Zealots to break with the general citizenry, held the inner court of the Temple. About twenty-four hundred men were in Eleazar's group. John of Gischala had a larger following—about six thousand—but a poorer position, the outer court of the Temple and part of the lower city on Ophel. The third party, headed by Simon son of Gioras had the largest army—about fifteen thousand—and controlled the whole of the upper city and part of the lower. Among Simon's army were about five thousand Idumeans who had remained in Jerusalem (*War* V.1–12, 248–54). Tacitus described the conditions in the following way:

> There were three generals, three armies: the outermost and largest circuit of the walls was held by Simon, the middle of the city by John, and the temple was guarded by Eleazar. John and Simon were strong in numbers and equipment, Eleazar had the advantage of position: between these three there was constant fighting, treachery, and arson, and a great store of grain was consumed. (Tacitus, *Histories* V.12.3; *GLA* II.30)

In this triangular affair each group sought dominance in the city. John's position, between the other two forces, meant that his group had to defend itself from two sides. None of the leaders was any longer from the moderate party. The number of the moderates had been decimated by murder, desertion from the city, and "conversion" to more radical positions. In the battles between factions, large sections of the city were burned and much of the stored grain destroyed (*War* V.21–26). The loss of grain was especially significant. The year October 68 to October 69 C.E. was a sabbatical year when crops were not produced and replenishment of supplies was difficult, if not impossible. By the time of the April–May 70 C.E. harvest season, the city was under siege.

Titus marched against Jerusalem at the head of four legions, the three earlier commanded by his father and the revitalized XII Fulminata. In addition, he had brought troops from the two legions in Egypt. The usual contingents of auxiliary forces from rulers in the area were also present (Tacitus, *Histories* V.1.2). The fifth legion approached via Emmaus, the tenth via Jericho, and the other two accompanied Titus from Caesarea. The procurator of Egypt and former prefect of Judea, Tiberius Alexander, was now a member of Titus's staff (*War* V.39–46).

As the troops neared Jerusalem, Titus and six hundred horsemen rode forward to reconnoiter the city. During this reconnaissance, Titus and a handful of men were cut off from the rest by a group of Jews sallying forth from the city. Although Titus escaped, the courage and close success of the Jewish contingent lifted the spirits of the city's defenders (*War* V.51–67).

Titus deployed his army very close to Jerusalem, the tenth legion on the Mount of Olives to the east and the other three legions on Mount Scopus to the north (*War* V.67–70). While the tenth legion was setting up camp, a combined force of the Jewish defenders sallied across the Kidron Valley and for a short time successfully attacked the Romans (*War* V.71–97).

Such cooperation among the Jewish factions was short-lived at this stage of the contest. At Passover, John's followers, disguised as ordinary worshipers, gained access to the inner court of the Temple precincts. John then assumed command of both his followers and those of Eleazar. This temporarily reduced the major factions to two (*War* V.98–105) but did not end the internal struggle, which continued until Roman battering rams were hammering away at the city's defenses (*War* V.248–57, 275–79).

Titus decided to encamp nearer Jerusalem and moved to a spot adjacent to the walls, leveling the ground for moving equipment between Scopus and the city. Terms of surrender were presented to the defendants by Josephus but fell on deaf ears (*War* V.106–8, 114), and the siege began in earnest. Because of the natural shape of the landscape, being surrounded on three sides by deep ravines, the city was attacked from the north, as throughout its history. Titus planned to take the third (Agrippa's) wall first and move from there to the Antonia fortress and then into the Temple. Siege works were begun under cover of artillery fire, near the towers of Psephinus and Hippicus. At the latter, Agrippa's wall had not yet been completed (*War* V.33–34, 258–60). In spite of efforts by the Jews to burn the machines and their sallies outside the walls, the battering ram, nicknamed "Victor," did its work. After fourteen days, the outer wall was breached (*War* V.266–302). The Jewish defenders fled, taking refuge behind the second wall, and the Romans occupied Bezetha, demolished a section of Agrippa's wall, and set up camp in the newly conquered suburb (*War* V.303).

The second wall was attacked and after only five days successfully breached. Titus and a picked band entered but were repulsed in severe fighting. Four days later a second assault succeeded, and control of the second line of defense fell into Roman hands (*War* V.331–47).

The northern wall of the inner city and the northwestern wall of the Temple enclosure now became the next objectives for Titus, but these he knew would be the most ferociously defended. The fortress of Antonia stood at the angle where these two walls met (*War* V.238–43) and first had to be secured. Josephus claims that Titus temporarily suspended the assault in the hope that the rebels would reconsider and surrender. Four days were said to be spent in a parade of the troops and in the distribution of the soldiers' pay (*War* V.348–55). Josephus provides a speech he claims to have given to the defenders, after the siege was renewed, outlining a rationale justifying surrender (*War* V.356–419).

This third phase of the assault on the walls focused on gaining access to

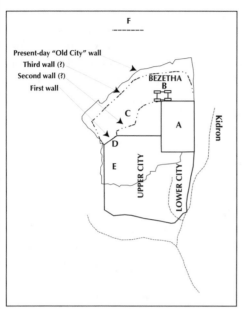

Present-day "Old City" wall
Third wall (?)
Second wall (?)
First wall

F

BEZETHA
B

C

A

D

E

UPPER CITY

LOWER CITY

Kidron

Josephus describes three walls that protected Jerusalem at the time of the First Jewish Revolt (66–70 C.E.)

FIRST WALL
Extended from the western portico of the Temple compound (A) around the "upper city" and the "lower city" back to the SE corner of the Temple. Archaeologists have discovered what may be small sections of this wall.

SECOND WALL
Enclosed the city's expansion northward beyond the First Wall. Extended, according to Josephus, from the Antonia fortress (B) to approximately the NW corner of the First Wall. Otherwise the line of the Second Wall is unknown.

THIRD WALL
Begun by Agrippa I (39–44 C.E.) and completed by the Jewish rebels at the time of the first revolt, the Third Wall included a still larger portion of the city north of the First and Second Walls. The exact line of this Third Wall also remains unknown.

A. TEMPLE COMPOUND
Herod refurbished and expanded the Temple, and surrounded it with a massive retaining wall. Some of this retaining wall survives today in the lower courses of wall surrounding the Temple Mount.

B. ANTONIA FORTRESS
The Antonia fortress, also built by Herod and named after Mark Antony, protected the NW corner of the Temple compound.

C. CHURCH OF THE HOLY SEPULCHRE
Presumably the crucifixion of Jesus would have occurred outside the city walls—that is, outside the First and Second Walls, the Third Wall not yet having been built. It remains uncertain whether the Church of the Holy Sepulchre marks the actual spot of the crucifixion.

D. FORTIFICATION TOWERS
Three towers constructed by Herod protected the NW corner of the First Wall.

E. HEROD'S PALACE

F. WALL REMAINS
Remains of an ancient wall have been discovered north of the present-day "Old City" and are interpreted variously by archaeologists: (1) Possibly this was the Third Wall, which means that the city extended further north than the plan above indicates. (2) Possibly this was a "Fourth Wall" constructed by the Jewish zealots at the time of the revolt and in anticipation of Roman attack. (3) Possibly this was the siege wall constructed by the Romans for the purpose of isolating the Jews who held the city during the first revolt.

MAP 5.
JERUSALEM AT THE TIME OF
THE FIRST JEWISH REVOLT (66–70 C.E.)

the upper city through the north wall and to the Temple precinct through the Antonia fortress (*War* V.356). Famine within the city was becoming severe; accusations, bickering, and atrocities to prevent desertions spread like an infection within the city (*War* V.420–45). Atrocities were not the special prerogative of the rebels (*War* V.446–59). The Romans sought to intimidate the Jews into submission by returning prisoners to the city with their hands cut off and by crucifixion of captives near the walls: "The soldiers out of rage and hatred amused themselves by nailing their prisoners in different postures; and so great was their number, that space could not be found for the crosses nor crosses for the bodies" (*War* V.451).

Gallant efforts were made by the defenders to prevent the battering rams from reaching and destroying the walls. The legions spent seventeen days building earthen ramparts. John's men, during this time, had tunneled underneath the mound built against the Antonia. When the ram was brought up, timbers smeared with pitch and bitumen were lit in the tunnel, burning the props and producing a major cave-in (*War* V.466–72). Simon's party led an assault on the other earthworks, setting fire to the battering machines and the timbers supporting the dirt fill (*War* V.473–90). Before commencing construction on new earthworks, Titus held a council of war at which it was decided to encircle Jerusalem completely with a guarded wall to blockade all comings and goings and thus heighten the famine in the city. The wall, almost four miles in length, not only encircled the uncaptured portions of the city but also was extended to include part of the Mount of Olives. Thirteen small forts at strategic points in the wall housed soldiers who patrolled the circumvallation day and night (*War* V.491–511). When work was resumed on the siege, reconstruction of the earthen ramparts was difficult because of the lack of timbers, which had to be fetched at a distance of nine miles (*War* V.522–23).

Famine in the city increased, and with it, the tendency to desert. Numerous persons were executed for treason by Simon, including the aged priest Matthias, who initially had secured Simon's admission to the city (*War* IV.574), and three of his four sons, the other having fled to the Roman camp (*War* V.527–33). A plot to surrender the city to Titus led to further executions (*War* V.534–40). Even deserters had a difficult time for a period. Arab and Syrian soldiers, discovering that some Jews had swallowed gold coins before leaving the city, began to kill and cut open deserters in the hope of finding money—a practice Titus soon halted (*War* V.548–66).

The legions rebuilt the siege works in three weeks. An increase in the Roman guard and a decrease in the effectiveness of Jewish sallies meant that the greatest problem was securing timbers (*War* VI.5, 15–23). In July, when the wall was finally breached, the Romans discovered that John and his followers had built a second wall behind the outer one. This inner wall was finally scaled and the Antonia captured, but fierce fighting prevented the Romans from gaining access to the Temple courts (*War* VI.24–32, 54–92). In listing the Jewish heroes in the effort to prevent the Romans from entering the Temple, Josephus mentions those in John's army, Simon's division, and those belonging to the Zealots (*War* VI.92). The various parties thus continued to claim a separate identity even in the last days of the war. (Josephus nowhere comments on the fate of Eleazar son of Simon; perhaps he had died in battle or at the hand of Simon. In *War* VI.148, he refers to four divisions among the defenders of the city, the three noted plus the Idumeans.) In order to provide an easier ascent for the troops and thus to facilitate attack, Titus ordered the demolition of the Antonia. Josephus reports that on the day the soldiers began to raze the fortress, the daily sacrifices in the Temple ceased for "lack of men" (probably an error for "lack of lambs") (*War* VI.93–94). The cessation of sacrifice produced despondency among the defenders, and Titus sought to use the situation for negotiation. First Josephus and then a body of aristocrats, the latter having recently deserted to the Romans, urged the rebels to surrender and thus to save the Temple from destruction. Although some Jewish nobles took the occasion to desert, the vast majority remained resolved to fight until death (*War* VI.94–130). When appeal for a negotiated settlement failed, the Romans attempted a nighttime assault on the Temple compound but failed to penetrate the Jewish defenses (*War* VI.131–48).

The Temple enclosure was a square surrounded by walls as heavily constructed as the city fortifications. A colonnade paralleled the insides of the wall. A second line of defense was formed by the walls surrounding the inner courtyard of the Temple. The Roman commander recognized that a full-scale assault would be required to take the Temple. Four ramparts were begun against the outer walls, two facing the north and two the west wall. Timbers now had to be brought from a distance of over ten miles because of the devastation in the region, and the defenders made construction work difficult (*War* VI.150–51). The burning of structures inside the Temple enclosure was begun when the Jewish defenders set fire to the covering of the northwest colonnade, which had adjoined the Antonia, since these porticoes produced an attack route against the Temple. The Romans responded by burning the adjacent portico (*War* VI.165–66). The Jews filled the space beneath the western portico with combustible materials, lured Romans on top by pretending to retreat, and fired the structure, inflicting heavy casualties (*War* VI.177–92).

When two of the ramparts were completed, the battering rams were brought up but proved ineffective against the walls. Other means of access were attempted—undermining the foundations of the northern gate and assaulting the walls and porticoes with ladders. When these failed, Titus ordered the Temple gates burned (*War* VI.220–28). The defenders watched as the fire spread from the gates to the adjacent porticoes and then took refuge in the inner courts of the Temple compound (*War* V.233–35, 244).

The next day, Titus ordered his troops to extinguish the fires and to construct a roadway to the burned gates. He then held a war council with his staff. The issue of what to do with the Temple was a topic of consideration. Two traditions about Titus's position on the issue have come down to us from antiquity. According to Josephus, Titus opposed the destruction of the Temple both in the council and in battle and did everything humanly possible to preserve it even after it was fired (*War* VI.236–67). A second totally contrary tradition, preserved by the Christian writer Sulpicius Severus (ca. 363–420/5) in his *Chronicle* (II.30.6–7), is usually but not unquestionably traced back to lost portions of the history by Tacitus:

> It is said that Titus summoned his council, and before taking action consulted it whether he should overthrow a sanctuary of such workmanship, since it seemed to many that a sacred building, one more remarkable than any other human work, should not be destroyed. For if preserved it would testify to the moderation of the Romans, while if demolished it would be a perpetual sign of cruelty. On the other hand, others, and Titus himself, expressed their opinion that the Temple should be destroyed without delay, in order that the religion of the Jews and Christians should be more completely exterminated. For those religions, though opposed to one another, derived from the same founders; the Christians stemmed from the Jews and the extirpation of the root would easily cause the offspring to perish. (See *GLA* II.64)

Suspicion can be raised about the historical accuracy of both traditions. Josephus presents Titus as a person possessing superhuman capabilities and as one who tried in every way to avoid the limits to which the war eventually led. Josephus was motivated by an apologetic concern to please and to make his patrons, Vespasian and his descendants, appear in the best light. The report of Sulpicius Severus states that the Temple was destroyed in the hope of eradicating Judaism and Christianity. More likely Titus's actions were based on the need to suppress the rebellion rather than the desire to exterminate two religions, one licit and the other illicit. This text too is apologetic, illustrating the survival of true religion in spite of human opposition.

According to Josephus, three options were discussed at the war council: (1) destruction of the Temple as part of the normal course of suppressing the rebellion, (2) destruction of the Temple if it were used as a fortress, and (3) saving the Temple even if the defenders used it as a last refuge (Titus's alleged position). The official position taken by Titus can no longer be determined, but it seems hard to believe that despite Roman *"religio"* he would have argued against destroying the Temple if it became a last bastion for the defenders.

With the withdrawal of the Jewish forces to the inner courts, the Romans occupied the outer courts (*War* VI.244–49). After two Jewish sallies attacked from the inner court, "Titus then withdrew to Antonia, determined on the following day, at dawn, to attack with his whole force, and invest the temple" (*War* VI.249). In the ensuing assault, the Temple was fired. Josephus says a soldier "snatched a brand from the burning timber and, hoisted up by one of his comrades, flung the fiery missile through a low golden door, which gave access on the north side to the chambers surrounding the sanctuary" (*War* VI.252). Titus and his commanders were able to enter the burning sanctuary, even the Holy of Holies, and to supervise the rescue of some of its contents (*War* VI.260). With the Temple aflame, other buildings in the area were set afire by the Romans (*War* VI.281–85). To celebrate their success, the Roman legionnaires set up their standards opposite the Temple's eastern gate and offered up sacrifices to them. With rousing acclamations, they proclaimed Titus *imperator* (*War* VI.316–17; Suetonius, *Titus* 5.2).

Even though the Temple had gone up in flames, the battle for Jerusalem would last another month. Many of the rebels, including John, whose special arena had been the Temple enclosure, escaped to the upper city (*War* VI.277). Simon and John requested and received negotiation with Titus, who offered them their lives in exchange for unconditional surrender but refused their counteroffer to surrender the remainder of the city in exchange for safe passage beyond the circumvallation (*War* VI.323–51). Indignant over their response, Titus gave his troops permission to plunder and burn the lower city (*War* VI.352–55, 363).

The rebel leaders prepared for their last stand. They and their troops set up headquarters in the solidly built palace of Herod, slaughtering the refugees who had congregated there (*War* VI.358). The Romans again had to construct earthen ramparts to attack the palace and upper city (*War* VI.374–77). The renewal of assault brought on a new round of desertions. The Idumean force sought to negotiate en masse with Titus, but their emissaries were caught and killed by Simon (*War* VI.378–86). A priest and the Temple treasurer, who had salvaged a number of treasuries from the Temple, used these valuables to purchase their freedom from Titus (*War* VI.387–91).

The preparations for the final attack took eighteen days. The rams breached the walls in one day. The defenders fled in panic, even abandoning the strong towers of Herod's palace without a struggle (*War* VI.392–400). Many of the rebels sought shelter in the tunnels beneath the city (*War* VI.370; 401–2). The Roman soldiers spent the day looting, burning, and slaughtering, withdrawing at dusk to return at dawn to the remnants of the city still aflame (*War* VI.403–8).

In spite of the killings and slaughter, thousands of survivors and earlier captives remained alive. Those found armed and offering resistance were killed. The old and feeble were slain as valueless. Those known to have been rebels were executed. Seven hundred of the most handsome and tallest young males were set aside for a Roman triumphal parade. Many able-bodied youths seventeen and older were sent in chains to labor in Egypt, while others were preserved for use in gladiatorial and wild beast shows. Women and those under seventeen were sold into slavery (*War* VI.414–19) "for a trifling sum per head, owing to the glut of the market and the dearth of purchasers" (*War* V.384). In addition, Josephus claims, with probably not a little overstatement, that so much plunder hit the market that "throughout Syria the standard of gold was depreciated to half its former value" (*War* VI.317).

The number of war victims and captives given in ancient sources seems excessively high. Josephus reports that for the entire war ninety-seven thousand prisoners were taken and one million one hundred thousand casualties resulted (*War* VI.420). Two that did not die were John and Simon. After seeking refuge and escape in the subterranean passages for several days, John was forced out of hiding by hunger and Simon gave himself up after futilely attempting to tunnel to safety with the assistance of some stonecutters (*War* VI.433–34; VII.26–36).

The city was further humiliated when Titus ordered the razing of the walls of both the city and the Temple enclosure with the exception of the western wall and the three towers of Herod—Phasael, Hippicus, and Mariamne. The former was preserved as a place of encampment for the garrison to be left behind and the latter "to indicate to posterity the nature of the city and of the strong defenses which had yet yielded to Roman prowess" (*War* VII.1–4).

After addressing his troops, awarding honors, offering sacrifices, and feasting with his troops, Titus entrusted the custody of the area to the tenth legion, dismissed the twelfth to service on the Euphrates, and took the fifth and fifteenth with himself to Caesarea on the coast (*War* VII.5–20). Since it was now October and not a time to sail for Italy, Titus cavorted for a time with Agrippa in Caesarea Philippi and presumably with the Jewish king's sister Berenice, who had taken a strong liking to Vespasian and had a passion for Titus, which eventually led to her temporary domicile in Rome as his mistress (Tacitus, *Histories* II.2.1; 81.2; *GLA* II.8, 15).

In Caesarea Philippi, Titus, using his Jewish captives, put on all kinds of spectacles, beastly shows, and gladiatorial contests (*War* VI.23–24, 37–40, 96). From a certain perspective, it was an incongruous, incredible time. A Jewish king was entertaining the conqueror of his fellow religionists while enjoying shows produced by the further decimation of Jewish flesh. While Jerusalem's ashes still smoldered, the passion of an uncircumcised future Roman emperor burned for one of the last of the Hasmonaean beauties.

After traveling throughout Syria with his "touring circus" of Jewish prisoners (*War* VI.23, 37–40, 96), Titus revisited Jerusalem in the spring of 71 C.E. before leaving Alexandria for Rome. Although some fortresses were still occupied by Jewish rebels, he left the conquests of these to others (*War* VII.112).

A triumphal procession for Vespasian and Titus in Rome celebrated the conquest of Judea. Seven hundred prisoners as well as Simon and John marched in the parade where floats illustrated scenes from the war (*War* VI.116–18, 123–47). Prominent spoils from the Temple—a golden table, a golden lampstand, and a copy of the Jewish Torah—were displayed in the triumphal march (*War* VII.148–52). At the temple of Jupiter Capitolinus, the procession halted and Simon was removed from the marchers and taken to be scourged and executed according to the traditional Roman treatment of captured generals (*War* VII.153–54). John was sentenced to perpetual imprisonment (*War* VI.433).

The Roman dominance over the Judean rebels was widely enshrined. Vespasian's temple of peace housed spoils from the Jerusalem Temple (*War* VII.158–62), coins depicted Judea as a dejected Jewess under a palm tree with the inscription *Judaea capta*, and the arch of Titus depicted the Temple spoils carried in triumphal possession.

Some Retrospectives
on the War

The general course of the first Jewish Revolt, as outlined above, is reasonably clear. Some features of the war and its causes, however, require further comment.

1. The extent and the ferocity of the intrafighting among the Jews are not surprising. Group competition, conflict, and slaughter were characteristic, even if intermittent, features of Jewish life from the time of Herod's death until the final days of the siege of Jerusalem. As we have noted, Tacitus, in describing the beginning of the siege, spoke of the Jews as possessing "three generals, three armies" (*Histories* V.12–13). There were, in fact, two wars: a multifaceted Jewish civil war with numerous forces striving for dominance, and a Jewish-Roman conflict. Similarities and parallels to this state of affairs can be seen in earlier periods, for example, at the time

of the second-century B.C.E. Jewish struggles with the Seleucids from which the Maccabeans emerged victorious.

Several factors may have contributed to this group rivalry: (a) The geographical regionalism of the Palestinian area historically contributed to sectional diversity and disputes. In a real sense, Galilee, Samaria, Judea, Idumea, Transjordan, and the coastal plain were distinct geographical entities with their own orientations and regional distinctiveness. Then, in the midst of these entities, there were free cities or cities with majority Gentile population. Regional competition and bitterness abounded. Even the leadership of the war effort in Jerusalem itself came to be dominated by persons and groups from outside Judea proper: John of Gischala in Galilee, Simon son of Gioras from Gerasa in the Transjordan, and the Idumeans. The main phase of the war was fought in Jerusalem, not the native region of either of the final leaders and thus where someone else's turf would be destroyed. (b) A history of sectarian parties and stringent competition between them had already produced a pattern of internal struggle. The disputes, rivalries, and conflicts between, for example, the Sadducees and the Pharisees had frequently been severe and brutal. Thus group conflict and struggle for power in the name of religious issues were old and indigenous components of Jewish life. (c) Tensions and struggles between socioeconomic classes were an important aspect in the inner-Jewish warfare: the lower-order priests against the ruling hierarchy, the indebted against the creditors, the rural against the urban, and the groups deriving substance from the Romans against those exploited by the Romans or nonparticipants in Roman administration. (d) Many of the paradigms of success drawn from the people's scriptures and traditions were heroes supported by minority movements who had risen to prominence and acquired dominance by internal warfare and violence: Phinehas, whose zeal burned in the slaughter of apostates (see Numbers 25); David, an outlaw who fought the house of Saul certain of divine election; and the Maccabees, whose civil war against compromising fellow countrymen led to their triumph and glory. One might say that such paradigms suggested that the slaughter of fellow Jews was a prerequisite for success against outsiders. A movement's or leader's lack of widespread support was no deterrent when viewed in the light of the biblical promise that a few true believers could overcome overwhelming odds (see Lev. 26:7–8).

2. A contributing factor, both to the outbreak of the revolt and to the intra-Jewish struggles, was the absence of effective and continuing leadership at the upper levels of Jewish society. The old aristocracy of the Hasmonaean era was depleted under Herod and new families graced with royal largess. Herod encouraged immigrants to return from the Diaspora. Some of these became prominent in Judea, such as the family of Boethus

from Alexandria, to whom he awarded the high-priestly office, and Hillel from Mesopotamia, who became one of the most influential rabbis of his day. After the death of Herod, the high-priestly office was almost totally politicized, with a constant chain of new appointees and dismissals from office at will. In the years from 6 to 66 C.E., twenty different appointments to the office were made. In addition to the rapid turnover in office, appointments were made after 44 C.E. by the Jewish monarchs Herod of Chalcis and Agrippa II. Neither ruler had any routine connection with Judean life and both followed strongly pro-Roman policies as the best means of securing their own advantages. This insecurity and instability in leadership no doubt produced a general sense of anarchy and encouraged groups to take the law into their own hands. Even after the revolutionary government was formed following the defeat of Cestius, the leaders selected to pursue the war proved ineffective and were replaced in authority. John of Gischala arrived in Jerusalem in the late fall of 67 C.E. and became the dominant figure of power until Simon son of Gioras arrived in the spring of 69 C.E. Both John and Simon were freebooting, self-appointed leaders. The fact that they could become the leaders of the war effort illustrates the absence of stable Jewish leadership at the top and the role of violence in moving to positions of prominence.

3. Religious issues and messianic/eschatological beliefs must have greatly influenced both the causes and the course of the war, but ancient sources do not make it possible to reconstruct their exact significance. Many of the would-be leaders and redeemers of the time were probably influenced by beliefs that the end of time was near, that the Romans would be driven from the country as part of the redemption of the faithful, and that they and their supporters were the chosen instruments of God's saving activity. Josephus, in comparing these redeemer figures with the assassin and terrorist groups, such as the *sicarii*, disdainfully noted that the former had "purer hands but more impious intentions" (*War* II.258).

Both Josephus and classical authors refer to prophetic oracles in vogue at the time which predicted the rise of a world ruler from Judea. In reporting on the capture of Jerusalem, Josephus declares:

> What more than all else incited them [the Jewish rebels] to the war was an ambiguous oracle, likewise found in their sacred scriptures [Num. 24:17–18 or Dan. 7:13–14?], to the effect that at that time one from their country would become ruler of the world. (*War* VI.312)

Tacitus, whose familiarity with Josephus's writings is far from certain, also notes that "the majority [of the Jews] firmly believed that their ancient priestly writings contained the prophecy that this was the very time when the East should grow strong and that men starting from Judea, should possess the world" (*Histories* V.13.2; *GLA* II.31). Suetonius notes that "there had spread over all the orient an old and established belief, that it was fated at that time for men coming from Judea to rule the world. This prediction . . . the people of Judaea took to themselves; accordingly they revolted" (Suetonius, *Vespasian* IV.5; *GLA* II.120). The expectation of the appearance of the Jewish messiah thus probably played an important role in the war, and various personalities, including John and Simon, may have seen themselves or been understood as this ruler. The family of Vespasian used the supposed prediction as propaganda for itself, since Vespasian was declared emperor in Judea, a view reflected in Josephus, Tacitus, and Suetonius.

The Postwar Years

Judean life following the fall of Jerusalem is far less documented than for the preceding period. Josephus continues his account to report on events immediately following the city's destruction. Otherwise the historian of this period is at the mercy of almost chance evidence: incidental references in classical authors, occasional Roman inscriptions, coins, archaeological artifacts, and references in rabbinical literature. Only the broadest picture emerges of the period once we move beyond the period of Josephus's discussion.

Two major immediate changes were made in Roman administration in Judea following the revolt; both were attempts to remedy weaknesses in the earlier policy. First, the province was made an entity unto itself and placed under an imperial senatorial legate of praetorian rather than equestrian rank. The governors were thus more experienced and competent officials than their predecessors, with fuller staffs including a procurator in charge of financial affairs. In the now independent province, the governor was no longer under the supervision of the Roman legate over Syria stationed in Antioch. He was thus capable of taking immediate action without the time-consuming process of appeal to a higher provincial authority. Second, major adjustments were made in the military. Troops stationed in the province were no longer drawn from the region; the Sebastian and Caesarean forces were moved out of the province. The size of the permanent military contingent was raised from a few auxiliary units to legionary status as part of Vespasian's restructuring of the Roman Empire's eastern defenses. Under the new system, the bulk of the military forces was stationed in Jerusalem, nearer to where trouble was apt to erupt, rather than in Caesarea, which, however, continued to be the administrative capital. The legion first stationed in Jerusalem was the X Fretensis, whose legionary emblem was the boar. Temporary command of the army of occupation was given to Sextus Vettulenus Cerealis, who had served as commander of the V Macedonica legion during the war (*War* III.310; VII.163). Sextus Lucilius Bassus became the first regularly appointed governor (*War* VII.163).

When Titus left Judea accompanied by the majority of the Roman forces, three fortresses and countless caverns and coves were still occupied by Jewish rebels. The task of removing these fell to Bassus. Herodium, Herod's burial place about seven miles southeast of Jerusalem, was taken apparently without much difficulty, probably in late 71 C.E. (*War* VII.163). Machaerus in Transjordan was a more serious obstacle. The Romans began the task of constructing a rampart across a 150-foot ravine, but the rebels surrendered the fortress in exchange for safe passage after one of their fellows was captured, scourged, and faced with crucifixion (*War* VI.164–209). A significant number of rebels, some having fled from Jerusalem and others from Machaerus, took refuge in the otherwise unknown forest of Jardes, perhaps located somewhere in the Transjordan or even in the Jordan Valley. The Romans surrounded these and massacred three thousand with virtually no casualties of their own (*War* VII.210–15).

A number of Jewish rebels, meanwhile, had fled Judea for Alexandria and Cyrene. In the former, their appearance led to intramural fighting in the Jewish community and then to Roman execution of the rebels (*War* VII.409–19). As a precautionary matter, the Jewish temple of Onias IV built at Leontopolis in Egypt (*Ant.* XIII.70) was destroyed (*War* VII.420–36).

With the capture of Machaerus, probably in the summer of 72 C.E., only Masada was left under rebel control. Bassus's death in Judea left this conquest to his successor Flavius Silva, who took up his post either late in 72 or early in 73 C.E. According to Josephus, Masada was defended by a force of die-hard rebels numbering, including women and children, just under a thousand. Commanding the group was Eleazar son of Jairus, a grandson of Judas the Galilean and relative of Menahem (*War* II.447; VII.253). Masada, in an arid, desolate area but defended by a small Jewish force, with its precipitous cliffs was more a natural than a military obstacle. Silva set up headquarters opposite the mountain citadel, surrounded the site with a siege wall to block escape, constructed garrison camps at several points, and conscripted Jewish labor to provide his troops with supplies and water (*War* VII.275–79). The Romans chose not to scale the fortress via the so-called "snake path" from the southeast but instead to construct earthworks across the ravine from the west. In this direction, a ridge abutted the cliffs about two-thirds of the way to the summit and could be heightened to allow the battering ram access to the wall encircling the plateau on top of the mountain. With the rampart completed, the ram broke through the fortification, but the Romans discovered that the defenders had constructed a second, inner wall of wood and dirt. Pliable against the battering of the ram, the wall was fired (*War* VI.280–84, 304–19).

Josephus provides the following melodramatic account of the defenders' last night. With Silva and his forces awaiting the dawn to renew their attack, Eleazar twice addressed his compatriots, eventually convincing them to commit suicide not only to avoid capture and slavery or horrible death but also to rob the Romans of the sense of triumph (*War* VII.320–88). According to their covenant of death, the men dispatched their families and burned their belongings. Ten men selected by lot killed the others and then one of the ten dispatched the remainder before killing himself. Seven people, two women and five children survived, hiding themselves in a cistern. When the Romans assaulted the citadel the next morning, they encountered only deafening silence and a mass of the slain (*War* VII.389–406).

Reasons can be found for doubting Josephus's version of the final hours: the speeches of Eleazar are surely Josephus's compositions; the survivors were said to be hiding as the killing began, which makes questionable their knowledge of the subsequent course of events; skeletons found in an isolated cave suggest the death of defenders perhaps from starvation rather than communal suicide; and his version glorified a willingness to die for patriotic reasons and apologetically freed the Romans from the embarrassment of having slaughtered families. Over against these objections, however, one can argue that Josephus hardly would have fabricated such a tale when participants in the siege were surely still surviving to counter such a story. At any rate, with the capture of Masada, in the early spring of either 73 or 74 C.E., the last Jewish stronghold was taken by the Romans.

In addition to the upper-level alterations in Roman administration, noted above, other changes were made in Judean life. Some of these were economic and political. (1) Josephus reports that Vespasian, "reserving the country as his private property (as an imperial province?) ordered Jewish territory to be leased out" (*War* VII.216–17). In all probability, this means that land owned by Jews who were captured or who surrendered was appropriated by the Romans and then rented out. Land owned by Jews not participating in the war was probably left undisturbed. (2) The process of urbanization in the region was continued. Municipal autonomous status was restored to some cities (Jamnia, Azotus, Antipatris, Apollonia, and Gaba) and extended to others (Joppa and Sepphoris). A military colony of eight hundred veterans was established at Emmaus, near Jerusalem, where they could be called on in times of emergency. A major new city, Flavia Neapolis (modern Nablus), was established near Shechem. Caesarea, where he was first proclaimed as emperor, was raised to colony status by Vespasian. (3) An annual tax of two drachmas was imposed on all circumcised Jews, replacing the traditional Temple tax. This requirement to pay for the privilege "to observe their ancestral customs" was applied in the Diaspora as well as the homeland—but only to those who were circumcised—with the proceeds going to the Roman god Jupiter Capitolinus (*War* VII.218; Dio Cassius, *Roman History* LXVI.732; *GLA* II.375). Not all Jews were circumcised, and therefore not all Jews had to pay the *fiscus.*

Enormous changes in Jewish religious life resulted from the consequences of the war. (1) With the destruction of the Temple, the animal sacrificial cult came to an end in Jerusalem. Along with the loss of the Temple, the priestly guilds lost occupational usefulness and prominence. Worship became concentrated in the services of the synagogue, devoid of sacrifice. Many ritual demands of the scriptures were spiritualized and sublimated so as to be obeyed without being observed. Ordinary life was reinterpreted to replicate aspects of the Temple service—charity and good deeds were understood as sacrifice and the table in the home replaced the altar. The teacher-rabbi replaced the priest as the religious authority and interpreter of the will and word of God. (2) A rabbinic school was established at Jamnia, a city that Vespasian had earlier used as a settlement center for Jews who voluntarily surrendered to the Romans (*War* IV.444). The founder of this academy was Rabbi Johanan ben Zakkai (ca. 1–80 C.E.). According to rabbinic tradition, he faked his death and escaped from Jerusalem in a coffin being carried away from the city for burial. His escape probably occurred early in the war rather than late, that is, before rather than after the Roman siege began. Johanan requested and was granted permission from the Romans to establish his school, which, with him as its *nasi* (prince or patriarch), replaced the Sanhedrin as the most prominent Jewish authority. The academy assumed many of the functions of the earlier priestly establishment—setting regulations for religious and festival observances and supervising the calendar.

Virtually no information exists on life in the province of Judea during the reigns of Titus (79–81 C.E.) and his successors, Domitian (81–96 C.E.), Nerva (96–98 C.E.), and Trajan (98–117 C.E.). The death of Agrippa II, sometime in the 90s, probably had no effect on Judea. After the war, he had been rewarded for his loyalty by the receipt of the district of Arca in Lebanon and had regained full control of his four districts in Judea. When he died unmarried and without immediate heirs, the four districts were restored to Judean provincial control.

Under Trajan, a widespread Jewish revolt against Roman authority erupted and lasted for three years (115–117 C.E.). Originating in Egypt, the revolt spread to Cyrene, Cyprus, and Mesopotamia. Even the fullest account of the revolt, which reached the level of a full-blown war, provides no discussion of the causes of the revolt (Eusebius, *Ecclesiastical History*

IV.2). The occasion for the uprisings was Trajan's campaign in Mesopotamia against the Parthians. Messianic speculation, the desire for nationalistic revival, and pent-up hostilities against Gentile overlords all seem to have been involved. In Cyrene, the Jewish leader took the title "king." It is difficult to believe that Palestinian Jews were not involved in this revolt in some fashion. Some disturbances may have broken out in Judea, but of this we have no information. That Judea actually was or was considered to be a trouble spot is indicated by Trajan's appointment of Lusius Quietus as Judean legate in 116 or 117 C.E. Quietus had suppressed the Mesopotamian revolt. His appointment, because of his rank, indicates that Judea was raised to consular status, a condition of provinces with more than one legion. The II Traiana-legion was apparently sent to the region; its name appears on milestones along a road built in 120 C.E.

The Second Jewish Revolt

Under Trajan's successor, Hadrian (117–38 C.E.), the Jews and Romans again engaged in bitter and lengthy warfare, lasting from 132 to 135 C.E. (probably spring of 132 to summer of 135). The sources for the war are extremely sketchy and sometimes contradictory (see Text 9). Archaeological materials from the time of this second revolt shed some light on matters. These include not only Jewish coins dated to the first and second years of the revolt but also documents of Jewish participants in the war, including letters from the leader of the revolt to his subordinates in the field.

Ancient texts suggest two causes for the revolt. (1) Dio Cassius says that Hadrian founded a new city on the old site of Jerusalem, naming it Aelia Capitolina, and built a temple to Jupiter on the site of the Temple. The Jews revolted as a consequence. That Hadrian arrived in Syria-Palestine in 129–30 C.E. and that he there pursued his program as the "restitutor," inaugurating various construction projects, would lend support to the theory that it was the rebuilding of Jerusalem and the "desecration" of the Temple site that triggered the Jewish uprising. On the other hand, Eusebius places the building of Aelia Capitolina in the period after the war, which, at any rate, may have been the case since the war would have halted construction in Jerusalem. (2) A second reason for the war is indicated in what is called the *Historia Augusta*, a fourth-century compilation of pseudo-biographical material about the Roman emperors. This document states that the Jews rebelled because the Romans prohibited the practice of circumcision (*Hadrian* 14.2). No other ancient source explicitly suggests this as a reason. At some point in his reign, however, Hadrian did seek to tighten the Roman laws against castration, and it could have been that circumcision was put under the same ban. Antoninus Pius (138–61 C.E.), Hadrian's successor, later made a concession to allow Jews to be circumcised but still considered circumcision of a Gentile as the equivalent of castration and thus subject to capital punishment. This could suggest that Hadrian issued a universal ruling against circumcision to which the Jewish revolt was a reaction. A universal ruling against circumcision is more apt to have been issued before the war rather than as a particular punishment of the Jews following the war, since circumcision was practiced by several other peoples in addition to the Jews although it had only been licit for Jews. Whether one or both or even some other causes led to Jewish armed rebellion must remain uncertain. Even greater uncertainty exists about the causes for the widespread uprisings under Trajan in 115–17 C.E. Perhaps the old issues, unrest, and animosities continued to smolder, only awaiting some precipitating factor to burst into flames. Some action by Hadrian served this function.

TEXT 9:
ACCOUNTS OF THE
SECOND JEWISH REVOLT

At Jerusalem he [Hadrian] founded a city in place of the one which had been razed to the ground, naming it Aelia Capitolina, and on the site of the temple of the god he raised a new temple to Jupiter. This brought on a war of no slight importance nor of brief duration, for the Jews deemed it intolerable that foreign races should be settled in their city and foreign religious rites planted there. So long, indeed, as Hadrian was close by in Egypt and again in Syria, they remained quiet, save in so far as they purposely made of poor quality such weapons as they were called upon to furnish, in order that the Romans might reject them and that they themselves might thus have the use of them; but when he went farther away, they openly revolted. To be sure, they did not dare try conclusions with the Romans in the open field, but they occupied the advantageous positions in the country and strenghtened them with mines and walls, in order that they might have places of refuge whenever they should be hard pressed, and might meet together unobserved underground; and they pierced these subterranean passages from above at intervals to let in air and light. At first the Romans took no account of them. Soon, however, all Judaea had been stirred up, and the Jews everywhere were showing signs of disturbance, were gathering together, and giving evidence of great hostility to the Romans, partly by secret and partly by overt acts; many outside nations, too, were joining them through eagerness for gain, and the whole earth, one might almost say, was being stirred up over the matter. Then, indeed, Hadrian sent against them his best generals. First of these was Julius Severus, who was dispatched from Britain, where he was governor, against the Jews. Severus did not venture to attack his opponents in the open at any one point, in view of their numbers and their desperation, but by intercepting small groups, thanks to the number of his soldiers and his under-officers, and by depriving them of food and shutting them up, he was able, rather slowly, to be sure, but with comparatively little danger, to crush, exhaust and exterminate them. Very few of them in fact survived. Fifty of their most important outposts and nine hundred and eighty-five of their most famous villages were razed to the ground. Five hundred and eighty thousand men were slain in the various raids and battles, and the number of those that perished by famine, disease and fire was past finding out. Thus nearly the whole of Judaea was made desolate, a result of which the people had had forewarning before the war. For the tomb of Solomon, which the Jews regard as an object of veneration, fell to pieces of itself and collapsed, and many wolves and hyenas rushed howling into their cities. Many Romans, moreover, perished in this war. Therefore Hadrian in writing to the senate did not employ the opening phrase commonly affected by the emperors, "If you and your children are in health, it is well; I and the legions are in health . . ." (Dio Cassius, *Roman History* LXIX 12.1–14.3; *GLA* II.391–93)

The rebellion of the Jews once more progressed in character and extent, and Rufus, the governor of Judaea, when military aid had been sent him by the Emperor, moved out against them, treating their madness without mercy. He destroyed in heaps thousands of men, women, and children, and, under the law of war, enslaved their land. The Jews were at that time led by a certain Bar Chochebas, which means "star," a man who was murderous and a bandit, but relied on his name, as if dealing with slaves, and claimed to be a luminary who had come down to them from heaven and was magically enlightening those who were in misery. The war reached its height in the eighteenth year of the reign of Hadrian in Beththera, which was a strong citadel not very far from Jerusalem; the siege lasted a long time before the rebels were driven to final destruction by famine and thirst and the instigator of their madness paid the penalty he deserved. Hadrian then commanded that by a legal decree and ordinances the whole nation should be absolutely prevented from entering from thenceforth even the district round Jerusalem, so that not even from a distance could it see its ancestral home. Ariston of Pella tells the story. Thus when the city came to be bereft of the nation of the Jews, and its ancient inhabitants had completely perished, it was colonized by foreigners, and the Roman city which afterwards arose changed its name, and in honour of the reigning emperor Aelius Hadrian was called Aelia. (Eusebius, *Ecclesiastical History* IV.6.1–4)

Dio Cassius notes that while Hadrian was in Egypt (following his tour through Syria-Palestine in 130 C.E.) and then again in Syria (where he returned from Egypt in 131 C.E.), the Jews remained quiet. With Hadrian's departure from the area, armed revolt broke out. The leader of the Jewish rebellion, whose name is now known from recently discovered documents, was a Simon Bar Kosiba, referred to in ancient texts as Bar Kokhba ("the son of the star"; see Num. 24:17) or Bar Koziba ("the son of the lie"). Nothing is known about his background. Coins of the revolt refer to him as the *nasi* ("the prince") of Israel. Rabbi Akiba, one of the day's leading rabbis, is reported to have accepted him as the Messiah and to have associated him with the "star" spoken of in Num. 24:17. Simon may have asserted messianic claims, but there is no evidence that he assumed the title of king. The title *nasi* had already been used by Johannan ben Zakkai and his successors at Jamnia, which might indicate that Simon only saw himself as their replacement.

Coins and documents from the period speak of the "freedom" and "liberation of Jerusalem" or of "the redemption of Israel." Both coins and documents indicate the belief that a new era was under way and are dated according to the year of the rule of Simon. This suggests that the revolt was understood as a national movement of liberation, as a war undertaken to restore independence to the Jews and to produce a Jewish national state.

The extent of territory held by the rebels cannot be determined. Dio Cassius notes that the Romans initially had little regard for the uprising but that eventually 50 fortified outposts and 950 villages were captured by the Romans. Even allowing for some exaggeration, this suggests that a sizable territory was controlled by the forces under Bar Kosiba before the Romans took the revolt seriously. Documents from caves on the western shore of the Dead Sea indicate that a civil as well as military administrative system was set up. Jerusalem was apparently captured, although clear evidence for this is lacking. Some coins were struck simply bearing the name Jerusalem, which could indicate that the site fell into Jewish hands. Some coins refer to "Eleazar the priest" and others show a star above the figure of a temple. Whether Eleazar was the priestly counterpart to Simon and whether efforts were made to rebuild the Temple and reinstitute the sacrificial cult remain unknown, although reference to "the priest" on coins would indicate the revival of the office of high priest.

The rebels seem to have pursued guerrilla tactics as much as possible. Dio Cassius speaks of advantageous positions, places of refuge, underground strongholds, and subterranean passages as positions occupied by the Jewish forces. The Romans committed several legions (or parts thereof), numerous auxiliary forces, and "their best generals" to the war. For part of the war, Hadrian himself seems to have been in Palestine.

The final refuge of Simon and his forces was the mountain fortress of Bethar, some seven miles southwest of Jerusalem. Naturally isolated from the surrounding terrain, Bethar was surrounded by a siege wall. The remains of two large camps indicate a sizable Roman army participated in its capture. A ramp was constructed to give access to the walls by the battering rams. With the fall of the city, the war was over "except for isolated pockets of resistance." Apparently Simon died in battle at Bethar.

Following the end of the second revolt, the Roman city of Aelia Capitolina was raised on the ruins of Jerusalem, both as a punishment of the Jews and as a symbol of Roman perseverance. Temples to the god Jupiter and to Hadrian as Olympius occupied the site of the temple to Yahweh. Other amenities of a Roman city adorned the new Aelia. Jews were forbidden by imperial decree and the threat of death from entering not only the city but also the territory of the city. (An exception to this rule may have allowed the Jews admission on the 9th of the month Ab, a day that commemorated the fall of the city, when they could lament the city's fate at the western wall of the old Herodian city.) Foreigners were resettled in the town. The province of Judea was renamed to bear an old title that in the fifth century B.C.E. had already appeared in Herodotus—Syria Palaestina.

Bibliographical Abbreviations

ANRW	*Aufstieg und Niedergang der römischen Welt*
ANW	*Ancient World*
BA	*Biblical Archaeologist*
BAR	*Biblical Archaeologist Reader*
BJRL	*Bulletin of the John Rylands University Library of Manchester*
CB	*Classical Bulletin*
CBQ	*Catholic Biblical Quarterly*
HSCP	*Harvard Studies in Classical Philology*
HTR	*Harvard Theological Review*
IEJ	*Israel Exploration Journal*
JJS	*Journal of Jewish Studies*
JRS	*Journal of Roman Studies*
JSJ	*Journal for the Study of Judaism in the Persian, Hellenistic and Roman Period*
JTS	*Journal of Theological Studies*
NTS	*New Testament Studies*
REJ	*Revue des études juives*

Bibliography

General Treatments of the Period

Abel, F. M. *Histoire de la Palestine depuis la conquête d'Alexandre jusqu'à l'invasion arabe.* 2 vols. Paris: J. Gabalda, 1952.

Barclay, J. M. G. *Jews in the Mediterranean Diaspora: From Alexander to Trajan (323 B.C.E.–117 C.E.).* Edinburgh: T. & T. Clark, 1996.

Boccaccini, G. *Middle Judaism: Jewish Thought, 300 B.C.E. to 200 C.E.* Minneapolis: Augsburg Fortress, 1991.

Cambridge Ancient History. Cambridge: Cambridge University Press. 2d ed. Vol. 7.1: *The Hellenistic World* (ed. F. W. Walbank et al., 1994); vol. 7.2: *The Rise of Rome to 220 B.C.* (ed. F. W. Walbank et al., 1994); vol. 8: *Rome and the Mediterranean to 133 B.C.*(ed. A. E. Austin et al., 1993); vol. 9: *The Last Age of the Roman Republic, 146–43 B.C.* (ed. J. A. Crook et al., 1994); vol. 10: *The Augustan Empire, 43 B.C.-A.D. 69* (ed. A. K. Bowman et al., 1996).

Davies, W. D., and L. Finkelstein, eds. *Cambridge History of Judaism.* Cambridge: Cambridge University Press, 1984–.

Eddy, S. K. *The King Is Dead: Studies in the Near Eastern Resistance to Hellenism 334–31 B.C.* Lincoln: University of Nebraska Press, 1961.

Feldman, L. H. *Jew and Gentile in the Ancient World: Attitudes and Interactions from Alexander to Justinian.* Princeton, N.J.: Princeton University Press, 1993.

Freyne, S. *Galilee from Alexander the Great to Hadrian, 323 B.C.E. to 135 C.E.: A Study of Second Temple Judaism.* Wilmington, Del./Notre Dame, Ind.: Michael Glazier/University of Notre Dame, 1980.

Grabbe, L. *Judaism from Cyrus to Hadrian.* 2 vols. Minneapolis: Fortress Press, 1992.

Harris, William V. *War and Imperialism in Republican Rome 327–70 B.C.* Oxford: Oxford at Clarendon, 1985.

Jagersma, H. *A History of Israel from Alexander the Great to Bar Kochba.* London/Philadelphia: SCM Press/Fortress Press, 1985.

Kuhnen, H. P. *Palästina in griechisch-römiscen Zeit.* Munich: Beck, 1990.

Nickelsburg, G. W. E. *Jewish Literature between the Bible and the Mishnah.* Philadelphia: Fortress Press, 1981.

Peters, F. E. *The Harvest of Hellenism: A History of the Near East from Alexander the Great to the Triumph of Christianity.* New York/ London: Simon & Schuster/Allen & Unwin, 1970/1972.

Rostovtzeff, M. *The Social and Economic History of the Hellenistic World.* 3 vols. Oxford: Oxford at Clarendon, 1941.

Saulnier, C. (with C. Perrot). *Histoire d'Israël.* Vol. 3: *De la conquête d'Alexandre à la destruction du temple.* Paris: Cerf, 1985.

Schäfer, P. *The History of the Jews in Antiquity: The Jews of Palestine from Alexander the Great to the Arab Conquest.* Luxembourg: Harwood Academic Publishers, 1985.

Schürer, E. *The History of the Jewish People in the Age of Jesus Christ.* Rev. G. Vermes et al. 3 vols. in 4. Edinburgh: T. & T. Clark, 1973–87.

Smith, M. "Palestinian Judaism from Alexander to Pompey." In *Hellenism and the Rise of Rome,* ed. Pierre Grimal. New York: Delacorte, 1968.

Stone, M. E., ed. *Jewish Writings of the Second Temple Period.* Assen/Philadelphia: Van Gorcum/Fortress Press, 1984.

Will, E. *Histoire politique du monde hellénistique (323–30 a.v. J.C.).* 2 vols. Nancy: Publications de l'université, 1979–82, 2d revised edition.

Zeitlin, S. *The Rise and Fall of the Judaean State: A Political, Social, and Religious History of the Second Commonwealth.* 3 vols. Philadelphia: Jewish Publication Society of America, 1962–78.

Introduction

Büttner-Wobst, T., ed. *Polybii Historiae.* 5 vols. Leipzig: Teubner, 1882–1904.

Livy, Titi. *Ab Urbe Condita.* Edited by W. Weissenborn and H. J. Müller. Berlin/Dublin/Zurich: Wiedmannsche Verlagsbuch-handlung, 5th edition = unchanged 3rd. of 1833 ff.

Polybius. *The Histories,* with an English Translation by W. R. Paton. Cambridge: Harvard, and London: Heinemann, 1979 reprint.

Chapter 1: The Jewish Community
under Ptolemaic and Seleucid Rule

Bagnall, R. S. *The Administration of the Ptolemaic Possessions outside Egypt.* Leiden: E. J. Brill, 1976.

Bevan, E. R. *The House of Seleucus.* 2 vols. London: E. Arnold, 1902.

Bickerman, E. "La Charte séleucide de Jérusalem." *REJ* 100 (1935): 4–35.

———. *From Ezra to the Last of the Maccabees: Foundations of Post-Biblical Judaism.* New York: Schocken Books, 1962.

———. *The Jews in the Greek Age*. Cambridge, Mass.: Harvard University Press, 1988.

Büttner-Wobst, T., ed. *Polybii Historiae*. 5 vols. Leipzig: Teubner, 1882–1904.

Cross, F. M. "The Discovery of the Samaria Papyri," *BA* 26 (1963): 110–21 = *BAR* 3 (1970): 227–39.

———. "Papyri of the Fourth Century B.C. from Daliyeh: A Preliminary Report on Their Discovery and Significance." In *New Directions in Biblical Archaeology*, ed. D. N. Freedman and J. C. Greenfield, 41–62. Garden City, N.Y.: Doubleday & Co., 1969.

Davies, P. R. *Daniel*. Sheffield: JSOT Press, 1985.

Hadas, M. *Hellenistic Culture: Fusion and Diffusion*. New York: Columbia University Press, 1959.

Hengel, M. *Jews, Greeks and Barbarians: Aspects of the Hellenization of Judaism in the Pre-Christian Period*. London/Philadelphia: SCM Press/Fortress Press, 1980.

———. *Judaism and Hellenism: Studies in Their Encounter in Palestine during the Early Hellenistic Period*. 2 vols. London/Philadelphia: SCM Press/Fortress Press, 1974.

Jones, B. W. "Antiochus Epiphanes and the Persecution of the Jews." In *Scripture in Context: Essays on the Comparative Method*, ed. C. D. Evans et al., 263–90. Pittsburgh: Pickwick Publications, 1980.

Lapp, P. W., and N. L. Lapp. *Discoveries in the Wâdī-el-Dâliyeh*. Cambridge, Mass.: American Schools of Oriental Research, 1974.

Mandell, S. R. "The Beginnings of Roman Hegemony over Judah and Jerusalem." In *Approaches to Ancient Judaism 3*, ed. J. Neusner, 3–83. Atlanta: Scholars Press, 1993.

———. S. R. "The Isthmian Proclamation and the Early Stages of Roman Imperialism in the Near East." *CB* 65 (1989): 89–94.

———. S. R. "Roman Dominion: Desire or Reality?" *ANW* 22 (1991): 39–41.

Mazar, B. "The Tobiads." *IEJ* 7 (1957): 137–45, 229–38.

Mørkholm, O. *Antiochus IV of Syria*. Copenhagen: Gyldendalske Boghandel-Nordisk Forlag, 1966.

Rowley, H. H. "Sanballat and the Samaritan Temple." *BJRL* 38 (1955–56): 166–98 (= his *Men of God*, 246–76).

Sherwin-White, S., and A. Kuhrt, *From Samarkhand to Sardis: A New Approach to the Seleucid Empire*. London: Gerald Duckworth & Co., 1993.

Tcherikover, V. *Hellenistic Civilization and the Jews*. Philadelphia/Jerusalem: Jewish Publication Society of America/Magnes Press, 1959.

———. "Palestine under the Ptolemies (A Contribution to the Study of the Zenon Papyri)." *Mizraim* 4–5 (1937): 1–90.

Wright, G. E. "The Samaritans at Shechem." *HTR* 40 (1962): 357–66.

Chapter 2: The Hasmonaeans

Badian, E. *Foreign Clientelae (264–70 B.C.)*. London: Oxford at Clarendon, 1958.

Bar-Kochva, B. *Judas Maccabaeus: The Jewish Struggle against the Seleucids*. Cambridge: Cambridge University Press, 1989.

Bickerman, E. *The God of the Maccabees: Studies in the Meaning and Origin of the Maccabean Revolt*. Leiden: E. J. Brill, 1979.

Bringmann, K. *Hellenistische Reform und Religionsverfolgung in Judäa*. Göttingen: Vandenhoeck & Ruprecht, 1983.

Bunge, J. G. "Zur Geschichte und Chronologie des Untergangs der Oniaden und des Aufstiegs der Hasmonäer." *JSJ* 6 (1975): 1–46.

Davies, P. R. "Hasidim in the Maccabean Period." *JJS* 28 (1977): 127–40.

Efron, J. *Studies on the Hasmonean Period*. Leiden: E. J. Brill, 1987.

Farmer, W. R. *Maccabees, Zealots, and Josephus*. New York: Columbia University Press, 1956.

Fischer, T. *Seleukiden und Makkabäer*. Bochum: Studienverlag Brockmeyer, 1980.

Gruen, E. S. *The Hellenistic World and the Coming of Rome*. 2 vols. Berkeley: University of California Press, 1984.

Habicht, C. "Royal Documents in Maccabees II." *HSCP* 80 (1976): 1–18.

Harrington, D. J. *The Maccabean Revolt: Anatomy of a Biblical Revolution*. Wilmington, Del: Michael Glazier, 1988.

Jones, B. W. "Antiochus Epiphanes and the Persecution of the Jews." In *Scripture in Context: Essays on the Comparative Method*, ed. C. D. Evans et al., 263–90. Pittsburgh: Pickwick Publications, 1980.

Learney, A. R. C. *The Jewish and Christian World: 200 B.C. to A.D. 200*. London and New York: Cambridge University Press, 1984.

McCown, C. C. "The Araq el Emir and the Tobiads." *BA* 20 (1957): 63–76.

Mandell, S. R. "Did the Maccabees Believe That They Had a Valid Treaty with Rome?" *CBQ* 53 (1991): 202–20.

———. "Was Rome's Early Diplomatic Interaction with the Maccabees Legal?" *CB* 64 (1988): 87–89.

Momigliano, A. *Alien Wisdom: The Limits of Hellenization*. Cambridge and New York: Cambridge University Press, 1975.

Sachs, A. J., and D. J. Wiseman, "A Babylonian King List of the Hellenistic Period." *Iraq* 16 (1954): 202–11.

Schwartz, S. "Israel and the Nations Roundabout: I Maccabees and the Hasmonean Expansion." *JJS* 42 (1991): 16–38.

Sievers, J. *The Hasmoneans and Their Supporters: From Matthias to the Death of John Hyrcanus*. Atlanta: Scholars Press, 1990.

Smith, M. "The Dead Sea Sect in Relation to Ancient Judaism." *NTS* 7 (1960/61):347–60.

VanderKam, J. C. *The Dead Sea Scrolls Today.* Grand Rapids, Mich: Wm. B. Eerdmans Publishing Co., 1994.

Vaux, R. de. *Archaeology and the Dead Sea Scrolls.* Rev. ed. London: Oxford University Press, 1973.

Vermes, G. *The Dead Sea Scrolls: Qumran in Perspective.* Rev. ed. London/Philadelphia: William Collins Sons/ Fortress Press, 1977/1981.

Chapter 3: The Herodian Period

Alon, G. *The Jews, Judaism and the Classical World: Studies in Jewish History in the Times of the Second Temple and Talmud.* Jerusalem: Magnes, 1977.

Bernegger, P. M. "Affirmation of Herod's Death in 4 B.C." *JTS* 34 (1983): 526–31.

Bickerman, E. *Studies in Jewish and Christian History.* 2 vols. Leiden: E. J. Brill, 1976–80.

Braund, D. C. "Gabinius, Caesar and the *publicani* of Judae." *Klio* 65 (1983): 241–44.

———. *Rome and the Friendly King: The Character of Client Kingship.* New York/London: St. Martin's Press/Croom Helm, 1984.

Hoehner, H. *Herod Antipas.* London/Grand Rapids, Mich.: Cambridge University Press/Zondervan Publishing House, 1972/1980.

Jeremias, J. *Jerusalem in the Time of Jesus: An Investigation into the Economic and Social Conditions in the New Testament Period.* Philadelphia/London: Fortress Press/SCM Press, 1969.

Jones, A. H. M. *The Cities of the Eastern Roman Provinces.* 2d ed. London: Oxford University Press, 1971.

———. *The Herods of Judaea.* 2d ed. London: Oxford University Press, 1967.

Kanael, B. "The Partition of Judea by Gabinius." *IEJ* 6 (1952): 98–106.

Levine, L. I. *Caesarea under Roman Rule.* Leiden: E. J. Brill, 1975.

Millar, F. *The Roman Near East, 31 B.C.–A.D. 337.* Cambridge, Mass.: Harvard University Press, 1993.

Perowne, S. *The Life and Times of Herod the Great.* London/Nashville: Hodder & Stoughton/Abingdon Press, 1956/1959.

Safrai, S., and M. Stern, eds. *The Jewish People in the First Christian Century.* 2 vols. Assen/Philadelphia: Van Gorcum/Fortress Press, 1974/1976.

Safrai, Z. *The Economy of Roman Palestine.* London: Routledge, 1993.

Schalit, A. *The Jews under Roman Rule: From Pompey to Diocletian.* Leiden: E. J. Brill, 1976.

———. *König Herodes: Der Mann und sein Werk.* Berlin: Walter de Gruyter, 1969.

———, ed. *Philonis Alexandrini Legatio ad Gaium.* 2d ed. Leiden: E. J. Brill, 1970.

Chapter 4: The Jewish-Roman Wars

Applebaum, S. A. "Judaea as a Roman Province: The Countryside as a Political and Economic Factor." *ANRW* 2, no. 8 (1977): 355–96.

————. *Prolegomena to the Study of the Second Jewish Revolt (A.D. 132–135)*. Oxford: British Archaeological Reports, 1976.

————. "The Zealots: The Case for Revaluation." *JRS* 61 (1971): 155–70.

Borg, M. "The Currency of the Term 'Zealot.'" *JTS* 22 (1971): 504–12.

Cohen, S. J. D. *Josephus in Galilee and Rome: His Vita and Development as a Historian*. Leiden: E. J. Brill, 1979.

————. "Masada: Literary Tradition, Archaeological Remains and the Credibility of Josephus." *JJS* 33 (1982): 385–405.

Cornfeld, G., ed. *Josephus, The Jewish War: Newly Translated with Extensive Commentary and Archaeological Background Illustrations*. Grand Rapids, Mich.: Zondervan Publishing House, 1982.

Fitzmyer, J. A. "The Bar Cochba Period." In his *Essays on the Semitic Background of the New Testament*, 305–54. London/Missoula, Mont.: Geoffrey Chapman/Scholars Press, 1971/1974.

Hamel, G. *Poverty and Charity in Roman Palestine: First Three Centuries C.E.* Berkeley: University of California Press, 1990.

Hengel, M. *The Zealots: Investigations into the Jewish Freedom Movement in the Period from Herod I until 70 A.D.* Edinburgh: T. & T. Clark, 1989.

Horbury, W. "The Beginnings of the Jewish Revolt under Trajan." In *Geschichte—Tradition—Reflexion*, ed. W. Cancik et al., 3.283–304. Tübingen: J. C. B. Mohr (Paul Siebeck), 1996.

Horsley, R. A. "Ancient Jewish Banditry and the Revolt against Rome, A.D. 66–70." *CBQ* 43 (1981): 409–32.

Jones, A. H. M. "The Urbanisation of Palestine." *JRS* 21 (1931): 78–85.

Kasher, A. *The Jews in Hellenistic and Roman Egypt: The Struggle for Equal Rights*. Tübingen: J. C. B. Mohr (Paul Siebeck), 1985.

Maier, P. L. "The Episode of the Golden Roman Shields at Jerusalem." *HTR* 42 (1969): 109–21.

Mandell, S. R. "Who Paid the Temple Tax When the Jews Were under Roman Rule?" *HTR* 77 (1984): 223–32.

Neusner, J. *First Century Judaism in Crisis*. Nashville: Abingdon Press, 1975.

————. *From Politics to Piety: The Emergence of Pharisaic Judaism*. Englewood Cliffs: Prentice Hall, 1973.

————. *A Life of Yohanan ben Zakkai*. 2d ed. Leiden: E. J. Brill, 1970.

————. *The Rabbinic Traditions about the Pharisees before 70*. 3 vols. Leiden: E.J. Brill, 1971.

Rajak, T. *Josephus: The Historian and His Society*. London/Philadelphia: Gerald Duckworth & Co./Fortress Press, 1983/1984.

Rappaport, U. "John of Gischala: From Galilee to Jerusalem." *JJS* 33 (1982): 479–93.

Rhoads, D. M. *Israel in Revolution 6–74 C.E.: A Political History Based on the Writings of Josephus*. Philadelphia: Fortress Press, 1976.

Roth, C. "The Constitution of the Jewish Republic of 66–70." *JSS* 9 (1964): 295–319.

———. "The Pharisees in the Jewish Revolution of 66–73." *JSS* 7 (1962): 63–80.

———. "The Zealots in the War of 66–73." *JSS* 4 (1959): 332–55.

Saldarini, A. J. "Johanan ben Zakkai's Escape from Jerusalem." *JSJ* 6 (1975): 189–204.

Schäfer, P. *Der Bar Kokhba-Aufstand: Studien zum zweiten jüdischen Krieg gegen Rom*. Tübingen: J. C. B. Mohr (Paul Siebeck), 1981.

Schwartz, D. R. *Agrippa I: The Last King of Judaea*. Tübingen: J. C. B. Mohr (Paul Siebeck), 1990.

Schwartz, S. *Josephus and Judaean Politics*. Leiden: E. J. Brill, 1990.

Schwier, H. *Temple und Tempelzerstörung. Untersuchungen zur den theologischen und ideologischen Faktoren im ersten jüdisch-römischer Krieg (66–74 n. Chr.)*. Fribourg/Göttingen: Universitatsverlag/Vandenhoeck & Ruprecht, 1989.

Smallwood, E. M. *The Jews under Roman Rule*. Leiden: E.J. Brill, 1981.

Smith, M. "Zealots and Sicarii: Their Origins and Relation." *HTR* 64 (1971): 1–19.

———. E. M. *Masada: Herod's Fortress and the Zealots' Last Stand*. London/New York: Weidenfeld & Nicolson/Random House, 1966.

———. *The Finds from the Bar Kokhba Period in the Cave of Letters*. Jerusalem: Israel Exploration Society, 1963.

Yadin, Y. *Bar-Kokhba: The Rediscovery of the Legendary Hero of the Last Jewish Revolt against Imperial Rome*. London/New York: Weidenfeld & Nicolson/Random House, 1971.

Index of Scripture

Index of Subjects

The Jewish People
in Classical Antiquity

DS121.65
.H39 1998

DATE DUE
